C. G.



Prayers and Words
Alethea

# *Message In The Wind*

*Alethea A. Adams-Wells*

MESSAGE IN THE WIND



Published by:
Unole Publishing Company, Inc.
P.O. Box 230
Salt Lick, Kentucky 40371

ISBN: 0-9645787-0-0
Library of Congress Catalog Number: 95-090233

Printed in the United States of America
First Printing

# AUTHOR'S NOTE
# MESSAGE IN THE WIND GWONISGESDI UNOLE

A "MESSAGE IN THE WIND", is a "KNOWING": perhaps not always the exact date or time of something taking shape, but just knowing it will soon come to pass.

When I was two weeks old I had contracted polio. Therefore, leaving me unable to walk until I was seven. Having two elder sisters as well as two younger ones, this left me sort of in the middle, yet in turn, allowed me to become more in-touch with myself and my sensitiveness.

Allow me to give you a few examples of "MESSAGE IN THE WIND"; I was about four years old and had been playing beneath our old cabin porch most of the day. Mama was doing her usual chores in the kitchen. The next scene I recall, I'm scooting across the floor searching for Mama's dress-tail. There's something I must tell her!

"Mama", I whisper. "Do you want to know what the wind said to me a little while ago?"

"Yes, my little Bead-Eyes, tell Mama your Message In The Wind!"

I gazed into her warm, dark brown eyes and shyly answered. "Mama, two Fancy-Mans are coming today! And they are really big mad about something!" Mama leaned over and gently kissed my face, thanking me for speaking of what the Wind had told me. I could feel the roughness of her hard working hands but her understanding and love was the bond that makes a crippled child and young Mother unite with Spirit. Within a few hours revenuers came to call upon my Father who was hard at work just up the hollow behind the barn toiling at his famous moonshine still! So from that day on, Mama was always eager to listen very closely whenever I whispered what the Wind was Speaking!

During these young years I would meet people and could

feel or know what they were feeling without having to speak a word. Once this real pretty woman came into our mountain shack and I felt immediately that she could sing. Turns out that she was a fine songstress and for many times to come she joined in our Mountain-Ballad-Concerts!

Another time this handsome man, all dressed in a black cowboy outfit came to buy some moonshine! I reached out and touched his fancy shirt saying, "Mister, you look like a cowboy! But you can't even ride a horse!"

"Well, can you?" insisting an answer he turned his head toward Mama yet keeping his eyes on me, and with a big grin, asked Mama, "How in the hell, does that child know that I can't ride a damn horse?"

Mama answered with her big pearly smile! "My little Bead-Eyes can always tell you what the unole (wind) speaks!" Cowboy just shook his head then tipped the moonshine jar to settle his nerves!

Being raised in these Kentucky Mountains to a Cherokee Indian Mother and half Cherokee-Irish Father, I was taught much about the History of struggle and sorrows of our Foremothers and Forefathers. I learned many stories about the Trail of Tears, that were often told around our old kitchen table. "I'll walk that Cry-Trail one day, won't I Mama?"

"Yes, my Bead-Eyes!" She would answer with her promising smile! Yet in her heart, she silently spoke, "No my child." Because she knew that my crippled right leg could never withstand a journey such as that.

But Mama taught me to always believe in The Great Spirit and to always pray, therefore, all Dreams would someday come true. Well, this teaching and belief has remained in my heart and I knew that one of these days I would walk that Sorrow-Trail, because I kept hearing that special "Messsage in the Wind."

# FIRST SOME HISTORY ON OLD HICKORY AND THE MAGICIAN

In 1829 the main public issue pertaining to Andrew Jackson becoming the newly elected President was only if he would promise to remove the Cherokee Indians from all States East of the Mississippi River. Winning the majority of electoral vote margin by 178 to John Q. Adam's 83, President Jackson headed for his new Mission of Glory! This new President had already well earned his nickname "Old Hickory" because his discipline was tough and he refused to take "NO" for an answer. He was a hot-headed duelist, a great fighting General, yet good to his armies. One of his famous quotes was, "I'll perish before I'll retreat"!

In November of 1813 he first defeated a small group of Creek Indians under Chief Red Eagle (Gigage Awohaʔli). At that time the territory was in Mississippi. By March 1814 the Creek War ended. Chief Red Eagle had to surrender. To punish the Creeks, General Jackson took twenty million acres in and around Horseshoe bend. Again, Jackson repeated this same War-Act upon the Seminole Indians in 1818.

So by the time he was ready for the White House he had aquired a taste for Indian-Blood. Many people, Indian and white, could be overheard speaking, "There goes Old Indian-Hating-Hickory!"

But at this time, bearing a High-Title, he also carried a heavy heart due to the recent death of his pipe smoking Rachel. She had been laid to rest just a few days before their White House move. Yet as she lay dying due to heart failure her last request was, "You are my precious niece, Emily Donelson. Will you take over for me in the White House?" This youthful niece did carry out her Aunt's great wish, but only to find herself an early grave at the age of twenty-eight.

The new President looked much older than his sixty-one years of age. Tuberculosis was taking it's toil as well as the Dueling-Bullets that still remained in his body. And he often quoted to his close friends, "With my Rachel gone, I have nothing to live for." So, with this new Mission on his mind as well as a promise to keep to his voters, he set in full force! Project? The "Indian Removal Bill" and he had this forced through Congress by 1830. But many moons would pass before this dark cloud would fall its heavy rains upon the "Cultured and Proud Cherokee Indians"!

Jackson was into his second term of being the "Great White Chief." When he called upon GOD to help him he spoke that he needed to make some changes in his administration, especially the National-Debt. In short, he was highly successful! By 1836 there was so much flow of "Paper Money" that he ordered that only gold and silver would be accepted for trade or Land-Payments! Simply because the Government had more money than it could spend due to Tax Collection, "Our Federal Union must be preserved," Jackson kept speaking. But when the Supreme Court shook him to reality pertaining to the Federally-Protected Cherokee Indians his answer was of no suprise! "What rights did they have or need anyway?" Yet he kept this Indian-Issue in the back of his mind due to his present task, "The Banking War Monster". And to the amazement of many, he completed that War-Task as well!

Old Hickory had a buddy, Vice President Martin Van Buren, whom Jackson had hand-picked himself. Jackson was growing tired of all these Political-Wars, so it was time they got down to real business of their own! Allow me to step back, in brief, for one of the many favors that Van Buren did for Jackson. It's recorded in history as "The Affair of Mrs. Eaton". I'm not involving you in this run-on affair story, but now the time had come for last minute "Political-Back-Scratching" time. Old Hickory was in the process of his "ASKINGS" to Van Buren when this message was brought to Jackson from his old friend Sam Houston, "Please acept Texas as a State because I just kicked Mexican President Santa Anna's ass here at the Alamo!" Andrew Jackson had no intentions of taking this neck of desert land as a State but on his last day of being the White-Chief (Unega Ugvwiyuhi) he accepted this Bloody-Battle-Ground as a new State!

Now, back to Hickory and the Magician's last minute deals! Remember, that Van Buren didn't like Cherokee Indians anymore than Old Hickory did! Being his last day in office he asked Van Buren to PLEASE carry out his orders to remove "Those Damn Red Ass Cherokees" to Indian Territory in Oklahoma. Van Buren promised that he would. A few days later Jackson left in a train enroute to his favorite mansion in Tennessee that he had named "The Hermitage". It was now June of 1845. At the age of seventy eight years, the much worn out, Indian Hating, man of many colors was drawing his last breath. He slowly tries to raise his feeble hand as he had done so many times to accomplish his victories. Calling all his house-staff and Family to his bedside to hear his one last talk. "I hope to see you all in Heaven, both white and black." Then he passed away. Old Hickory died without a penny. His adopted son Andrew Jackson, Jr. spent it all!

## THE MAGICIAN

Since Old Hickory formed the Darkened-Clouds over our Cherokee Nation, the Magician intended to show the Indians how he could make the Rains come.

Martin Van Buren became the eighth President of the United States by being carefully chosen by his friend the former President Andrew Jackson. Martin Van Buren was born in the State of New York in 1782. His ancestors had come from the Netherlands, therefore Van Buren could speak Dutch better than he could speak English. His greatest desire was to become a lawyer. He performed quite well in this field and was admitted to the Bar Association at the early age of twenty.

In 1807 he chose to marry his distant cousin pretty Hanna Hoes! Her health was always a bit unstable yet she bore him four sons within five years. But this left Hanna far weaker and at the young age of thirty-five, with her body overtaken by tuberculosis, Hanna lost her life, leaving her Husband to remain a widower. He would never remarry.

Now, as he stepped into this great position as a President, he was in need of a White House Hostess. So he chose his Daughter-In-Law Angelicia Singleton Van Buren to fill this position. At President Van Buren's Inauguration in 1837 he spoke, "I intend to work in the shadow of my predecessor, Jackson!" Then he immediately reassigned all of Jackson's Cabinet Members!

Within two months he reversed the payments of gold and silver back into Paper Money. This prosperity was only to be temporarily. Next, after many cries from the Government workers about too many hours of labor, Van Buren reduced the number of work hours to ten hours per day. Due to Slave States, he had both sides pissed off. Anti-slavery supporters didn't agree with his plans for the new war upon the Seminole Indians and the Pro-slavery supporters were angry because he didn't want to choose Texas for a slave state.

The people kept giving Van Buren new names, from "The Magician" to "Martin Van Ruin" and the "Lily-Fingered Aristocrat"! He loved to squander money from the public to make his baths be hot and this would cost much to install a hot water tank into his bath chambers. Still that wasn't enough! Perhaps the reason he turned gold and silver back into paper money was to make sure he could drink fine wines from silver goblets and eat his food upon fancy golden plates!

Since his term was growing near the end he had to keep his deal with Old Hickory! First, all former Peace-Treaties that had been signed and the many promises were to be broken. Now the "Great White Chief of Washington" pointed his "Golden Magic Evil-Finger". He sends Major-General Winfield Scott to "Cause the Tears".

## PRIOR TO RATTLESNAKE SPRINGS TEARS

The Cherokee Indians had lived many years with the White people. Many Councils were called by both parties. But in the year of 1815 someone found some gold. This treasure remained in the back of the white man's mind until they could figure out a way to have every ounce of dust or lump, whichever it may turn out to be. Dahlonega, Georgia would never remain the same concerning harmony and peaceful living between the Cherokee and Whites.

Gold finding repeated itself again in 1829. Sadly enough, the Cherokee were not "Gold Diggers". Our People preferred SILVER. But this second find raised the white man's eyebrows and made his heart beat much fast with "Gold Dreams" in his head. Therefore a quick pencil-push had to be drawn up. President Jackson passed several Acts of the Georgia Legislature through the State of Georgia, annulling all the laws of the Cherokee Nation, meaning the Cherokee People could not have any Political gatherings and their land was to be divided amongst the Whites. All the gold and silver mines were seized by the Government. Next they closed all Indian Courts and didn't allow any Indian to testify in court if there was a white person involved. And these "Laws" were "BACKDATED" to 1828 and "SEALED"!

I personally must speak my "No Understand" here. Upon the second finding of gold in 1829 came the Old Hickory Removal-Act which became active in 1830. Remember now, in 1835 a Great Treaty of Peace was drawn up by the White Chiefs again.

## "THE UNITED STATES AND CHEROKEE NATION TREATY OF 1835"

Perpetual "peace" and "friendship" shall exist between the citizens of the United States and the Cherokee Indians. The United States AGREE to PROTECT the Cherokee Nation from DOMESTIC STRIFE and FOREIGN ENEMIES and AGAINST INTERNECINE WARS between the several tribes. The Cherokee shall endeavor to preserve and maintain the peace of the country and not make war upon their neighbors. They shall also be PROTECTED AGAINST INTERRUPTION and INTRUSION from CITIZENS of the UNITED STATES who may attempt to settle in the country without their consent. And all such persons shall be removed from the same by order of the President of the United States.

Perhaps I didn't read this Treaty correct, or Old Hickory was on some bad drugs the day he sent this notice to our Cherokee People!

This confused many of our Cherokee Chiefs and Leaders. The Nation Land of the Cherokee ranged from South Alabama; East to the Grandfather Water, Mississippi; and North to Kentucky River, Hunting Grounds.

After that gold-war in Georgia, the Cherokee moved their Council-Gatherings to Tennessee, never to trust the Georgia territory again. All the while NEW LAWS were thrown at the Cherokee Nation and the fairly decent laws would tend to be cast aside. As the many Chiefs had councils they would ask amongst themselves, "What is this dark cloud falling upon our people? How is it that our children cannot play with the white children anymore? Once we lived and shared with the white Fathers. Have we done wrong to prosper as they have insisted us to do?"

It was mandatory that Cherokee learned the white man's Christian way of life. And the Cherokee did. In fact the young Indian children learned the Bible better than the whites. This caused anger amongst the white parents. The Cherokee men built fine log homes for their women. Many Cherokee teenaged daughters and sons went off to North Eastern schools to become GREATLY EDUCATED. This also made problems with the whites because their pretty young daughters chose to marry the handsome Cherokee young men when they returned from school. The interracial marriages became very high in numbers and this caused more tension!

Ironically enough, even George Gist, better known as Sequoyah, invented the Cherokee Alphabet and was praised so greatly for this that in 1825. Chief John Ross of the Cherokee Nation presented a piece of silver medal to Sequoyah that had been inscribed bearing Gist's name and ingenuity.

Other Indian people like Major Ridge, Joseph Van, and John Ross all were Cherokee. They lived in plantation homes, owned many black slaves and rode in fine carriages. Whenever the more wealthy Cherokee rode their horses they were usually accompanied by a mounted black servant in imitation of their white neighbors.

Yet all this advancement was to no avail. In late 1835 the more wealthy Cherokee were advised to sell what they wished to and take their families and slaves toward the West to Indian Territory. If they disobeyed this Gentle-Order much sorrow would be the picture because the REMOVAL was going to happen. Many did take the advice and head West, mainly the wealthy ones, including their slaves and family members. There were about seven hundred in all. As they departed they prayed that many more would follow since the official voluntary removal date had been POSTED and ANNOUNCED, that day being May 23, 1838.

Many pleas for the Cherokee poured in from all directions. Ralph Waldo Emerson wrote a letter to Van Buren reminding him of the "Treaty of 1835". And Emerson spoke of the gloomy opinion he had of the United States Government. There was no reply from Van Buren.

On May 10, 1838, Major General Winfield Scott, of the United States Army, sends a MESSAGE to the Cherokee that still remained in North Carolina, Georgia, Tennessee, and Alabama; the speaking that will be heard forever in Cherokee Hearts.

## "LETTER TO THE CHEROKEE PEOPLE FROM WINFIELD SCOTT"

"Cherokees! The President of the United States has sent me, with a powerful army, to cause you, in obedience to the Treaty of 1835, to join that part of your people who are already established in prosperity on the other side of the Mississippi. Unhappily, two years which were allowed for the purpose, you have suffered to pass away without following, and without making any preparation to follow, and now, or by the time that this solemn ADDRESS shall reach your distant settlements the emigration must be commenced in haste, but, I hope, without disorder. I have no power by granting a further delay, to correct the error that you have committed. The full moon of May is already on the wane, and before another shall have passed away, every Cherokee man, woman and child, in these States, must be in motion to join their brethren in the far West.

My Friends! This is no sudden determination on the part of the President, whom you and I must now obey. By the treaty, the emigration was to have been completed on or before, the 23rd of this month, and the President has constantly kept you warned, during the two years allowed, through all his officers and agents in this country, that the Treaty would be enforced. I am come to carry out that determination. My troops already occupy many positions in this country that you are to abandon, and thousands, and thousands are approaching, from every quarter, to render resistance and escape alike hopeless. All those troops, regular and militia, are your friends. Receive them and confide in them as such. Obey them when they tell you that you can remain no longer in this country. Soldiers are as kind hearted as brave, and the desire of every one of us is to execute our painful duty in mercy. We are commanded by the president to act towards you in that spirit, and such is also the wish of the whole people of America.

Chiefs, head-men and warriors! Will you, then by resistance, compel us to resort to arms? God forbid! Or will you, by flight, seek to hide yourselves in mountains and forests, and thus oblige us to hunt you down? Remember that, in pursuit, it may be impossible to avoid conflicts. The blood of the white man, or the blood of the red man may be spilt, and if spilt, however accidently, it may be impossible for the discreet and humane among you, or among us to prevent a general war and carnage. Think of this, my Cherokee brethren! I am an old warrior, and have been present at many a scene of slaughter, but spare me, I beseech you, the horror of witnessing the destruction of the Cherokee. Do not, I invite you, even wait for the close approach of the troops, but make such preparations for emigration as you can, and hasten to this place, the Ross' Landing, or Gunter's Landing, where you will be received in kindness of officers selected for the purpose. You will find food for all, and clothing for the destitute, at either of those places, and thence at your ease, and in comfort, be transported to your new homes according to the terms of the Treaty.

This is the address of a warrior to warriors, May his entreaties be kindly received, and may the God of both prosper the Americans and Cherokees, and preserve them long in peace and friendship with each other!

Winfield Scott,
Cherokee Agency
May 10, 1838."

Winfield's own soldiers called him "Old Fuss and Feathers"! Now I choose to agree with them in addition to my personal opinion! "If one could mix, "Some Old Hickory," with a dash of "Golden Magician" then stir well. Now serve your mixture upon a heaping of "Fussy Feathers" note this must be roughly tossed onto a gold platter. There! It's all perfect, because you would be consuming the food of the damn-devil himself!!!"

Yet sadly enough, there were about fifteen thousand Proud Cherokee rounded up and treated like cattle, instead of the educated and white-man ways Christians they had become. When these soldiers (aˀyosgi) fiercely and un-Godly attacked! Beautiful and hard working Cherokee women were busy cooking and cleaning their log homes. singing songs and thanking Our Great Spirit for another warm Dogwood-Moon day The aroma of corn (selu) and beans (tuya) filled her cabin and teased the nostrils of her husband (uhyehi) that was working at their nearby barn! Her baby (usdi) was in the yard playing with the family dog (gila). How would a child know what would take place in a short while, when in fact the roundup was in progress just down the road. Suddenly evil invasion of the white-soldiers appeared! First the Father (Udoda) was facing the soldier's guns, the Mother (Uji) dragged from her cooking in the midst of screaming. This once peaceful Family, the cursing soldiers found more easy to run thundering horse-hooves over the crying child than to contend with such a small matter.

Some of the Cherokee were of more luck. The few that found a hiding place prayed to The Great Spirit, their Thanks, intending to stay in the deepened forests until all would come to pass. And others were in such a fear they poisoned themselves, finding reason that death by choice was better than death by the gun and sword of the dog soldiers. "Why?" (gadohv) came the mournful cry (adlohyida) from the Cherokees. But they received no answer. On this day of May 24, 1838, there was just the sound of a whip slicing its way through the hot air, finding its place to rest and bringing blood from their quivering bodies.

## RATTLESNAKE SPRINGS STOCKADES

The STOCKADES had already been built at Rattlesnake Springs and thousands of Cherokee were herded in from rifle point to sword point. All the fine provisions that were promised by General Scott were another of already many untruths promised to the Proud Cherokee Nation. Their clothing was whatever they had on and many weren't wearing shoes the day of the roundup. The promised food was maggot-infested meat that even a starving dog (gila) wouldn't even eat. The shelter? Log cattle stockades. No overhead or a simple lean-to, just the sky for a roof. Many families were separated in the different stockades never to see their Mother, Father, Sibling, or Husband and Wife again.

The Cherokee People could see their blooming crops that now lay unattended in the cultivated fields. As the Spring turned into a hot sweltering summer, the stockades turned into powder dry floors. Just a handful of wood was thrown into their prisons for a small fire to prepare the maggot-meat. With as many as 800 to 1000 Indians thrown in each stockade, the bad meat and night dampness started the weak and young ones to find death as their mercy and Spiritual Journey into the Heavens of Our Great Spirit. These becoming much more fortunate because the unknown journey that laid ahead would be far worse than their present dwellings.

Young mothers, sickly with fevers, flux and foul smelling from their mouth due to the infested meat, gave birth to still-born children. Many mothers died along beside their child. Chants could be heard by the Shamans through the many stockades that imprisoned more than thirteen-thousand Indians and Black slaves. "Oh Great Spirit, send us rain to wet our dried throats and to cleanse our bodies."

When night would fall, the Dog-soldiers would make their nightly routines. In promising the young women a blanket or a fresh piece of bread, being naive, the young woman would take the dog-soldier up on his offer. The fresh breath of air would be much welcomed to her. The stench of feces and death amongst the many prisoners was far more than anyone could withstand. But she didn't get that promised bread. Instead she had to fight the rough hard hands of the dog-soldier only to lose her virginity and her pride. Afterwards, he cast her back into her prison like a person would throw away a chicken bone. She would then bow her once proud head in shame as she faced her people.

Due to the stockades becoming so infested with urine and many tons of excrement, General Scott thought it best to start the removal West. When at least a hundred prominent Cherokee Leaders asked of the General to wait until fall to finish the removal because diarrhea, soldier-given gonorrhea and rotting teeth were taking their toll upon their people, Old General Fuss agreed! He would await until the air became cooler and perhaps sickness by then would subside. After all, the General felt the "Indians weren't arrested, they were just in temporary confinement! This is the Law," as he could best figure and his reports of the former three departures were losing a lot of Indians due to the heat and fatigue. So September 1 will be arranged for the fourth removal.

Ready now for the Fall Removal, the first one was on the 28th day of August. Cherokee Chief's nephew Bill Coodey oversaw the first Fall removal detachment and Chief Going Snake, many moons old, took the lead.

On September 1, 1838, the second detachment was herded Westward. Next detachment removal was on the 3rd day of September and this is the exact date that "I" personally chose to begin my long trek Westward and retrace the very Bloody-Steps my Foremothers and Fore-Fathers were forced to.

Their forced removal began on this exact date, one hundred and fifty four years earlier. Allow me to introduce my readers to another kind of Wisdom my Cherokee Indian Mama taught me. "Numbers" in Cherokee is "Disesdi", and the reason this is needed to share my story begins with the number of our Cherokee People that were forced Westward on September 3rd, 1838.

The Cherokee Leader, John Ross, spoke the removal count of "950". This is added by a simple form: Take "9"+"5"+"0" which gives you "14". Now add "1"+"4" and this gives you "5"! And in Indian Numerology the "5" means "Surprise"! So what I'm trying to relate here is I chose the September 3rd date, because "3" means "News." In turn, this date and number of my people, turns out to be, "News of Surprise!" And this you will see, these "Words of Truth" come to pass.

## LEAVING RATTLESNAKE SPRINGS

Dark clouds hovered over Rattlesnake Springs as the Dog-soldiers herded the Cherokee and black slaves. Seemed the sky threatened to give a great pour down upon "The Just and Unjust." As the Dog-Soldiers looked above them with much fear, the Cherokee smiled within their hearts.

Only Dry-Land-Lighting pierced across the sky as the Dog-Soldier cursed at the Indians, the Mothers-to-be with swollen bellies praying their unborn child would make this Tearful Walk. While some of the women were due to give birth at anytime.

The young men were kept under the sharp watchful eyes of the soldiers. And the Elder Indians just shuffled slowly forward, staring aimlessly through glazed eyes, not showing the pain inflicted upon them from the dog-soldier's lashing whips nor the point of their swords or the aim of their guns. Tears rolled down the cheeks of the little children. "Where is my Mama? Where are we going? Have you seen Daddy?"

"Shut your big mouth, you little red-ass, before I give you a good licking with my whip." screamed the soldiers.

Scared, hungry and already tired, the children would search for an Elder Cherokee's hand in fear of the dog-soldiers and this journey they couldn't understand. Hospital-Wagons and food-wagons brought up the rear. Only the soon-to-die would get a ride just before death. The Slaves were not even allowed to ride and the ones left behind were sold. Presently the clouds are dark. They give a promise of rain.

It's September 3rd, 1992. I'm standing here at the Sacred Grounds of Rattlesnake Springs looking toward the Heavens and Praying. No rain comes, just the Dry-land-lighting pierces the sky. Just as it did over a hundred years ago on that darkened day of Our Cherokee History. My people asked to bathe and have prayer before their tearful removal. They were denied. Here in the Sacred Rattlesnake Springs I bathed. The cold September water seemed to hold me warmly as I prayed for my People that had perished on that trail. And I prayed that I would be safe upon this life-long dream journey.

"Oh, Great-Spirit, allow me to live so I may speak and teach about this awfully darkness that fell upon our Proud Cherokee Nation. And I want to thank you for this beginning I've long awaited for. Thank you for my devoted Mr. Bill, that has made this journey possible. Great Spirit, please give me wisdom and knowledge to walk safely with care. Show me the route when I get lost. Teach me to stand upon the rock and not the sands when I come to strange water crossings. Teach me to be a better person today than I was yesterday. Bless all my Friends and Relatives. And guide Mr. Bill safely back home to Kentucky. Will you see that my little kitten, Bandit, doesn't miss me so much that he may grieve? And about Nellie Bly, my horse here! Will you show her how to avoid the broken glass that we're bound to come across? Great- Spirit, I thank you kindly for all that you have given me. And if its at all possible, would you tell Mama I miss and love her dearly. And if you permit, will you allow her to just get a quick glance down here so she can see my smile? Hope I haven't asked you for too much. And thank you for my warm moccsasins. Only you know how scared I am and just how heavy my heart is for the passing of this once forced journey, and how heavy it is now for the many troubles upon my mind. Well, Great Spirit, I pray that I haven't kept you too long, and my one last request is; You know how you've always guided me that special way. Will you grant this? Always speak and guide me with your everlasting and wonderful MESSAGE IN THE WIND?"

After my prayer, I looked across the Sacred Springs to where once the many stockades stood and I chilled, allowing my imagination to wander and see as it may have been the very night before this September 3 removal in 1838.

While the August moon hung full and low over the Rattlesnake Springs stockades, the young mother to be lay withering upon the dew dampened but powdered earth amongst nearly one thousand other Cherokee Indians and Black slaves, her swollen stomach aching with her first child promising to come two moons early. "Why?" she moaned as the fever ravaged through her. Spells of delirium and cold sweats continued. Foul bile of the maggot-infested meat still spewed uncontrollably. "Oh, Great Spirit, where is my husband-man now? Where is my Mama? Why must we be here awaiting our death when we've done nothing wrong?"

As the Elder women tried soothing her, chanting, praying, crying and singing, assuring her she and the baby would be fine. "All will be well," they softly spoke. Then silence fell upon her crying throat and quivering bleeding young body. The small lifeless baby passed through in gushes of blood. No sound of a cry. The young mother's body ceased chilling and quivering. Her waiting was over.

Low whimpers were heard in the cattle stockades. The whispers passed quickly. All prayed quietly so as not to disturb the guard-dog soldiers. Young and elder men alike begin digging into the arid land. There beside and atop others, she and her bloody child lay together. This sad way of death had been going on now since the warm moon of May. The Dogwood Moon.

Denise Mantooth interviewed me just before departing the Sacred Rattlesnake Springs. This nice young smiling woman worked for the Cleveland Banner Newspaper. Ms. Mantooth shared her feelings and respect for The Cherokee People pertaining to the past and to the presence of us today. Speaking "I'm enjoying this interview and as a child, when we played cowboys and Indians, I was always the Indian." I was elated with her stories and felt privileged that my departure date was also her Birthday!

This tall, lanky, handsome poised man photographed me. He worked with the Chattanooga television station and he followed me and Nelly-Bly up the road to our turnoff, Nelly's pack needed readjusting. He helped Mr. Bill with her two-hundred pound pack. Then the camera man wished me the very best of luck as we parted ways! Both of us vanishing into our own paths and worlds.

The old Trail from Rattlesnake Springs, Tennessee, is now route "58." Mr. Bill drove just ahead of me and Nelly just to make sure we got across the I-75 overpass. But the darkened sky gave a sure warning that she was destined to give us rain. Our first day the journey ended after about a five mile walk.

Mr. Bill had driven ahead to locate lodging for me and Nelly. He came upon this big red barn on the right side of the road. Next, he finds out who the owner is from a secretary that works at Mr. White's business building. And many thanks to Ms. Tresea Cook, we were granted permission to spend the night in the big red barn! Just as me and Nelly came dragging hooves and moccasins in, the clouds opened wide and gave one of her best performances. I'd gotten Nelly into a perfect smaller barn with a picture perfect corral, but she chose the hard rain instead of the shelter. No doubt the rains felt soothing upon her sweated-back and tired legs! Me and Mr. Bill sat in his truck and admired the beauty of the storm! Later when it subsided, we decided to go out for food. (Alsdayhdi).

Found this cozy little restaurant that sat upon a knoll back about four miles just off my trail. We settled in a window booth and started talking to the nice waitress! Her name was Melba Rice. Then the Owner-Lady of the establishment talked with us. I ask for their autographs and they obliged me! We four had an enjoyable conversation about the "Trail of Tears." The ladies promised to pray for my journey to be a safe one. We thanked them kindly as we left the Maple Grove Inn of Charleston and we promised to return one day to enjoy their great steaks again! Darkness was falling by the time we made our bed in the back of Mr. Bill's truck, "Ol' Blue". The rains had taken a rest too. I kissed Nelly goodnight and we just sat there on some lumber, not wanting to let the other one know that we were both just wanting to bawl our eyes out.

"Mr. Bill?" I said real softly with a grin." The Wind speaks that we are gonna have company!"

"Well, Princess, just who did the wind say was going to visit us?"

"Why, Mr. and Mrs. Happy Hiwassee!"

"Well, I've learned to never doubt your Messages in the Wind." He answered with his deep Kentucky husky voice. And sure enough, they pulled in the barnyard within the next twenty minutes!

We four enjoyed laughter and tears for a couple of hours. We recalled how their driveway up River Road along the Hiwassee River has all these "Don't come up here" signs! And it was way after dark! I kept saying to Mr. Bill, "Go on honey! Don't worry about those old signs. I can feel the Wind speaking that its alright. You'll see, just go on, its only a dead end road!" Mrs. Happy Hiwassee really laughed now!

"Yes, you all did! And when we heard a vehicle come in our drive and you Alethea, bounced out with a big smile and talked a mile a minute, saying who you all were, wanting to turn your truck and horse trailer around. Plus, you were walking the Trail of Tears. This really blew us away! Especially the way you dress. That big long skirt, ripped-up man's shirt and your white bandana with your long dark hair, I thought to myself, "this is a 1990's Indian!" Yes, you got our attention and that's why we had to come down to the Park where you all were camping!"

"That's my Woman-Princess!" Mr. Bill said, soft and low.

"You never know what she's going to say. She can curse a person out and smile at them the same time! Loves adventures, likes to ride her horse and shoot her guns! But that's why I love her dearly. She's all fire, but will cry if a butterfly hits the truck!"

At this time I again thank Mr. Hiwassee for introducing me to Mr. Cattle Man. I felt grateful that he allowed us to stay a few days upon the Sacred Rattlesnake Springs Ground. And I feel that since the Removal his seven generations of families have protected and taken good care of Sacred Grounds. I feel the many bones of our people that lay beneath the farm land are kept warm by the milk cows when they bed down.

"That's a nice was to look at that situation, Alethea!" Mr. Hiwassee warmly replied. "Now!" He asks, with a grin! "How did you name us Mr. and Mrs. Hiwassee?"

That was easy for me to quickly answer! "Ya see, Mr. Hiwassee, I can't remember peoples names the very second after they speak it to me. One reason, their name doesn't seem to match their face and spiritual personality. The second reason, seems the majority of people have the same name. A person can call ten different numbers in a phone book and ask for a Sue, Joe, Betty, a Bill, James and John, and if its not one of them answering, the person will speak to hold on for a minute, or they're not here right now, but will be a little later! And finally, my mind just doesn't think like the majority's does. I feel that a person's Spirit must match his name! I can't remember ya'lls name and you folks have a happy face every time I've seen you so your names are Mr. and Mrs. Happy Hiwassee!"

"Thank you, Alethea, we like our Indian names you have given us.!"

Rain was setting back in so we called it a night and embraced farewells. They drove away, we crawled into the covered back of Ol' Blue, and tired bodies found sleep quickly!

Next morning, still the rain kept a steady fall. We took this opportunity to rearrange my pack for Nelly. Met the Mr. Bull-man that leased Mr. White's property there. Such a jolly, full of laughter kind of man! Mr. White arrived with his family. We all had such a nice visit and they were proud of my strength to attempt such a journey.

Me and Mr. Bill went to the Ponderosa truck-stop for a late breakfast. I'm hooked on cheeseburgers and milk real bad, so I just had to have a double with extra, extra cheese! I didn't prepare for this trip. I'm forty-three pounds of lard clinging to a five feet five inches of frame. No excuse, but I figured my people didn't get to prepare for this trek either. They where confined moons before the removal, thin no doubt, with much sick and weakness. Therefore, I'm not giving myself any breaks or excuses for this fat ass, belly and chin. I thank our "Great Spirit" for whoever designed my 18-hour bra! Although I'm not sure where it goes sometimes, my belly, my boobs or my chin!

Another night in the Red-Barn and rain steadily coming. Finally, the next morning still holds darkened skies but just a mist is falling. Me and Mr. Bill worked in silence. Today was the day we knew that upon this departure, it may be a long time before we see each other again, Had Nelly all packed and Bonnie, my nine-shot, nine-inch gun is loaded and all ready to go. As he hitched that big white-horse-trailer to Ol' Blue, my heart grew as heavy as my lead bullets. We embraced for a long while, then I began to lead nelly across the rain-drenched grass toward the roadside heading Westward.

"Oh Great Spirit, I'm scared plum to death, but I feel all this Cleansing Rain of your's presents a Blessing. Thank you (Wada)."

Nelly was feeling really spunky and didn't want to obey me this morning! I felt just the opposite. Then a couple of cars pull up and this glamorous Black Lady gets out of her car. Her friends or family follow. She greets me with this beautiful grin asking if they could take some pictures of me and Nelly. "Sure!" I reply with a smile but shaky voice, 'cause I'm trying to look behind me, towards Mr. Bill. Now Nelly has some attention. Its performance time! Switch of her tail, arch that muscled neck, and holding her head in a way that has her rolling those big brown eyes up like the photos of Princess Diana of Wales! They take many pictures and thank me kindly! And the glamour-woman looks back at me as if she could feel what I was feeling. I'll pray for your safe journey," Her words flowed softly as the misty rain. I'm trying to give her a much appreciated "Thank you Miss," but Nelly was rushing me since her photo session was over! Throughout the rest my journey I kept thinking of that woman and I just knew that she had to be half-Black and half-Cherokee. I also felt that someday we'd meet again.

As me and Nelly started to cross the overpass of I-75, she refused. "You're too intelligent Nelly, to act this crazy." Was my gentle scold. Here comes Mr. Bill, my hero and rock! "Nelly, what is the matter girl?" He questioned her in his deep gentle voice. Taking the reins, Nelly crossed the overpass and looked back at me like, "What's your problem, mama? Can't you handle me this morning?" I just answered her with a little bow, "You are the boss your Royal High-ass!" Then Mr. Bill handed the reins back and told Nelly to be good to me. One last kiss, both fighting tears, and he walk's back toward his waiting empty-haul Kentucky Bound. Just above the Truck-stop upon a knoll, me and Nelly stood there in the yellow clay. I could see the Big-Road from here easily. She seemed to know because she stood there like a lady, looked toward the big-road, seeing her white horse-trailer heading North out of our sight. I commenced to crying.

"Goodbye, my Mr. Bill. Will we meet again? Will you be careful as I promise to be? When this journey is over, will you still be waiting for me with open arms? Will you marry me as you said you would, just as soon as you get that divorce over? Or will you go back to her or maybe find someone new? I adore you Mr. Bill, with every ounce of my body. Please allow me to feel the warmth of your strong arms again and I will never leave on an adventure again. Don't forget to see the doctor, you promised. And Mr. Bill, don't forget to pray for us. I need you so, I just need you so. Don't leave me, please. AKTIYA AYV" (wait for me).

Wiping my tears away, this elderly woman pulls up in a brand new pickup truck. "Saw you on the news honey, mighty proud of you. I became a widow here recently and I know what it feels like to be alone. I will pray for you and I'll always feel the White-man did the Indians wrong. Now, hang in there, and give it all you got. I'm a Christian Believer and I know you're going to make this Trail of Tears walk. May God bless you." Waved her strong looking arm and drove away. I just stood there in awe! She knew how I was feeling. That's a Message in the Wind.

Me and Nelly was getting our walking pattern together, when a young lady and her thirteen year old son stopped. "Saw you on the news and I just had to find you! My husband is Cherokee Indian. I'm going back to the house and get him. Because if he doesn't get to meet you, he will be upset. Besides, he's in bad health." As she turned around, the cloud's gave a gentle sound of thunder, a promise of more than just a misty rain! But, within a few minutes they returned.

"Hello there!" The handsome Cherokee softly greeted me!

"And a howdy to you sir!" quickly replying!"
"Miss, how about me walking to the top of this hill with you and your horse? Now, I'll have to go pretty slow, cause I'm not in good health, But, I believe I can make it!"

"Sure you can, and we'll take it slow if you want. Hold on to Nelly's bridle, she doesn't mind!" As, he reached for the side of her bridle, I could see from the looks of his unsteady and swollen hands that he wasn't a well Man. Taking short and slow steps, I admired this elderly Indian as we both tried to talk between our puffing breaths. He could be home in his bed, where its warm and dry, yet he chose to walk a little ways with me upon Our Foreparent's Trail of Tears. His wife and son waited for us in a Church driveway at the top of his destination. I was dying for a tobacco about then, but I dared not to mention this. I knew these were good Christians, my vice could wait. Then we four, and Nelly making five, stood there and talked of the sorrow that was brought upon our people. The missus suggested that we have prayer. As we stood there in a Circle, the Cherokee Husband spoke the prayer, chills went through my body as the skies let out a loud roll of thunder! "I thank you all so much for this special time you've given to me to show how much you care and understand," speaking softly as one would speak in church.

"You are so welcome, child, and we want to offer you our home to get in from the rain. It will probably set in for the rest of the day," the husband spoke between gasps.

"Thank you much anyway, but me and Nelly best try and get a few miles more.

"Well, " the wife answered softly, but with firmness, "Here is our gift. It's not much but there's our phone number and directions to our house. I'll come any time, day or night, should you need us." Then her words almost gave a hint of sadness about them. We all embraced once more. They patted Nelly then we parted.

"I will see that sickly man again one day," I spoke out loud to Nelly. "And it may be over a year or so but I just know that he will be alive I just know it." Took a tobacco break at a turn-off we needed to take. "Oh, those Virginia Slims never tasted so good! Right now the next best thing to a double cheeseburger, with double extra cheese and at least a pound of grease, would be a gallon of milk, Yea!" Nelly munched on tree limbs and I decided to look in the envelope. "This is unreal," squealing, to Nelly! "Those nice people gave us a ten dollar bill!" Nelly looked at me as if to say, " Mom, you just better save enough to buy me a root-beer." "I'm shaking that bush Nelly, and they don't deliver root beer to spoiled horses out here in the back roads. Let's go!"

A few miles later this young teenager roared his hot-rod by slightly swerved toward Nelly's rear end as to see if he could spook her. It didn't scare Nelly, but it surely pissed me off! The first time I tried to ignore this rude action but the second time was too much. "You crazy bastard!" I yelled. "Don't you have any better sense? If you harm my horse, I'll kick your ass in so many ways, you'll like every damn one of them." Now, as he speeds off again in the opposite direction. I actually felt a little better from that un-lady like outburst! Me and Nelly were both tired, yet this little episode just gave a much needed revitalizer! This fancy white car kept passing us real slow. Thinking to myself, "Well this is going to be higher class butt-hole!" Turns out it's the local High-Sheriff! I gave him a one line description of what just happened!

"Ah, hell," he lowly growled. "You can take that long gun you got there and shoot his ass, throw him in the back ditch, and I can pick him up after dark."

"You've got yourself a deal buddy," answering with a serious grin! We talked for a short while; he offered us his barn for the evening, but I still needed to gain a few more miles. Yet, much appreciation.

"Dying for a cold drink of water aren't we Nelly?" Her nudge answered me. Then just ahead I saw this elderly lady walking across the road to gather her mail.

"That's a pretty Bay horse you have there honey! Would you all like a good cold drink of water from my old well? I know that you're tired, and it's getting late and all, so if you want, you can use the barn for rest as well." These words of such a sweet offer sounded so good! And her voice was so sincere and fragile-like.

"Thank you so much, Ma'am,but we'll take you up on that water offer though the sun is now on the lower side of the sky, I'd like to get a few more miles in." She wished me and Nelly the best of luck as we slowly walked out of her drive. The sun was growing just as tiresome as me and Nelly were. I could hear her hooves dragging as loudly as my moccasins. Soon we'll find a barn, I prayed. Then I heard what sounded like songbird hello's. Upon the right side of the road in a pretty picture house sat two smiling winter year ladies! They offered refreshments and their nice shade trees for Nelly. Thanked them, but declined. We spent a few minutes of talk and I learned that they were sisters! They informed me that just over the small bank was an Exxon station, "Bless you and your horse both, child. And we pray that you make that journey with GOD'S speed!"

"Thank you my Ladies and do keep me in your Prayers!" I tried to answer gleefully, but I think my reply sounded more like weakness. "Words of truth!" I thought. "The Exxon intersection!" Me and Nelly walked around to the back of the store and this handsome man about my tender age of forty was about to get in his truck. "Hey mister?" I asked in my best Indian-Scarlet voice! Whenever I really want something this manner of asking always worked for me. Especially with Mama, Daddy and now with Mr. Bill! "Me and my horse, Nelly, we're dry as a bone! So would you be so kind as to return to that store and bring out three rootbeers?" With a grin as big as an opossum's he obliged me! I gave him a five-dollar bill, and he quickly returned with the ice-cold rootbeers and the money change. "I do thank you sir!" grinning big too! "And my Nelly thanks you too!"

"You mean that horse is going to drink a rootbeer?" he asked with a bit of confusion.

"She sure is!" I answered. By demonstration Nelly didn't waste any time putting down two bottles quickly! Afterwards she turns out her upper lip to show off her big horse-laugh!! About the midst of Nelly's performance, this lady pulls up and with a big smile, hands me the biggest peach I've ever seen!

"Oh, my child! I read about you in the paper and your desire to retrace your Ancestor's walk has really touched my Christian Heart!"

"Thank you ma'am!" reaching, as she was handing the peach.

We talked for a spell, but the sun was hugging the top of the timberlines now so we had to make our farewells! I got two whole bites of the peach! Miss Nelly savored the rest, without any hard feelings, of course! Crossed the narrow hard-top road and within a couple of hundred yards, we turn to the right to follow an old gravel road, when this nice, serene looking lady about my age stops. "Honey, you and your horse just have to be exhausted! I don't have a barn but just down this gravel road about a mile I think you can find a place for the night. I'm a Christian and my heart speaks that I should help you. Now I've got these groceries I need to get home right now, but I'll come back and find you. Now don't worry about a thing!"

"Thanks lady. We are so very tired and I'll be waiting for you." She gave effort to keep the gravel dust low as I watched her drive out of sight.

On this straight stretch of dusty gravel, Nelly was tending to stumble from tiredness and sharp stones piercing the frogs of her hooves. "Hold in there Nelly, a barn will show soon. Don't give up baby, not now."

Approaching, was three "Tom-Salyers" of the nineties! "Young fellows, could you all help me find a barn for the night?"

"Sure can," they all replied at once! Nice horse you got there ma'am. We been riding ever since the rain stopped. We have mean ponies, but we're tougher than they are! You gonna ride yours?

"No," I barely answered. "She is just to carry my pack. Are ya'll sure that you can find me a barn?" sounding impatient, knowing there was about a half an hour until darkness fell.

"Here's the place, ma'am! The old feller that lives here; well, he's just the care-taker and he can't hear very good, so we'll do the talkin' for you!"

Thinking to myself, this is a first! I'm allowing kids to do talk for me! Because I'm one of the world's worst to ever let someone else to do my speaking. But this time I'm just too darn tired. From around the little rundown weathered house came this elderly, small and wiry looking man bearing a wide, toothless smile. He asks, "Ma'am, that there hoss for sale?"

"No," I tiredly, answered.

"What's that?" He half yells, "I can' t hear too good, but I have the best barn around. It ain't mine, but I'm the care-man of it and you and your hoss sure can bed down here!" Me and Nelly followed the old man and three boys around the house to this old rusting, sagging barbed-wire gap. I chilled for a second when I saw the old gap all covered with poison-vine! Checking out the area, I couldn't figure out why there was a gap when there wasn't a fence around the pasture!

"Hush your crazy question's, Alethea," thinking to myself. "Just be thankful you and Nelly have a barn!" They led us to this greenish cattail pond so Nelly could get a drink. She spooked like she had been shot at, as if to inform me, "Excuse, me Mama, but I'll pass on the thirst quencher!" Now we check out the barn! Three-fourths dilapidated! Part's leaning in all four directions. Once there had been a roof, well, at least some sagging rafters without a tin-roof gave promise to withstand the night! No stall or door, but lots of old hay! "Thank ya'll so much! Now we need to rest." I watched the old man and boys head back toward the house and I started crying! "Oh, Nelly I'm so tired and hungry. Aren't you?" But these tears weren't going to fix this problem, First, I got the thirty feet of my rope and made her a make-shift door and stall. Took the load from her sweaty back, led her into the stall and rubbed her down real good. "We'll be alright, Nelly," I assured her!

Then I saw that lady that promised to find me! She approached with a big smile and open arms and had brought her daughter and grandson. We bid new greetings as we chose a cool seat upon the ground,

"Here, I thought you would be hungry," gently handing me a brown bag that held two bologna sandwiches and two cans of ice cold colas!

"Oh, how can I thank you enough?" answering with my mouth watering at the same time!

"Just enjoy honey. And be watchful here. Don't think I'll forget you. I'll return in the morning. Now try and get some rest. I know that you and your horse are completely given out."

"You're right," I agreed and we embraced. Cried again as I watched them slowly cross the field, fading out of sight. "Thank you, Our Great Spirit," I prayed out loud as I begin feeding Nelly her corn I'd brought along and myself at the same time! Had my flashlight out as I made last minute checks on Nelly and found my place upon the old dry-rotted hay, too tired to remove my moccasins. From the haystack I leaned over to give Nelly one more kiss goodnight. "Good night my horse! Osda usvʔi my sogwili!"

Laying there upon the old hay listening to Nelly breathe, going into a much needed sleep. I wanted to but I was too tired to sleep and just lay there and gazed at the silver, three-quarter moon. A great view with no roof! Now rested, with a full belly, I was glad there wasn't a roof! Wondered what Mr. Bill was doing right now? Is he missing me this bad too? Tears came into my eyes again, then I started praying hard to keep those tears at bay.

Just as I started to doze I felt such intense heat! "Now what is this? How can hay be so darn hot! Oh, that's just because it's so old! Shit! Me and Nelly could blow up! I've heard of old hay setting a barn on fire! Great! This is it. Haven't even started the Trail good and I'm going to die! Calm down Alethea, just get ahold of yourself, okay? Okay! Good! Got that mind-shock under control. WWWhat's TTThat!!!?? Something is biting me! Is it a flea? A bed-bug? In hay? Never heard of it! Ok, It's lice! Hell, it's all of them!"... I lost the battle. Tiresomeness overtook and sleep came, finding me with my hand up in the air trying to remove these mystery-bugs one at a time!

---

*Sat. Sept 5, 1992 - Left Princess at Red Barn around 10:30. Got home around 4::pm Tried to call Bull-man to find out where my woman was, but he didn't know. Probably camped in Woods.*

---

Early morning sun and Nelly licking my moccasins awakened me. "Am I alive Nelly?" Then checking myself I hadn't had a nightmare. Here is the living proof! Red bite places all over me. The bugs even found their way up my old long skirt! "Now what's the other itch? Oh no, poison vine!! This can't be, no! No, no!" Then I heard foot-steps!

"Ya got ya clothes on?" the little wiry-man whispered,

"Haven't had them off," I firmly answered.

"Are ya good and awake?" he hyena-laughed!

"Never have been asleep and what do you want?" keeping my voice steady. Then silence. I watched him scurry like a ground squirrel, crossing the heavy-dew field toward the house. Eased off the mystery-flea hay giving my personal opinion to the unwanted bed-mates and tried to stretch and scratch at the same time! I gave Nelly a good-morning kiss, seeing she was as stiff and looked as bad as me! Was well under way of repacking when my Angel-woman appears again!

"Good morning! Brought you some hot coffee and some egg sandwiches. Enjoy them while they are hot!"

"Thank you a thousand times!" answering with a tired grin and going for the coffee! Then I told her about my early-morning visitor! We had a good laugh and she remained there with me until my chore was completed. Walking with me back to the gravel road, she bid farewell again, speaking that she would meet me somewhere again right after she attended Church. Now, I'm in search of a creek so I can remove some poison here! Me and Nelly had walked about a mile when I heard the beautiful sound of fast moving Ama, (water)! Music to our ears! We then found our way down to this fast-moving creek. Time to strip again. As Nelly was filling her thirst, I was in search of the right spot for a healing process! First I had to look closely for many broken bottles and cast them aside. The cold water felt so refreshing as I shampooed my hair first! Next I tied Nelly just above me where her pawing and playing in the water would give me the muddy-stream I'd need to soothe and to medicate myself for the bites and poison vine! "Thank you,

Great Spirit, for the wisdom I have learned from my Mama to know that your muddy-ama is soothing medicine!"

Back to repacking, I choose this pretty long tan skirt that Mr. Bill had gotten for me at Wal-Mart just before leaving the Sacred Grounds. Refreshed, and I feel like a new woman! Then it dawns on me! "Wasn't that poison ivy me and Nelly just walked through heading back up to the gravel road?" My own positive answer, "Yes!"

Enroute again. Come to this intersection we're to turn right. Grandmother Sun (Ulisi Nvda), is growing hotter now! Nelly is stepping high again and I'm beginning to start scratching from the quick-to-work poison ivy! As we're turning this sharp corner onto another narrow hardtop road, I failed to see this partially covered hole! Down goes me, down goes Nelly and over the steep bank goes all her pack! We re-upright ourselves, then wait a second before we search each other's eyes, asking ourselves if we're Alright?! Shaken mostly, but I've torn this new skirt and it doesn't even have a mile on it! Nelly waits as I retrieve her pack. Nothing to it! I'm just out of breath, more dirty, and two more fresh tears in my Sunday Skirt! "We're even Nelly. I'm itching, new skirt torn and you have some red scratches showing there!" A firm nudge in my back was a fair reply!

After a couple more miles, we were crossing this concrete bridge that a beautiful swamp flowed beneath. There was the nice Peach-Lady and her husband-man! Delighted to see each other again and to meet her husband-man! She asks if she could take some pictures of me and Nelly! "Sure!" Then I was caught by surprise! This was one of those moving-kind of pictures. But it was fun and Nelly did her usual movie star routine! We chatted for awhile then they headed on to Church.

For the next several miles we met many nice people that

wanted to talk and take our pictures and pose with me and Nelly! Met an old Farmer looking for his cows. Reaching inside his pocket he pulled out a one dollar bill.

"Here lady, this is all I have on me, but I want to give it to you; can't tell, it may come in handy and I'm sorry for what the white people did to The Cherokee Nation."

"Thank you Mister, and if you like, I'll help you find your cows. I can take Nelly's pack off and she can climb that hill better than you can walking besides it's awfully hot!"

"No child, you be on your way. It will be a long journey. Just be careful and keep that gun you got on you close by." I watched him walk into the woods until he was out of sight. He reminded me of my Grandpa Adams, bib overalls and slow walk. My heart grew heavy for him. I remember our old cow would get out and I'd always go with pa to find her. Just to ride the cow back home was worth the limping walk to find her. "Goodbye Pa," I whispered, as me and Nelly went onward.

The Angel-Woman finds us again and brought along her brother and nephew. The men folk wanted to walk with me and Nelly to the Big-Water, "Blythe's Ferry." I spoke that they were most welcome to join in the Walk. Her brother could out walk my Nelly and she's a Tennessee Walker! We had many laughs and kept our spirits up by trading stories of our lives! Angel-Woman drove just ahead in her truck. Then we'd take breaks, so I could enjoy that good coffee she brought me! Much tired, we came upon this nice manicured Goat-Farm. Nelly seemed to want a drink real bad. The young man that lived there went over into his goat pasture and retrieves Nelly this five-gallon bucket of cold water. She takes two swallows and turns the bucket over with firm intentions! I gently scolded her, as she just gives a big horse-laugh, as if to say, "Excuse me, but I think I smelled goat's breath in your cold water Sir!" Much laughter, and moved on.

Finally! We have made Blythe's Ferry but kisses, lies, threats and love, weren't going to persuade Nelly to get on that Ferry!

She won! So the Angel-Woman made a quick trip. She knew this man back down the road, and he came to our rescue in his cattle-truck. Now she won't load! No, Mama has to walk in first. I do, And I make a grand slide into the fresh cow manure! "Thanks Nelly, I owe you one!" We bid farewells through the cow-truck-windows!

## BLYTHE'S FERRY

Cherokee detachment commander Choowalooka spoke in a letter to Captain Sam Henegar that all the Indians in the removal crossed the Tennessee River at the same location, called BLYTHE'S FERRY. This information was published in a Frankfort, Kentucky, newspaper on October 25, 1897. Reason for this documented information was due to many beliefs that the Cherokee-Removal had been crossed just north of Jolly's Island. This Cherokee Leader named John Jolly had adopted a white boy. He had ran away from his home in Tennessee. Reason? Nobody really knows for sure, but Samuel Houston found comfort and freedom in his new Indian Father's home on Chief John Jolly's own Island. Chief Jolly taught Sam the many ways of the Proud Cherokee. Gave him freedom to follow his dreams. The noted Chief also gave Samuel Houston an Indian name, "The Raven". Becoming of truth to live up to his Indian Name, Raven would play many parts of his life; everything from an admired Raven to a great politician.

Blythe's Ferry was built and operated by John Blythe. He began this Ferry business in 1809. Passed on for his son John Blythe to continue his father's business. The Ferry still bears the same name today. Though as I crossed in 1992, the owners were kind and didn't charge the fare to me and Nelly. At the present tense of history of the Blythe's Ferry, a huge bridge is being built. thus ending the long standing life of "BLYTHE'S FERRY".

After the Cattle-Truck-Man unloaded me and Nelly on the other side, we slowly made our way up the narrow winding road looking forward to reach the top of the mountain. Finally! As I rested and gazed behind us, overlooking the big-water we had just crossed, I felt this sadness come over me. Shaking the mystery-chills off, we walked slowly, dragging our feet. I'm praying for a place to find rest. The first dwelling we come upon gives off this energy of such strong warmth! This small little old-fashioned house set just off to the right side of the road. Many moon's old trees graced the yard. and well manicured, tall rose-bushes joined in harmony of color that adorned the picture of sweetness! "You sure have a pretty horse!" came this sweet little voice out of nowhere.

"Why, thank you!" answering, yet still searching, for this soft speaking of a woman. Then I spot her! Immediately she reminded me of Mama. I felt sad and happy at the same time! She was petite like Mama was, had her hair up in bobby-pin curls, a plain pair of slacks with a simple blouse. This woman I'm looking at puts me into a daze, allowing many pictures of Mama to blend in with the view.

"Where are you going?" Her question was as warm as her voice.

"Oh, I'm walking the "Trail Of Tears," replying quickly with a smile!

"Well, stop and rest awhile. I bet you have had a long day! So tie your pretty horse up there to that big tree and I'll get you something to drink!"

"Thank you ma'am, I'd love to take a good rest! And since it's getting late in the evening, do you know of a barn where me and Nelly could hold up for a few days? I have poison ivy really bad and would like to find a Doctor-Man and maybe get a shot and some Medicine?"

"Honey, you see that pretty fancy barn and that Big-House? Well I know the man that owns them and I'll go make a phone call and see about getting you all Fixed up! Now, I'm just the care-taker here but just relax and let me see what I can do!"

Quickly as a little Quail she dashed out of sight! I stripped Nelly down, loved and talked to her, assuring that all would be fine 'cause we have just met a nice lady that reminds me of a beautiful, "White Arrow!"

While resting, the Peach-Woman finds us again. This time I meet her Son and Daughter! They took more of those moving-pictures and we enjoyed each others company again! She had brought me a supper and Nelly Bly some corn! How thoughtful. And I thanked her and the family over and over! Then the Happy Hiwassees found me! Next, this pretty yellow haired woman arrives, She had been looking for me along the Trail. Introduced her Husband-man and their fourteen year old son. I gave her an autographed news-article that some one had given to me. After all my visitors had a prayer for me and Nelly they soon departed.

White-Arrow being a shy person, had remained in the background, then appears to inform me that the Big-House owner's secretary would soon be here to unlock the barn! "Thank you Great Spirit, and thank you White-Arrow!" I spoke loudly.

This secretary was a fancy type of woman as well as pretty. She brought along either her child or grandchild, I don't recall, but I do remember that the little two year old was in need of good manners in a bad way! Loaded with questions which is great, but the way she rudely asked them was pushing my nerves! "Stay calm, Alethea!" speaking to myself. I could easily lose a fancy, Raddison Hotel style barn here!

Now, the fancy woman has a deal! "All you have to do is sign this paper here. In turn it would relieve the owner of any responsibilities if you should get hurt and be held in response if anything should be damaged!" saying with this big smile yet avoiding my eyes; just keeping her stare toward the paper.

"Lady, do you mean to tell me that this white-man's paper is the MUST in order for me and Nelly to doctor and rest? What in the hell would I want to destroy anything for? Plus, I think it's all bullshit, but give it here," reaching for the little piece of hand-written white-man's paper with a firm and cold stare. She kept her fake smile as I signed then reached for the little spoiled brat's hand and sped away in her fancy sports car.

Again I thank White-Arrow for making this happen for me. She invites me to stay in her house after I get Nelly put up. I spoke of the appreciation, but felt it best that I stay with my Nelly. So, tired, elated, and pissed-off I drag me and Nelly to the Raddison-Barn and cuss as I struggle to unlock the big stall doors. "Nelly, honey, if you are going to smoke in your stall and it should make fire? Well, kick the water-bucket over on it!"

"WOW!" To my surprise, I figured the barn was nice but this was unreal! I turn on the lights! Much aglow! Turning Nelly loose to choose the one of five stalls for herself, she does, the one most close to where I threw all her pack down including my sleeping bag. That particular stall has a wasp's nest the size of a small hornet's nest! "Okay, Nelly, go ahead and choose that one but you better not stir them all up and cause me to have bee stings on top of this poison-ivy!" She answers with a big snort and bursts out of the stall kicking wildly with freedom!

Found two huge water-troughs. Nelly got one for drinking and I have the other to soak my itching body in. Just as soon as darkness falls, I make my pallet upon the clean and sweetest smelling hay I've enjoyed in a while. I'm reciting a poem I had written as I'm getting everything laid out, trying to keep my mind off that fancy-woman and the itch that is now turning into pain. Took a big swig of the Medicine Water, K&M. Now that darkness had come, its bath time! Off to the fancy bath-trough, AHH, yea, this is it! The cold ama felt so soothing, thought I'd just sleep there in it for the night. But what little sense I do have left warns me better! After about an hour of soaking and trying to keep Nelly out, I return to the sweet-hay and make the perfect barn-bed! Nelly was right there to keep an eye on me, so I give her a big kiss and hug, bid goodnight, and crawl upon my own special pallet! Said my prayers, thanking our Great Spirit for this Raddison-Barn in comparison to the flea-bug hotel we'd had the night before! Pain returned and sleep would not come. Sleep has always been an enemy for me, never a friend. "Why?" I ask myself. Will this problem ever leave me be???????

I'm so tired! I should be soundly asleep by now. Hell with this. Got up, went outside past the bathing-barrels and on over to the edge of the wooded pasture. This is much better! With Nelly right beside me we gazed toward the other side of the Tennessee River. The Moon shown brightly but left the banks far across lost in the shadows of darkness, allowing me to wonder how my people felt when they where driven to this point, waiting for the Blythe's Ferry? I started to get these certain mystical chills again. One could just see what it was like on this river many moons ago. On moonlit nights like this, young Cherokees met to plan when they would become married and what part of the village they would live in. Feeling freedom of life before them, she would tend to their home and garden. He would plan to hunt for their food and protect her from any enemies of other Tribes. Didn't the handsome Raven (Ka/Lanu) play along these banks and swim the river many times just to show his strength and display his adventurous disposition, bringing the maidens to such admiration and full of laughter just for him? Seems the water (Ama) still ripples with the frolics that Raven and Chief Jolly's niece, beautiful Talihina, made as they swam about the shores! "We shall always be together, Talihina," Raven would closely whisper in her tender ears!

Did Sequoyah often ponder along these water ways to rewrite or figure a better way to develop the Cherokee Alphabet? Are the Spirit's of our Cherokee People restless tonight, perhaps wanting me to know that they, long ago on this River Shore, sat quietly and heard "The Message In The Wind"? Just perhaps the SHAMAN'S does .... and their Spirit's still do....

After a real good cry, tears for my people, tears for friends and family, and tears for my Mr. Bill, my heavy heart grew much lighter and me and Nelly slowly walked back to our lodging.

---

*Sun. Sept. 6, 1992 - Called Bull-Man. His wife said Princess was seen Sat. afternoon on Hwy 58. That's all I can find out. At 9:pm Mr. Hiwassee called, said Princess stayed in barns Sat. & Sun. night. Got Nelly across ferry in stock trailer. Staying in barn with fire-wires and running water. Said Nelly wouldn't go onto the ferry, so some man took them across in his stock-trailer.*

---

White-Arrow's gentle knock upon the barn door awakened me, bringing hot coffee and a bright morning smile! "I couldn't sleep at all, for thinking of you up here in this barn and me having a good bed, so I just slept on the sofa!"

"Sorry, White-Arrow, was quite a spell before I could sleep too! But, thanks to much praying, Sweet-Sleep did finally come. And Wada (thanks) for the coffee!"

"Make a deal with you," she cheerfully spoke while bidding Nelly good morning with a gentle pat. "Come on down to the house and accept a gift and I won't complain anymore about you sleeping in the barn with your horse!"

"Okay, you got it," answering with a forced smile, due to the ivy-pain that now felt like a broken bone.

Fed Nelly, kissed her, then we headed toward the house. Already I could smell real home-cooking just like Mama's! But I couldn't keep myself from reaching out to touch the morning dew that adorned her handsome roses that gave the appearance of an ocean of diamonds! Entering her home was like being home. First I noticed the large picture of Jesus on the wall, many family pictures and treasures about the way leading into the kitchen. White-Arrow's home had all the energies of warmth, love and memories never to be forgotten... As she directed me to the best seat at her kitchen table, tears clouded my eyes. Just as soon as we were seated she gave one of the most touching Graces I've ever heard.......

We embraced each other as if we'd known each other all our lives. Then we started trading our many stories. She spoke of how much her husband-man adored Indians. Oh, how I felt so much at home! I told her of my life-long dream to walk the Trail Of Tears, and how I liked to paint pictures and write poetry, Then she asked me if I could recite one of my poems! "Sure!" delighted that she wanted to hear one. So I searched my mind to find the poem to fit this special occasion. "White-Arrow, this is one that was inspired by Mama and its called the "Old Kitchen Table."

"OLD KITCHEN TABLE"

At the old kitchen table,
Mama, first said to me,
"Life ain't a bed of Roses
And don't take nothing free."

At the old kitchen table,
We'd shove as we set down.
All first for Mama's biscuits
Then we'd pass them all around.

At the old kitchen table
we laughed and we cried
Once we made a bed there,
When my favorite puppy died.

At the old kitchen table,
For ironing, it was handy.
And Daddy, he found room there
Just to make us 'tater-candy.

So now, that you are here my friend,
Won't you hear a joke, or a fable?
And pull yourself up a chair
At our old kitchen table.

White-Arrow was in tears, "Oh, honey, that's so pretty!" she cried! "Thank you White-Arrow! and I'll never forget this morning as I walk through this world!"

She wouldn't allow me to help her with the dishes but asked me to get my dirty clothes and she would wash them for me. I couldn't decide if this woman was an older sister or a new Mama. After clothes were busy cleaning themselves, she took me up to the Big-House and we walked toward the back yard. There, a perfect view of the Island! We traded more stories. She told of the many thieves that robbed graves from Jolly's Island and I tried to set real still so I wouldn't hurt so much, then recited another poem.

ROBBERS OF OUR GRAVE
SPOKE THE SHAMAN

In Northern Tennessee, out in a field
To visit a grand old mansion and a man.
His woman cooking a meal.
They spoke of the Spirits
Evil stories they told
But I laughed with the Spirits!
An' found the living ones cold.

'Cause a spirit Shaman appeared
To give me wisdom from the past.
We admired the Shaman's treasures
Through the white man's locked glass.

We gazed about the big walls
Adorned of platinum, silver and gold.
"No understand?" the Shaman pointed
An' this lesson I softly told!
It's all of music as you once sung
But in forms of roundness, not of the tongue.

Then we strolled down to the river
"Laughing", as he pointed where we walked.
"This is the place child,

I heard the Ama first talk!"

Next to a distant and deserted yard
with a wigwam out back.
"Now here's all the right poles,
but what is this cover sack?
No hides of Ani-Kawi or buffalo back?"

Child, please bring me my pipe
From that fancy chest.
I must share you more wisdom
As we smoke tobacco and rest.

I then bowed my head
With shame I couldn't understand
When I had to admit
We would need a key from the white-master's
hand.

With those hurting words
Brought tears to our eyes
Then the white master appeared
to appoint me Good-bye.

But one quick last touch
With our spiritual embrace
I cried to the Shaman
"They still rob your grave!"

"Yes, that I am seeing."
As he looked toward the sky,
"Hear the Great Spirit Calling?
Child please dry your eyes."

"Yes, my Shaman." as I was pulled away
My heart feeling heavy and low.
"My child I see them cast you from this sacred
place,
But wisdom shall forever flow in your soul."

"You're in too much pain" she said, wincing as if she could feel it too. "Why don't you let me take you into Dayton, just a few miles away, and we'll go to the emergency-room. Now come on!"

No fight here, "Yes, big-sister, I'll go!"

Made it! Eighty-five dollars later, including a shot and pills to go, we head back to her home. "White-Arrow, I have a feeling, the Wind speaks there is someone at your home."

"You're probably right my dear. Now relax, we'll soon be there."

Upon our arrival, there in front of the barn sat, Mrs. Hiwassee, Medicine-Water Woman, along with other friends I'd made along the Trail so far! We all had a nice visit. Then White-Arrow's son arrived. It had been awhile since she had seen him! After all company departs, we rest, while I'm soaking my pain-itching body in her water-hole (bath-tub)!! As the sun was fading from the September sky, I was preparing for my night in the Raddison-Barn when White-Arrow ask if I would like to meet the Lady-Owner of the Big-House? "Sure!" though still feeling poorly. I walked up to this mansion on the hill! There I meet the Lady-Owner. Seems she and her brother inherited the old home-place when their parents passed away. What a friendly and warm face she bestows upon our greetings. "Seyo," I spoke to her.

"This means "greetings" in Cherokee!"

"And Seyo to you," warmly replying. She lived elsewhere but returned to the old home-place, as a summer visit. On this occasion many of her friends had joined her. Everyone was most nice. We talked and laughed out on the veranda for quiet a while! White-Arrow was down at the barn within seven-hundred feet of the veranda trying her best to keep Nelly calm. I could hear Nelly squeal each time that she heard my loud laughter! I was really enjoying these nice people until this one woman must have had too much to drink. She spoke something I felt a bit uncouth. I bid goodnight and went back to the barn, but still thanking the nice owner-lady. White-Arrow was waiting for me. Informed me how Nelly would run whenever she heard my voice and true tears would come from my Nelly's eyes.

As I was climbing onto my sweet hay-pallet, White-Arrow made the statement that she had never slept upon hay before! "My sister, you must try it sometime in your life! And it's the best bed a crazy, wandering, Indian woman could ever have!" As she left the barn, I thanked her for all she had done for me today, and she is for sure in my prayers (Adadolisdi).

"You are so welcome, Alethea, and I've never met anyone quiet like you. Don't forget. Hot coffee in the morning!"

"You have a deal!" I promised, already growing sleepy.

After early morning coffee at White-Arrow's warm kitchen, she had to depart for work. Told her I'd be there when she got home but I must start re-packing. I was healing well, Nelly was quite rested, so we must journey on. We felt sadness as she left for work. I tended to Nelly, re-packed and straightened up the house for my friend. Then someone knocked on her door around eleven a.m. This nice good-looking elderly gent identified himself, spoke that he had been looking for me on the trail, and as he crossed the Ferry, they informed him of my where-abouts. I served him coffee, spoke of my holding-up reason and we crossed many Fields and Streams in talk. He asked me to autograph an article for him. I did. Though I still feel sort of an oddness about this. "Who am I? Nobody famous, just a determined woman making a lifelong dream come true." Yet he insisted I take the gift of twenty dollars, and he took pictures of me and Nelly! Such a gracious man. And as he left, I prayed that he would make it safely back to Cleveland, Tennessee. "We'll meet again Mr. Harcourt," I spoke with a big smile!

When White-Arrow comes in from work, she ask if I would stay one more day to make sure that I was healed well from my poison ivy. She would go into work late! "I'll try," answering. "I have the walking fever. Now I know what the term really means!"

"Thank you, Great Spirit, I'm ready to go!" In front of the barn were Mrs. Hiwassee, Medicine-Water woman and a few others who helped me ready for my journey! White-Arrow had informed the Sheriff of me going across his county so they could help watch for me. We ladies were just laughing and holding tears too, as the Sheriff and his Deputy pulls up! I was refilling my K&M jugs, and Nelly was putting on her horse laugh downing her share!

"Hello there!" smiled the Sheriff and his partner, extending their hands to greet me! What are you ladies doing this morning?"

"We're boot-legging!" I answered with a big grin! "And I have some real tasty medicine-water here, want a little taste?"

"Well," he stutters, as if to ask himself, 'Is she joking, or does she maybe have a bit of fire-water! "Yea, give me a little snort!" I handed him the jug, and he took a big swig of the K&M.

"Not bad. Really its good!" He chuckled as he passed it to his Deputy for his approval. Don't think the Deputy liked the taste. His smirk and grin at the same time gave his opinion away!!! But we all had a big laugh and the Sheriff was kind enough to Deputize me and gave me this card to carry should I have any problem's with anyone.

"Thank you kindly sir, I'll be sure to mention about this in my book at the end of my journey!" answering, with a soft and admiring smile,

"Lady you are the only woman to attempt this long trip by yourself. And I just want to speak that I admire you. Also, it's sad for what happened to our Cherokee People. Just please be careful and keep your gun handy at all times. I hope you do write a book about your trip. With your personality, its bound to be real good story!"

"Thanks again Sheriff, and I bet you five dollars that you really did think that I had fire-water a while ago!" He just grinned, shaking his head as we shook hands again. Then he and his Deputy slowly drove away.

Was noon by now. Sun was much hotter but I didn't mind because I had the upper-hand on that damned poison ivy. Mrs. Hiwassee and Medicine-Water Woman was going to follow me and Nelly as far as Dayton. Know that town! "They serve good Ivy-shots!"

As me and Nelly took the lead, I waved to White-Arrow as she eased by heading to work. Kept thinking about her suggestion on Nelly's behalf. She had spoken that she felt it would be best if I had Nelly sent back home because it would become awfully much of danger once I started over the Dayton Mountain. I'll know my answer by the time I reach Dayton. Prayers and the Wind tell me.

Took one break with my friends during the walk to

Dayton. The Mail-Woman stopped me. Wanted my autograph on many little pieces of paper. "Sure." I answered, but still, in my mind I can't figure out just why people want it. Still think it should be the opposite way. "I should be getting their autograph." Nelly is doing fine. By now we both have learned to match our walk and she has learned to avoid the bottles, on the narrow road shoulder. We are working so well together. I'd miss her company and help.

Once, when I had to pee real bad, she blocked the view of the road traffic while I stood there to find relief! There is an advantage to not wearing those damn panties! Several! Well, the road-view for one, never had an infection they call a yeast. Plus, just think of all the money a woman will spend on those pretty little matching panty-sets? And just two years ago, when I was living back in the mountains for the last seven years, I'd go Raccoon (Kvhli) hunting with the good-old boys, took a leak just like them, standing up!

Rambling in my mind again just seeking all the excuses I can to keep Nelly with me, a non-autograph-seeker comes to a halt and just about puts me and Nelly against a fire-wire-fence!

"Hey there pretty woman! Would you like to go out on a date with me tonight? I'll, buy you a big steak if ya want it. Now what do you say about that?"

"I say, you nasty, dirty looking ass-hole, you better get that damn rattle-trap car and wire a muffler on it, and get the hell out of my face before I take this fire-wire that's trying to kiss my ass, and tie you up with it. Plus that will be done when I strip you naked! GET outta here. NOW!" I hollered! He took off like Grant took Richmond! What makes it even worse he didn't even speak of Nelly! Probably didn't even see her! The foul smelling gila (dog) dung!!!!!

Nelly is a Tennessee Walker, and right now I'm a Red-neck Walker! Boy I'm pissed! Now who's this? Turned out to be this woman I call Leather-Jacket. She wanted to have council with me when I got to Dayton, "Fine," I firmly answered. Something doesn't feel right. "I'm listening, GREAT SPIRIT, for your "Message in the Wind."

## DAYTON, TENNESSEE

In 1820 this small town was called "SMITH'S CROSSROADS". The engineers of the Cincinnati, Ohio Southern Railroad had built a bridge across the swift moving creek, therefore, feeling they had the right to change Smith to Dayton. Just as the pre-stages of removing the Cherokee People, the white-man had his own foul taste in his mouth concerning his own rights, the pre-stages of North and South, Civil War, which would come years later. And still devoted Cherokee would lose their lives in this Battle too, fighting for the South.

Another interesting change took place here in this town and is still spoke about today. The Monkey-Trial! I found this title of words quite interesting, and inquired about the original off-spring concerning Smith's Monkey-Town! Appears a Biology Teacher was trying to project to his class that the evolution of Man came from a monkey! This caused a great up-roar amongst the parents and the Town's folk. Now a political-posse was rounded up to bring in this crazy teacher, Mr. John T. Scopes, to a trial of sorts. This took place in the moon of hot July, 1925. The trial lasted eleven days. The Rhea County Prosecutor, William Jennings Bryan took the stance against Mr. Scopes. The monkey-evolution-man lost. But in his own way he won. Because five days after the trial was over the silver-tongued Procecuting Attorney Bryan died. Five years later, 1930, the town built a small college high upon a hill overlooking the community, this being their dedication to this man, thanking him for removing the evil thoughts from the Monkey-Teacher's mind!

Today the town has a population of about seven thousand and the working people's income takes long, hot hours each day in the many small manufactures ranging from textiles, electrical appliances to sewing factories, or making those big Easy-Chairs (Gasgilo). Mr. Bill has been wanting one of those! I'll keep this in mind.

Thought Nelly might spook a little as we crossed the busy intersection. Wrong! She strutted as if she was the Lead in the Rose Bowl parade! Found the industrial park alright. Mrs. Hiwassee, Medicine-Water Woman and Blossom were waiting for me! I stripped my Nelly Bly down so she could rest and cool off. Then came Leather-Jacket and some photographer friend of her's. I tied Nelly to a tree right beside the table where we all gathered. But had to visit the bathroom which was only a few yards away. But just as soon as I was out of her sight she began to twist, squeal and make circles around the tree! Upon my return, we all had a good laugh.

Kept feeling this Bad-Message and we were all trying to talk when this elderly woman that lived just across the ditch outside of the park was mowing her grass. Actually, I was admiring the woman because I am afraid of a lawnmower and pray I never have to use one! Quite suddenly she stopped and yelled at me over the noise of that machine, "Woman, does that park owner know that you have a horse in his nice park? You know its going to mess up his park! And use the bathroom in it too!" Waiting for my answer, with a hateful stare from her eyes of coldness, I stood up to address my elder!

Putting my hands on my hip, "Lady, I'm tired and my horse is too. Personally, I don't think the owner-man knows if we are here! And for your information, I don't give a shit what you think or anyone else thinks. So you turn off that damn machine and hush, or mow you grass and leave me the hell alone!" I kept standing, waiting for her reply, hands on my hips, legs parted, indicating stance and my big long skirt and long hair blowing in the wind, looking wild as a woman of the West, with my long gun strapped to my right side! She quickly turned her machine off and went inside her house, never to be seen again!

After the scene, I made the remark out loud, "That woman might have liked me, or at least my horse!" All laughed.

Then Leather-jacket asks if we could have council. "Sure, speak here in front of my friends."

"Well," she began slowly, "We have a real good deal for you. Me and my photographer here would like to take some moving-pictures of you and follow you on the trail from time to time. We can make a real good moving-documentary of you! The thing we would need is about eight thousand dollars to make this for you. So, what do you think? Mr. Bill would pay this for you, wouldn't he?"

I took my time moving my eyes towards her's. Then prayed for the wisdom to stay out of jail, 'cause my patience was over, between the Lawnmower woman and this leather-jacket-leech; and knowing that "8" speaks "BEWARE! "Leather-Jacket? Do I look like the biggest and dumbest fool woman that you've ever met? Now, look close. Hell, I'm the one Walking the Trail Of Tears, you're riding around in a fancy car. If you want to take those pictures, then tough it out the way my People did and walk too. Plus, where in the hell do you get the idea I or Mr. Bill should pay YOU money when if anybody should get anything, YOU should be paying ME! Now, get the hell out of my face before I go on the war-path, MOVE-IT-NOW!!!" Grabbing their bags and displaying red faces, they departed with speed of a common thief! "Does anybody see the law coming for me?"

Everybody laughed, answering "No!"

Calmness returned. Then this pretty golden-haired woman shows up with her husband-man. She had Lupas and was now taking the K&M. Sweetness was all about this woman of youth. They had gifted me with an Indian-print shirt and earrings that he had made for me. I thanked them so kindly! As the evening wore on, I asked for a vote concerning Nelly. Are the mountains really steep and no shoulder to walk upon. They all assured me that's truth. So Mrs. Hiwassee calls Mr. Hiwassee and he and the Fancy-Horse-Trailer Man show up to take my Nelly and a lot of pack to the Hiwassee's farm back near Rattlesnake Springs. They will keep her safe for me. I had to load her and in doing so I knew this was the best for her but my eyes swelled up with tears. As I kissed her good-bye, I promised to return.

In between the escapades that took place earlier, a young lady from the newspaper had shown up at the park to take pictures of me and Nelly! So I would at least have the picture of her to carry since she had to return. Then this older lady shows up to interview me. "Fine," I speak. "Just make sure that you write with truth!"

We got half of the interview finished then planned to meet at the park at the same place tomorrow morning. Many people invited me to spend the night with them, but White-Arrow had arrived by now and she made it happen for me. Tired and lonesome for Nelly-Bly, finally sweet sleep overtook the sadness in my safe little corner of an old deserted room that White-Arrow had arrainged for me. I would be safe!

---

*September 8, 1992 - Princess called from Dayton, Tennessee. Afraid Nelly can't make the mountain narrow shoulders. Poison ivy getting better. Good night Princess and I love and pray for you.*

---

By 7 A.M. I was at the park, waiting on the lady to finish the interview. Meanwhile I condensed my packing. Just had the bare necessities all crammed into a small back-pack that Mrs. Hiwassee and Medicine-Water Woman had gotten for me at Wal-Mart the evening before. Called Mr. Bill at the phone that was attached to the picnic table. Damned thing was messed up and we kept getting cut off. Being irritable, nervous, and lonesome, I gave the operator my opinion of that telephone!! Finally got to update Mr. Bill and tell him how much I loved him and missed him something awful. We both cried and laughed!

---

*Called Princess this morning in Dayton, Tennessee. Had a Bad connection. She leaves Dayton this morning heading up her first mountain. Dayton police made her a deputy. Said she would call if close to phone.*

---

Mrs. Hiwassee calls me at the phone booth. Just wanted to make sure that I was alright. Had my Indian-Blanket around me. The air was a bit cool yet I figured this cool air would make it more easy to climb that Dayton mountain!

Still upset about that thieving Leather-Jacket and getting restless waiting for that Reporter. Finally she shows! Was kind of her to bring me some donuts and coffee! Sad thing is, I can't eat the donuts due to my low blood- sugar. This is all I need, to fall asleep while walking! But I thanked her anyway and we had a comfortable interview! She spoke that she was an artist too and would like to paint a portrait of me. I was most obliged!

As I head across town toward the mountain, my right knee begins to hurt. "Oh, no! You can't go out on me now!"

This being the leg I had polio in. I would have to relearn how to pace myself to walk. It was different when walking with Nelly and she was my security blanket (Unegvhaʔi) too.

Damn this pack is heavy! I then came upon a sign that spoke this was the "Trail Of Tears Route". That made me feel a bit less burdened! Wow! That mountain looks long! "It is dummy", I'm talking to myself as I prod onward.

Took a break at the half-way point. Two young gentlemen pulled over to wish me luck and said a prayer for me! Thanks, I thought, as I moved on up the mountain. I can see the top now! "Thank you Great Spirit!" Now a van pulls to the opposite side of the road. Out gets this beautiful, tall and soft speaking woman that's about my age.

"Howdy!" she begins with a big smile! "My name is Pearl, and I have been looking for you everywhere! Are you alright? Is there anything I can get for you?"

"I'm fine, but thank you for caring, and your name, Pearl, fits you!" My answer brought tears to her eyes. Felt sorta bad for a second.

"Now, just a ways from here, my aunt lives, and we want you to visit and eat with us!"

"Okay, I would be glad to!" answering with a returning smile! Watched her turn around and head back up the mountain. I got this second wind now, due to this Beautiful Pearl of a woman! Imagine how my people felt as they were driven like cattle up this mountain. Nobody asked if they needed anything...Just a lash of a whip, or a kick from a soldier's boot. A young woman being jerked aside and raped by the soldier. "Prayers" their own "Silent Prayers" were all they had. Adadolisdi (Prayers).

Just as I topped the mountain this young, red haired man rode a four-wheel machine across the road towards me. I was on guard! Then suddenly I felt good energies coming from him.

"Miss, my parents saw you walking earlier today and I saw you on the television". As he was speaking, he reached out his hand to offer a shake. I offered mine as well but thinking, "Was I on the television"?

"I admire your courage, ma'am. And I'm ashamed for what my race has done to your Foremothers and Fathers. Please allow my Prayers for you and you will make the journey, I just know that you will."

"Thank you sir!" as our hands released. "And thank you for your Prayers, I will need them. Bless the way your heart beats for my People," I know sadness was in my voice, but had no control. Waved as he drove away. I blinked back tears.

The sun was beating down upon me with all its heat! Thinking, I really need a recharge! I'm hungry and I need to take just a little break when this long station wagon pulls to a stop. I'm eyeing these shiny red and yellow tomatoes when this older friendly man speaks!

"Howdy! Would you like a good juicy tomato? I know who you are!"

"Thank you sir! Yes, I would love one of your big juicy tomatoes! If it's alright, I'll take one of those big yellow ones!" My watering mouth was trying to out-do my growling stomach!

"Honey, take all you want, and here's you some salt too!"

"Oh, thank you sir. Just one will do. Okay, I'll take two yellow ones!" This left my whole body happy, I kept waving until he was clean outta sight! "Thank you, Great Spirit!" Much Wada!

Now, a body gets one desire filled then needs another! I needed to pee, real, real bad! Saw this old country store and spied the toilet out back! This was a fancy Threads and Lace Store. So I inquire to this petite, laughing-face type of elderly woman. She reminded me of a Curly-Maple-Leaf!

"Ma'am," I speak kinda quietly! "May I use your toilet?"

"Why sure honey! " Her voice was even curly!

"Thanks" Then I made a dash toward the back!

Afterwards we talked awhile. Felt great to rest. I admired all the work she had put into a million stitches of dolly clothes and quilts! She spoke of her son, wished he was here. He and his Cherokee Indian woman just live down the road a ways. "Well ma'am, thanks again! "And I moved on.

I see the beautiful Pearl again! She was out beside the road waiting for me in front of her aunt's house! We made our introductions. The aunt had just gotten out of the hospital that day but had made this good homemade vegetable soup that she wanted me to share. We all prayed, then ate. I met the Aunt's husband and her brother too! All such nice people! We talked much about the Trail Of Tears and they spoke of the wagon-train that went by there a couple of years ago. They took many pictures and really liked my gun, Bonnie! Many thanks, and after warm farewells, I started out again.

Just back on the road, keeping a steady pace and watching the skies that were giving a promise of a shower. Suddenly, two men pulled over facing me. They had me in a ditch and bellowed out, "Indian where's your horse and whiteman?" Noticed they were migrant workers and as he nastily spoke, I could smell his rotten teeth. By now I'd fallen backwards in the ditch due to the weight of my pack. Trying not to show how scared I was, I replied as I eased my hand toward my gun, "Do I look like I need a horse and a whiteman?" firmly answering,

"Yeah, bitch, you need what we have for you!" laughing

and starting to open his truck door.

"Listen up men and move it, or I'll blow your frigging heads off your worthless bodies! You better make it easy on yourselves!"

The passenger hollered to his buddy, "Fool, that damn woman has a gun. Let's get the hell outta here!"

I stayed put as they sped away, looking back at me then giving me the finger-sign.

Took a few minutes to collect myself. Saying my prayers I got up slowly and moved on. My legs were quivering and my body drenched from fear.

Cloud's getting darker! Noticed this country gas station but didn't feel good energies from it. Gotta take a chance, I thought. It's going to rain, hard!"

"Howdy ma'am!" smiling to this grim-faced woman about my age.

"Could I wait out this storm that's coming? Already three big raindrops have hit my face and I think it's going to be a real one!"

She gave me a stare that matched her stale moon-pies, then began to answer. "Well, er, well, its a free country, er I, er."

"Forget it woman," interrupting her, "I've had my share of bullshit today and I don't need anymore!" Gave her a fake smile and slammed her screen door.

Walked about one eighth of a mile and saw Morgan's Body and Gas Shop. Thought of the Justin-Morgan Horse story and tried again! Saw the two young men sitting there seemed of warmth! "Sir there's a big storm coming. May I sit it out here in your business place?'

Answering with an honest smile, "You sure can lady, and you're right. I think it will be a real storm, come on in!"

I had no more removed my pack and gun belt when all

cut loose! Within ten minutes I was helping them mop up the water that was rushing through under the door. We got flooded out of that part of the station! Then in runs the owner's missus and we all head for the mechanic part of the station. At least its ten inches higher! As the storm grew more wild, more people were on their way to the mechanic room! Then much hard hail-balls started falling! I wrapped myself in my Indian Blanket and found about five-tire stack to crawl up on. I'm in the back and as the other people pour in, nobody really noticed me for a while.

But the two old-timers that stood near the open kept saying, "Hell, I've lived in these parts all my life and I ain't never seen a hail and rain storm like this. Have you?"

His friend agreed that he hadn't either! "But what the hell did bring this kinda storm, you reckon?"

About then one nudged the other and nodded his head toward me there upon my tire-perch all Indian-Wrapped!

"What do ya make of that?" The first one spoke with an unwelcome look, "Maybe she brought this big storm! Hell, I don't know, do you?" Keeping his stare on me he just shook his head to give a "no" for an answer.

"Great Spirit, help me, please!" I prayed to myself!

Within a few minutes the hail and rain stopped. Only the thunder left a promise to bring another one, shortly. I made the move toward the Entrance, when the nice owners said, "Just stay here, and wait the next one out, besides its getting late!"

"Thanks, I really mean this, but I'll take my chances. Again, I appreciate the shelter." Gave a wave and a smile but felt the eyes of the two old-timers upon my back that left an inside chill!

Trenchers of ama had poured mud across the road. There was no shoulder for me to walk and my moccasins were flopping leather. Thinking to myself, 'Lord, I'm due for a change!" So to ready myself for the next one, I started singing a song I had written when I was in the Air Force!

LORD I'M DUE FOR A CHANGE

Like a ragged leaf in the wind,
and like a beggar on the street,
Just like a child, that has no name,
Lawd, I'm due for a change.
Just like a train with endless tracks,
An' like a night, that has no end.
Like too much time spent in the rain
Lawd I'm due for a change.
The way lonesome cries in the night,
A wayward soul begs for a friend.
Like muddy water over-flows it's banks,
Lawd I'm due, yes I'm due, for a change...

This calmed me down a little. Then I saw this handsome looking gent just standing there in front of his van. He greeted me with a smile and said, "You met my mama earlier! She owns that store where one can buy quilts and etc., looked for you due to the storm coming. Thought I might find you during this storm-break! Hop in, we just live off the road here a couple of miles!" As he was opening the door for me, I thanked him kindly. After a few miles, we came to their home. They had added on to a trailer nestled back into the woods. A place of serenity.

His Cherokee woman came out to greet me with a warm hug and a big smile and I met all the animals! The storm had started again so we barely made it inside! We talked of our life ways, and after the storm passed we walked about their property. He said the old Trail Of Tears went right by this area. I feel there were many Trails, don't you?"

"Yes," he agreed, "Over the years of time many things change." It was growing much later now and at their insistence, I agreed to spend the night. The man prepared this B.L.T. like I have never tasted! He spoke that he enjoyed cooking! His woman said she was only fourth-Cherokee, but would like to learn the ways of old again. My suggestion was, go into the mountains ALONE and much knowledge will come to you. I added that I had done this, and remained in the mountains alone for seven years. The fragile, dark skinned and tender looking lady just looked at me with her forlorn eyes. "I'll never get a chance to do something like that but I wish I would have the nerve and guts to do just what you are doing now."

"One just has to believe and Pray. Then all that you ask for will come in time," speaking gently and patting her arm. After supper and long conversation, my body was shutting down, I asked if I could bathe? Afterwards a sofa never looked so great!

Next morning she dropped me off just where he had picked me up. We prayed there in front of the Church. Was still dark and she had to go to work, I think in a sewing-factory. I thanked her again and waved as she went out of sight. Even though she couldn't see me, I know she could feel my waving. I somehow felt sad for her. "Odalvˀi (mountain), remember the odalvˀil," I spoke into the darkness alone.

Since I was right there in front of a Church, I had a good long praying. I prayed for the young woman I had just met, I prayed for everything and everyone I knew. I felt spellbound to pray. This is a Message in the Wind.......

But Nature called so I walked on above the Church and

strained my eyes to spot any poison ivy as I stepped through a wire fence, Now, I need Nature's toilet paper! Let me scan the sky-line here, select the leaves from a tree. Therefore I won't have that ivy plague again!! Yeah! I found a good looking tree. Chose some cool leaves from it, and all's fine. Well, I thought, it will be about twenty more minutes or longer before its daylight enough for me to see to walk. I pulled out three of my Virginia Slims! Oh how I love that tobacco! Knowing I wouldn't have another one until the end of today's walk, I might as well enjoy these!

Think of all our Cherokee People that loved their tobacco (Jola) But couldn't have any when on this Death and Tear Walk? Jola is not only for one's pleasure, but its a Sacred and Blessing plant. Whenever we would move to another mountain shack, Mama always blessed the shack with her jola. "This will keep the evil spirit away," she would whisper, as if not to awaken them until she had the jola sprinkled. Then the spirit of darkness was helpless.

Ayv ganvdiʔa nihi Uji. (I miss you Mother.)

## PIKEVILLE

It's all down hill I heard. This will be an easy walk going to Pikeville! I feel great body-wise, but something is upon my mind just lingering there.

Whoa! What's that? Never had an itch like this before! Yes, I had an itch where the sun doesn't hit very often! I know I didn't use poison-ivy so what is it. Stopped to give myself a real good scratching! That's better. Again? Shit, here comes a truck. Hurry truck-man if only you knew how bad I got to scratch! I hugged the rock cliffs as I slither around them. There's no place to walk except in the narrow winding mountain road and traffic is growing heavy now. So I'm in and out of the back-ditch and rubbing my behind against a rock every chance I get! Then it dawns on me! Mountain Laurel, that's the only tree that I'm allergic to. Might as well take it like a man! So I start singing! "She'll be itching down the mountain when she comes! She'll be itching 'round the mountain when she comes. Yeah, boy!!!!!

Finally reach the flat-land! When you are walking down a steep mountain you have to readjust your body due to the heavy backpack. New walkers don't know this, especially me! The flat land is another adjustment one must make. I'm learning by now! The Pikeville sign comes into sight. Oh! I'll have a cup of coffee somewhere, then head on. Its still early in the day and this is a beautiful state. Just like my old Kentucky!

"Good Morning, Pikeville, Tennessee," I find the little town filled with much history. Saw a sadly deserted mansion. There was a neat looking elderly lady sweeping off the porch at her Bed and Breakfast establishment. I wave and speak a big hello! She looks at me for a second then turns her back. "What did I do!" I thought. Must be the way

I look! There! A real little cafe! Oh! I can just smell the coffee! Fumbled my way through the door. Everyone seems to be friendly! "I'll have coffee please," as the smiling waitress quickly served me. Then we got to talking and I told her what I was doing. This really touched her. Then my tummy decided it was hungry, so I ordered the nine-yards breakfast! Biscuits, gravy, three eggs, and a large order of bacon! Kept squirming in my seat to relieve this constant laurel-itch, hoping that nobody detected! Had my feet propped up in the other seat of a booth all to myself and I'm going to eat like an old coon-dog that's been out running all night! Much better! "Where is your bathroom ma'am?"

"Honey, just walk outside and turn to the left."

"Thank you!"

As I let my feet down to move. They wouldn't! Oh, my right foot just went to sleep on me, that's all. But I had to literally shove my foot to make each step. Immense pain set in and this worried me now. A sleeping foot doesn't behave this badly. But I fought the look of pain from my face. Didn't want anyone to see just how bad I was hurting. Was all I could do to get back to my seat. Paid my bill and stiffly stumbled out the door.

Ugodi agihliyi! Much pain! That's all I could think or mumble to myself. Ugodi agihliyi. Please Great Spirit, help me! Still I force my right leg to move. Then it just stops. I take a look around me and I see this laundromat across the street. I'll go over there. Perhaps I'll find someone to help me, or I can call Mr. Bill.

This little fragile elderly lady appears, "I saw you on the television and I hoped that I would get to meet you!"

"Thank you ma'am, but I'm in real pain. Do you think you could help me in any way, like find me a motel? But first take my moccasins off my feet? The right foot is swelling badly."

"Yes, honey, I will help you. There's a motel just a block back up the street. I'll take you there too!"

As she helped me into her sedan, she reached to pick my pack up and it being so heavy with my gun and all she nearly went down. By now, I'm out of my head with pain. I give her some money to get me a room, then she drives me right to the door. Helps me inside and puts me to bed. I gave her some more money and she departs to get some pain medication.

Quick to return with Tylenol-Gel Caps which I'd never had before. I take three. Within a few minutes I'm stoned! Don't even feel the itch anymore! But I'm scared, embarrassed and confused about all this hitting me all at once! She had to leave, but made sure that I had her phone number and had my medicine and the phone right beside me.

"Bless you honey, you will be safe. You're at the Dinner Bell Motel and Restaurant. I'll check on you soon!" Then she leaves.

Walkers keep in mind that when you are walking a distance as I am your transportation is your FEET! There's no difference to planning a long trip in your car knowing that you have four bad tires. So I am stranded beside the road with a flat tire and I can't even get a re-cap!

With a trembling voice I call the front desk..."Am I in a safe place?"

The pleasant reply of a man's voice reassures me! "Honey, don't worry about a thing, you are safe. And we know about your walk that you've set out on so just let me know what you would like for supper! Because me and the Missus will Doctor you and take care of you, okay?"

"Thank you Sir. I appreciate this, really I do!"

After a long nap, I awakened to the telephone ringing! Was the voice of the owner! "We are on our way!" Then in walks his wife carrying a pan of red vinegar with many towels! She embraced me to calm my fears and he's right behind her, carrying a big serving tray. With a big smile, he says, "Ma'am, this is room service! Where would you like this fine steak!?" We all laughed and I pointed to an area like I was a star!!! We talked while she checked my right foot and leg out "I think you have a pulled tendon my dear!"

"Oh no," I whimpered. I don't have time for this. I need to move on!"

They both spoke that nevertheless, I wasn't going anywhere for awhile! Sadly, I had to agree as they left me to soak and eat...!

Slowly, I helped myself out of the bed then put my hind-end in that cool red vinegar!! "Yes, that's it," I spoke out loud to myself! "Yes, that's it (sgidv)!!"

After eating and soaking, I called the Hiwassees. Needed to have them close. We had grown much used to each other's company and they felt more like a family! Then I called Mr. Bill. He soothed me over the telephone even if it was only his answering machine. And I wanted to see the Beautiful Pearl so I called her too. I don't suggest anyone eat Gel-Caps and have a telephone card!

The next evening the Hiwassees arrive and get a room for the night. Indian-Joe, the owner, with his ever so smiling face, and Mr. Hiwassee, helped me out to the back of the motel to the Gazebo! There we four get more acquainted and have much laughter! Then Beautiful Pearl arrives with a little of her home-made wine! That can just about cure anything! Forget the Gel-Caps.

---

*Princess left message on answering machine. She is in a*

*motel in Pikeville, Tennessee. Has a pulled tendon and can't walk. Happy's are going over to visit her. She must stay there a couple of days.*

---

By the third day I'm half walking. Indian-Joe suggests they take me to Fall-Creek Falls just for a pre-trial walk. Pearl, her sister, the Hiwassees, Indian-Joe and myself all went in Pearl's van, Indian-Joe at the wheel.

We took it slow and had the time of our lives! At a yard-sale I found these two old chenille bed-spreads. Figured they would make perfect skirts to wear on the trail and absorb the sweat!

"Well honey, I can make them for you!" Pearl spoke in her mountain brogue! The cloth-woman wouldn't even take a dime for the spreads.

"They are free to you lady. I'm really impressed with what you are trying to keep in people's mind in concern of what the white people did to you Indians. So please, take this as a gift!" Her face filled with warmth and sincerity as she gave me a strong hug!

Indian-Joe is a great didahlilosdisgi (photographer)! He takes many pictures of me that day and allows me to take one of him! I have the eye for picture-taking but not the mechanical-hand! Had a nice lunch at the Falls and stayed until sundown! That was the last picture Indian Joe took; the setting of the nvda (sun). I had studied the road closely, looking for the best sides for me to walk on. We stopped at this one farm so I could get Barn Reservations in advance. When I hobbled up to this pretty house to inquire, this elderly man replied, "Lady, I've had a lot of things asked to me in my life, but I've never had a woman to ask if she could sleep in my barn!" But he confirmed that I was welcome and went back to his supper just shaking his head in disbelief!!

---

*Called Princess around 10:00 a.m. Her and Happys just left for breakfast. She called me back, saying she was getting her pack all ready for tomorrow. Don't know when I'll hear from her again. Princess and new friends going to "Falls" and maybe find a barn to stay in tomorrow night. Good luck, Princess. I love you woman.*

---

All my company disbands, so the missus that "never smiles by nature" washes my clothes. Later, me, her, and Indian-Joe eat hotdogs and talk late into the night. We admire the stars in the darkened purple sky as I set wrapped in the bed-sheet when Pearl arrives with a beautiful skirt made out of that bed-spread! I model it, then decide its too pretty to wear on the Trail! I gave her ten hugs for that home-made skirt and a thousand dollars couldn't buy it!

---

*Called Princess 7:00 a.m. to wake her. We talked a long while. She will be leaving Pikeville, Tennessee sometime this morning. Probably won't hear anything more from her today. I miss you Princess.*

---

All ready to rear and walk again! My flat tire is fixed. Must I bid farewell to the aging lady in her nineties that still does 100 leg-lifts before she even gets out of bed? Indian-Joe gave me a big hug, and the "no-smile missus" wanted to walk with me a ways. Indian-Joe said he would pick her up around noon where ever that time may find us.

We walked very slowly heading toward the mountain. I was still slightly lame, but I knew this woman couldn't make that mountain! She was far too heavy and her heart wasn't into this. But I did admire her for asking to walk, yet I knew it was just so she could talk instead. Her heavy heart needed much council.

"Am I too hateful looking, Alethea!" She even sternly asked.

"Actually, you are a woman of beauty outside but inside you are very un-pretty because you are so unhappy with your life," answering her with the best tone I could muster.

"How could you tell that I am miserable?" she softens a bit.

"One, by just feeling your energies and the other, your body language. You show no warmth when you are around you husband-man, therefore, you can't be happy because nobody can stay mad that long!" touching her arm gently.

"You are right, and I must do something with my life and I will!"

During our walk we observed two young boys gathering these worms from a tree. They use these pretty looking worms for fishing!

"That's a handsome sight," I remark. "One boy is White and the other is Black! This is the South and more people should get along like that. They are more interested in fishing than they are of race!" She nodded her head. Then I reached down and picked up a big pretty one with a leaf, "You fellers won't take this one to the death-waters, will you?"

"No," they laughed and went on about their worm-picking!

High noon found us at the foot of the mountain and Indian-Joe did too! We bid our tearful farewells and went opposite ways.

Taking a long breath, I look up at that mountain and get mind control. First, I tell my right foot that I'm the boss! And I know there's two mountains, for truth, but I'm gonna make it!!! Secondly, I remind that foot again who's boss, "So, kick it out"! I start wearing rather quickly on the middle climb. There's no place to walk; a back-ditch again when a big log truck goes speeding by!

At one of my low periods when this logger slows down just enough to holler, "You can make it Indian. We're all counting on you!" And roars on, giving me a thumbs up!

"That's just what I needed!" waving and smiling back to me and I'm puffing and smiling as he speeds out of sight.

A young woman with two children stops. She explains the history of my walk and we all embrace! Two roughnecks decide to do a little dirty-talk, until I smile at them and pat Bonnie! They sped away cursing! Then a State-Patrol pulls over just to see if I need anything and compliments me on my choice of gun!

Just as I top the first mountain, there's a tomato-stand on the right side of the road. There is a young man and an elderly one. Directing my attention to the elderly one, "How much are your tomatoes sir?"

He smiles real big and says, "To you not a red-cent. Ya see, I am some Cherokee too and we need to stick together. Cool-off there and I'll be right back!" He returns with salt and the coldest glass of water I have ever had! The young man says he will give me a ride and won't even tell anyone!

"Thanks friend, I won't cheat. The only thing I cheat on is my diet!" He laughed speaking that he had to attend a night-class in some town. So me and the Grandpa man enjoyed talks about the old-ways. Thanked him and pushed on.

The nvda (sun) is on the down side of the galvloʔi (sky) and I'm growing weary with each step though much aliheliga (happy) to know my leg knows just who the boss really is! Had just finished the straight stretch, ready to attack the second mountain when this beautiful Cherokee woman about my age pulls to a stop. This must be the year for the forties women!

"Why don't you call it a day, and hop in?"

"Sorry ma'am, but I can't do that!" returning her smile!

"Well," she goes on, "Lets at least compromise! I own a Bed and Breakfast, so I could take your pack to the top of the hill and leave it at the country store. Then you can call me as soon as you get there! I live about twelve miles from the store!"

I agreed to that! "You made a good deal Lady, and thanks a lot!" "Boy, did this feel great," I thought, as I climbed the second mountain with hardly taking a second breath! Wish I could make this whole journey with only my gun! "Keep on dreaming, Alethea!"

Just as I top the mountain there stands a warm face gentle looking young woman. "Hello, I've been waiting for you! I'm a fourth-grade teacher and have many questions to ask!"

"Thank you lady!" answering and returning her smile! I met her Man-friend and we talked for over an hour. They invited me to spend the night but I told her of the lady that had offered a place earlier and I needed to get my back-pack over there at the country store. Other people stopped to say hello but soon the edge of darkness parted our ways.

The store-owners were really nice people. They offered me dinner, cola and a free pack of Virginia Slims! I thanked them so kindly and then called the B&B woman. She arrived in no time! Her establishment is just a mile inside the entrance of Fall-Creek-Falls!

She makes me feel welcome in this beautiful mansion, then gives me a tour. I meet her husband-man and daughter, Heather. After dinner we talk much. She washes all my clothes and as I bathed, I just knew these towels where so soft my rough skin would tear them up if they didn't melt first! Called to update Mr. Bill and soon found sweet slumber in her private guest-room!

---

*Had message when I got home to call Princess at a Bed and Breakfast or something like that. Its at Fall Creek Falls. Princess is staying there a night or so. Princess called me around 10:00 p.m. went to some meeting with the woman.*

---

Next morning I had to retrace the twelve miles from where she had picked me up at the store. Heather asked if she could go along! This would be great to have company and not have to carry a heavy pack. Her Mama informed me, as she dropped us off at the store, that a teacher had called last night and wanted me to stop along the route and speak to her class!

As Heather and I walked along, we shared stories and we both enjoyed tobacco! She spoke that she enjoyed her job at the Nature-Center down at the Falls. Seems the miles just eased beneath our feet as we shared many Indian stories. A young gila (dog) found us and tagged along until we reached the school! Gila went in with us to learn but some teacher ran him out the door. We find Mrs. Bitterman's class and we all enjoyed much! The students learned of the Trail Of Tears and all about animals too! Heather invited the class to visit the Wildlife Center anytime they chose. We answered questions to three different classes!

Afterwards we were introduced to the lunch-room ladies! They had prepared us a brown-bag lunch! We bid good-bye and went in search of our little gila-friend to share lunch with him, but to no avail. He was much angry 'cause he was expelled!

As we ate the brown-bag lunch, we tried to remember the last time we'd had one. Both agreed it must have been in the eighth grade! I laughed and informed her that my brown-bag in grade school was a lard bucket. She being in her early twenties found that most interesting! "A Lard Bucket?

Walking again, carrying just the left-over of the honey-buns we heard this pitiful cry. Right there at our feet a little stray kitten looks up at us! We take it far from the road and the last we saw of that little kitty, it was growling and chowing down on those honey-buns! I taught her, a cat in Cherokee is called "wasa"!

Soon the sign of the Falls entrance comes into view! Just beyond that sign is a home-style hamburger place! We just look at each other and smile real big. Both have a weakness for hamburgers! We eat again like two starved gilas, and being so full, we dread walking on to her house. It was about three P.M. when we arrived. Her step-father had done all the cooking for the guests and had the kitchen filled with many aromas. He looked at us a bit strangely when we turned down a piece of his fresh baked bread!

Instead, we retire to the sun-porch and she brings out two of her pets. I'm loving one, the older black-snake, and she's teaching the new one not to be afraid. Then in walks some guest. They become very scared, so Heather has to put them up! The one lady said that she had spent the night over at the Falls Hotel and got to speak to the Governor, but was thrilled to meet me. She was so proud of me and wanted a picture with me! I ended up posing for many pictures; including Heather and her family.

That night I repack my things and prepare to leave the next morning, so Heather invites some friends over. I meet this one teenager that was so enthused about meeting me he had an Indian Woman tattooed on his back! This touched me deeply. We all talked into the night even though I was tired and had attended an action community meeting earlier with the Owner-Lady. I spoke at the meeting and informed them; "I now know what all has to take place before any kind of sign is put up!" They gave me a loud applause.

Was midnight before we all parted for bed. Tomorrow's walk was on my mind and sleep didn't come easy. Next morning I had to be in a rush because the Mrs. B&B had to work early and her corvette didn't want to start. We bid our farewells as she drops me off at the Fall-Entrance. Waving goodbye, we head in opposite directions. "Don't forget to visit my Mama and please return," she yells.

B&B's Indian Mama lived about a mile from the entrance and was expecting me to visit for coffee. What a beautiful Woman. She looked so much like my Mama, I had to compose myself and fight tears as I did when I met White-Arrow. "Mama, you are walking with me, aren't you?"

I enjoyed the Family-Album she showed me and this one picture of her Great-Aunt still lingers in my mind. The Aunt rode a big Black Tennessee Walker and carried a gun on her side! This photo was taken in the late 1800's, but it looked like a picture of me when I lived in the woods those seven years. I rode a big black Tennessee Walker too! The big, long skirts and a gun strapped on my side! This I found chilling! But we enjoyed our visit and shared stories. Then I had to move on. As I was walking out her drive I met her son. He came to load some cows. Just one thing I couldn't figure out! "Why does her children allow the grass to grow so tall in their Mama's yard?" Making my way across the high grass and heavy-dew, I Prayed for this woman. Plus, her health was real bad. If I could have and knew how to work a lawn-mower, I would mow her grass myself...

As the day wore on the heat was about to overcome me! I

had nearly completed the flat mountain walk when I spotted this golden haired, handsome man. Suddenly, there was such a heaviness upon my chest! He held his head to one side and grinned like he was guilty of eating all the candy!

"I thought it was about time you passed this way," he spoke in almost a whisper. He was on the opposite side of the road but I was looking for an escape route for some reason.

"How did you know that?" I questioned him just as low.

"Walk with me, I know the best way of darkness."

I knew now why I had this heavy feeling. This handsome piece of man was the devil's disciple himself. With one hand on my wooden cross and the other on my gun I answered. "I walk the way of the Light. But if you walk your ass across that road, I'll send you back to hell a little sooner than you planned!" keeping my pace slow and searching for his vehicle I couldn't find. Being opposite of his belief and feeling his energies so strongly, I felt a strong wave of dizziness attack me!

"Look at me!" he demanded almost sweetly, "You are so beautiful and we can walk together the rest of our lives. You will never need for anything! "

I stopped, turned, and trembled as I faced this evil force with only the narrow road between us. Placing my hand upon my gun, allowing him to see the movement, I prayed as I made my last speaking. "I don't need anything from you mister, and I feel your powers but you're not stronger than a bullet the Great Spirit gave me!"

He just stared at me more with a hateful look then turned to his left and walked over the steep embankment, gone as quickly as he appeared!

"Thank you Great Spirit!" I spoke out loud. "Wada, with my every breath!"

I quickened my pace as I headed down the steep-winding mountain. Saw where the REBEL log-hauler was taking his logs from! GOOD-BYE Reb, thanks for all the thumbs-ups you've given me! And I like your truck!

Kept thinking about that asgina (devil); wondered how long he had been following me. I'm scared. Its hard to tell what your enemy may be. Our People did know theirs. The dog-soldiers were their main enemy. Starvation and sickness and death plagued them daily and the weather went from a drought to torrential rains to severe cold. My enemy in the nineties could be anything from a drive-by shooter or the damn asgina himself; not counting the rapist, which our Cherokee Women dealt with daily...

Reaching the foot of the mountain, I decided to rest awhile. Didn't really know just how far it would be on into Spencer. I hid beneath this finely constructed concrete bridge called the Measle Bridge and redirected my thoughts to that curious name of the bridge! It reminded me of a bridge we all played at when I was about sixteen, only our Carter's Bridge wasn't as fancy! There was a twenty foot jump down to the water. If you went to the right there was only about three feet of water. But straight over, the water was much deeper. One Sunday I get in line to jump just as the mountain boys did. Made my jump perfect. Then this boy I did have a crush on was too drunk on moonshine. We all yelled at him from the water, "please don't jump!" His reply was, "If that pretty Indian can jump, then I'll be man enough to get her!" He went to the right and all one could see was bloody water and his bones sticking out of his skin. The other boys rushed him to the hospital twenty miles away. Since I lived far into the mountain, it was two days before I found out if my friend was alive. He was, but to this day remains in a wheel chair and his Mama always blamed me, never allowing me to ever see his face again. Yet, his handsome face always comes to my mind when I see a high bridge and flowing water. "I still adore you, Brucey."

Still have the shakes but I've got to climb that mountain. I need to find a place to sleep tonight and though I just had a bad experience, I still have another Message In The Wind.

## SPENCER'S MOUNTAIN

As I start my climb to Spencer's Mountain top, a cross-country Bicyclist passes me like I'm standing still! "Hey, Jack, do you want to trade legs?" I was growing stronger by each mile but this made me have a complex! Plus I've lost several pounds now. "Oh, shut up Alethea and keep climbing!" I keep climbing, going around stiff curves, take a minute's break then continue. I swear this is the steepest mountain yet! I'm looking down upon treetops and this Mountain top still isn't in sight! "Help me Great Spirit." Then I feel bad about asking the "Maker Of Breath" a favor like this. "What about the little Cherokee children that were pushed up this mountain by lashing whips and the elderly that didn't even get to see the top?" With these thoughts, I hushed my whining.

I'm so thirsty! Then looking to the right side of the road I see a natural spring that someone has been kind enough to rock a small well-box around! And there sets a huge kanuna (bullfrog). "Howdy, Ududu Kanuna (Grandfather Frog)! Will you share your ama (water) with me?" He gives a loud crrroak and I take that as a "Nihi talugisgi (you can)!" So I drop my pack and bury my head all the way to the bottom! There, we meet again akta to akta (eye to eye)! Then I fill my canteen, splash, and play like a child!

Guess Ududa Kanuna can't hold his breath any longer, so he comes up for a chat! We have a great one-sided conversation while we both take our time to refill our lungs! "Well, I've got to be on my way!" breaking it to him gently! He promises to write me but wants to know how much a stamp costs with a frog discount!

Finally! I reach the top! The sign reads, Spencer, Tennessee! Elated again! The sight is beholding! Everything looks like a picture! Neat little houses, assorted flowers gracing the lawns and the narrow mountain road is spotless and flat! I needed this!

Then a bright red truck stops. A handsome, smiling face man gets out and says, "Howdy, Miss. You met a lady at the action meeting the other night and she instructed me to meet you with a cold cola!

"Why, thank you sir!"

"Which flavor would you like?" showing me his assorted selection!

"I will take the real thing!" laughing, as I reach for the Coke.

We sat in a shade and talked for awhile. I asked about the Measles Bridge! "Miss, my name is Measles and that bridge was named after my Father. He used to be the Road Commissioner and the Community liked the way he did his job so well that they named the Bridge after him!"

"That's an interesting story, sir!" answering in between the long drinks of that sugar water, knowing I'm not supposed to have it! But I'm not about to let this nice man know it!

Then he went on to say, "Dad's gone now. But we used to go off this mountain about every evening and fish. My dad and my Grandfather both told me of many stories of the Cherokee Removal. I really admire you Miss. You sure have to be a brave person to take on this Journey. Especially being a woman and crime as bad as it is now days."

"Yes, Sir, you're right. But this is a life-long dream that I have to make happen!"

"Well, my Prayers are with you and I best be getting to work. It was nice talking to you and I hope one day you can write a book about your journey." As he prepared to drive away, I waved and smiled, giving a promise that I would write that book!

Just as I got my pack on, ANOTHER CAR PULLS UP! Its two real nice women. They spoke that they were sisters and the little girl in the back seat had told them, "There is that woman I met at the Action meeting the other night when I was with my Grandmother." Turning my attention toward her, I remembered her pretty little face!

"This is wild," the driver spoke! She is a nurse at the Murfeebourgh's Veterans Hospital and a friend of hers told her about this woman walking the Trail Of Tears and as she was telling her sister the story, they see me at that very minute!

Taking a short second rest, she informed me to give her a call when I reached her territory! "I will be glad to ma'am, and thanks again for being nice and inviting me!" Me and the little girl waved until they where out of sight! I tucked her phone number into my bra and headed for the stretch!

After a few miles, I came upon this sign that pointed to the left, reading "Pole Bender's Restaurant"! "This sounds good," I thought. From climbing that mountain, I felt like a Bent Pole! But I didn't expect to walk that far. It was almost half a mile! "Don't judge distance from a sign!"

Deserted! Just the way I like to dine, alone! There were two young gents, one cooking and one serving! I spoke for a large order of meatloaf, green beans and the whole works! After serving my food, they joined me for conversation. The younger one said he wanted to tour the United States on a Harley! I agreed that would be a great adventure! I have a Lady-Friend back home in Kentucky named Willow and she wouldn't weigh one hundred pounds soaking wet and she toured the most part of the United States on her Harley all east of the Mississippi! So, if a small young woman like her did this, then surely a strong young man like you can. But I did encourage him to finish high school then take his adventure. College can always wait, for awhile anyway! This brought a big smile to his face!

"What do you think or feel about me?" The older one asks!

"Well, I think you have already been to town a time or two and your heart is not into this Country Enviroment. You would rather be in the depth of a big city, taking every danger that it has to offer and loving every minute of it!"

"Hey, Lady. You're right! But how do you know these things about people when you have just met us?"

"It's really a Gift that Our Great Spirit gave us all. I'm sure there are many names this fits under, but my Mama taught me, "It's a Message In The Wind!"

"Wow!" They both spoke! "Hey, the dinner is on us!"

"Thank you Gents," smiling as I prepared to leave, "But here is a healthy tip!" I gave them ten dollars.

Just as I had my pack in place and my gun on, a tall slender man walks in for dinner. He stops quickly looking me up and down, then asks, "What are you, the new Deputy?" as he was eyeing my gun.

"No, I'm Alethea, and I'm walking the Trail Of Tears! Who are you? "

"Oh, I am one of the local Historion and I've taught many people about the Trail going through here!"

"Great, now you should have one of those Action-Councils and have more signs put up to better mark this famous trail!" He agreed. We then shook hands and I made my way through the door that the gents already held open for me, just smiling and bowing with their arms stretched, "This way, Ma'am!"

Admiring the little town as I walked through, I kept my eye on these two men about my age. They kept making turns and would be at every stop sign that I was, yet look away as if they didn't see me. Saved by a carpenter that yelled at me from across the street, approching with a big smile and holding his hand out to shake mine!

"I've been watching those two. Be careful. I'm not from around here, just doing a job here. But I saw you could be in danger."

"Thanks Mister, I know they aren't showing off that damn truck they are driving but my gun, Old Bonnie, will take care of me!"

He admires my gun then asks if I need any money or food? "I've read all about the Trail Of Tears." he goes on. This man gave me comfort. As I started to leave he said that he would check on me as he left for home and the mountain leaving Spencer was much dangerous, just please be careful!" I promised as we embraced and departed.

## SUNDOWN OVER SPENCER

That hot nvda (sun) was slowing going down just as I was about half way down the curvy mountain. I'm exhausted but I must find a barn somewhere. The man was right. This area is really isolated! Just as I get around this stiff curve, I find this old daksi (terrapin) and he looks about as tired as I am! Take a short break, have my Virginia Slims, and ask him if he knew of an old barn I might could sleep in tonight?

"No," he replies in a voice with wisdom, "That's why I carry my house with me so I don't have to ask anyone of such a favor!" I rubbed his old house top again and thanked him for his advice.

"Wish I was as smart as you daksi," then moved even more slowly down the mountain. To my left I saw this dwelling, looked to be a trailer at one time then covered with boards. There wasn't any barn but I did spot a good sized wood shed! Three gilas ran toward me, two wagging their tails. The older one growled as if to warn me not to take another step! I scolded them, "Either bite me or hush!" They felt no fear so they quietened. Hollered, but nobody was home. So I just sat in the driveway loving on the dogs, smoking to help fight off the mosquitoes. Seemed the folks weren't going to show and it was getting much late, so I reshift my pack and head out the drive, bidding thanks (wada) to the dogs.

Finally I reach the foot of that long mountain! But I'm too tired to rejoice with a kick of my heels, but thankful for the flat land that lies before me! Only walk about a mile and I see this antique barn! This lifts my spirits! There's two horses grazing in the small pasture and they seem to welcome me! I speak my seyo (greetings) and ask where their master may be? So I walk on across the road to this white-stone house and knock upon the door, no answer. "Oh well," I'm thinking, "I can just set here awhile and wait because it's starting to get dark and Mr. Bill told me never to walk after dark. This I promised to him." I can hear their telephone ring and the answering machine does it's duty. Still nobody shows.

Two wasas come to play with me. One is a tom-cat, the other, a little female! He is being gentle but she's trying to claw my back-pack! I begin Praying to Our Great Spirit! "Please let somebody come!"

Shortly, a nice pickup truck pulls in. An older man speaks that his son and family live here. "Well sir, do you think they would mind if I just climbed in their loft. I'm so tired and I've come all the way from Fall-Creek-Falls since this morning?!" Avoiding my plea and question, he just keeps picking his teeth.

Then this elderly couple pulls up. "Have you had any supper honey?" The man asks gently.

"No sir, I haven't. What I need most is a barn to sleep in!"

"Well," he goes on, "We have been seeing you walk all day and the Missus has fixed you up a mess here if you want it!"

"Oh, yes I'll take it and thank you both so kindly!" As the elderly couple pulled away, I heard the older man speak words to the tooth-picker, something about him allowing me to sleep in that barn. To myself I thought, "Yeah buddy tooth-picker listen up, pay attention and allow me to smell the hay!

Tooth-picker just keeps going at his non-professional dentistry then speaks "I don't know where my son went, don't know even when he'll be back. Ya know, woman you've come almost thirty miles today?"

"Sir, my feet tell me I have walked many miles today. Now can't you just give me the O.K. to stay in their barn?"

Ignoring my question, he picks some more and speaks,"Well, its dark now and I better get on home. See ya!"

Tears well up in my eyes, then I get mad at myself for being so weak. But I speak out loud even if it's just the cats and the horses hear me! "It's folk like you, old tooth-picker, that made the Cherokee Removal and I hope you get clap-of-the-mouth for doing this to me!" There! I felt a little better! I tell all the animals good-bye and go into the darkness! I am much scared and I Pray every step! In the far distance I can see house lights and they are on both sides of the road. So, if the one side turns me down, maybe the other side neighbor will allow me their barn! I had walked about a mile when this truck came to a halt beside me. "Well!" I sneer.

Then old-tooth-picker says, "Aw, now, just walk back to my boy's barn. It's plum dark out here and there ain't no telling what might happen to you!"

"Hey, tooth-picker, you can go to hell! I make a habit of walking forwards not backwards. And you could have let me stay in that barn an hour ago. So kiss my pretty brown ass and get out of my way. Better yet, you ain't good enough to kiss it!" He sped away.

Now I'm crying and I'm really mad! Got to calm myself down here and think good thoughts. "Let's see. What would Mama suggest I do if she were walking with me?" Why sing, of course! Back in the mountains of Cherokee, Kentucky, when we didn't have anything to eat, Mama would say to us five girls, "Girls, Mama doesn't have any food for us tonight, but I have a song for you all!" And we'd gather around Mama's feet and listening to her sweet mountain Ballads. The aching for food would become lost in some pretty song that she was singing!

Okay, I'll sing a song I wrote about this good-old-boy, back home that spoke untruth about me once." I named him Poncho!"

SOME KIND OF FRIEND

The last time I saw you was at the end of the road,
When our backs grew weary, from a heavy load.
Last time I saw you we had our faces to the wind,
And you sure are some kind of friend.

If thunder was held just for you
You'd ask for a rainbow before lightning pierced thru.
But I just walk the mountains. Whippoorwills ask
Where I been?
And I just tell them about some kind of friend.

Well, there's times I look behind me,
To places where I've been.
And let it remind me
To never go back again.

I'll just walk the mountains,
And whipporwills, ask where I've been?
I'll just cry and tell them,"You're some kind of friend.
Yes, my tracks are cold now, and you're some kind of friend.

By the time I'd finished singing, I was near the house lights on the left side of the road. Took a deep breath, tried to shake a cold chill from inside me and went for the door. I had to knock ten times before this elderly man comes to the door. The big door was open and I could see through the screen door a television at a full blare! He gave me a big smile but couldn't get the screen door open!

Then the missus shows up. "What do you want?" She yells through the screen door.

"Ma'am, I want to know if I can sleep in your barn. Is that yours across the road?"

"Yes it is, and no you can't! Who are you anyway?"

"My name is Alethea, and I'm walking the Trail Of Tears. I just need to sleep" trying to sound as soft as possible.

Then the Man spoke, "There ain't no use of this talking through a door. Come on in child!" smiling with much warmth!

"Thank you sir!" I replied as I followed them into the sitting room.The man offered for me to have a seat, the lady spoke, "NO!" So I just stand there like a Cherokee Slave up for inspection, pack on my back. They jibbered back and forth at each other for thirty minutes. I'm growing weaker with this pack of fifty-two pounds that's getting to me! Drilled with many questions from the old She-juktajisdahli (copperhead), and still I remained standing but about to lose what little class I had left!

"You got any identification?"

"Yes ma'am, I do. Here is my Kentucky drivers license and copies of interviews along the Trail. It's all here!"

Old She-juktajisdahli ignored my idenification papers as I handed them to her but the nice, gentle Husband-man kindly reached for them.

"Why, everything is right here that a body would need to see," he softly replied to her as he tried to hand them to her.

"I don't need to see them" she answered sternly, ignoring

him, and not missing a stitch as she sewed away on some little doily she was making.

"Well, piss on this Ma'am. I'm going outside and pull up your porch. I won't put up with this kind of ignorance and you can call the Law for all I care. They already know me!" Tiredly I hobbled toward the door and found the cool night air much welcome and far warmer than old She-Copperhead!

Inside I heard him scold her a bit then he came after me. "Come on back in child. You can sleep here. And let me help you take that pack off. It must be a heavy load!"

I thought for a minute then followed him back to the sitting room. She never even looked up. Thinking to myself "If I was you I'd hold my head down too!"

"I called my daughter," she begins, looking toward her husband-man and she suggests that, "Old Man, you best hold a gun on her all night if you're going to let her stay!" I jumped from the sofa in plans to pull that porch up again as she interrupted me! "Well, you could be a rapist or a killer!" looking up at me with a smirk,

"Woman," I yelled, "You remind me of an old copperhead! And a killer ain't going to be carrying fifty two pounds on their back. Plus, if I was a rapist, how in the hell could I rape you? We are made alike you know! Answer that for me!? Or are we?"

With a new shape of another smirk, "I'm a good Christian Woman and we belong to the JEHOVAH witness belief."

"YOU DO!!!" I emphasized with a loud holler, "Well, I'm an Indian-Christian and believe in the GREAT SPIRIT! And if we read from the same GOOD BOOK you will find, "Don't turn a stranger from your door."

This got her attention just a bit and she looked at me so cold I forgot all about my tiredness for a minute. Then she jumped up mumbling loud as she headed for the back of the house!

"If anybody is going to stay in my house all night, they ain't going to sleep on MY porch!" The Husband-man motioned for me to follow her. As I walked into this elegant, antiqued bedroom decorated in a dusty-rose, I thought I'd faint! It's beauty and art of her choice, I had to respect and admire! But her manners and her taste don't match. Yeah! Copperhead Rose!!

"Now girl, there's you a bed! And I still don't like the way you look. Nor am I into Indians" kept mumbling as she slammed the door behind me, muffling out her last words!

"Why, bless you too, old Copperhead-Rose! Sweet dreams. Watch now, I might rape you tonight!!" I took a seat in this big antique rocker! Thought how could one have such good taste yet not a touch of compassion? Started to undo my moccasins, too tired! So I just pulled those fancy covers down, crawled in moccs, clothes and all! A big smile crosses my face! "Guess who has a blacker behind copperhead?" Then before my Prayers were said, sleepness overcome!

Awakened to the delicious smell of bacon and coffee! No dressing to do so I washed my face in the private bath and headed for the sitting-room. The Husband-man greeted me with a good morning and I thanked him for winning the sleeping war for me!

"You are welcome child. Would you like a good hot cup of coffee? The missus has everything ready. Go on into the kitchen!"

It took every bit of strength I had to steer myself toward the back door. Oh, how I wanted just the kahwi (coffee)! "Thanks just the same but I best be going!" giving him a big smile!

"Don't hold it against the Missus. She just has an odd way sometimes. Can you understand that?" speaking as he followed me out to just beneath the kitchen window.

"Mister, I don't hold hard feelings toward anyone. The only suggestion I have for her is to get on her knees and Pray to Our Great Spirit that he doesn't hold her to harshness!" I saw her peering through the kitchen window as I passed, smiling, making my way across the heavily dewed, manicured lawn, looking forward to the road.

At the road, stretched my legs and could feel the thirty miles I had put underneath my feet yesterday! Looked up and saw this odalvʔi (mountain) that I had to climb first thing! Then I took a look back to that stately brick copperhead-house and that utana (big) odalvʔi (mountain) never looked more beautiful!

I was blessed. Turns out the mountain wasn't too long after all and I had it cleared in a short while! A sign at the top reinspired me! It read: McMINNVILLE, TENN. 14 MILES!! Inhaled the fresh morning air, admired the well kept hay fields that were laden with dew! Birds darted about me showing no fear and sang their favorite morning Hymns so I shared one of mine!

WAKE UP MAMA

Two fancy men came calling at the house today,
What would they want at our house anyway?
Wake up mama, wake up mama, wake up mama...

One had sandy hair, looking long and mean,
Other smoked an ol' cigar, had the devil's gleem.
Wake up mama, wake up mama, wake up mama...

Chickens won't go into the chicken house tonight,
An' that ol' chicken hawk ain't flying very high!
Wake up mama, wake up mama, wake up mama...

Well, the hoss is fed, and my work is all done,
An' my Prayers been said, with the evening sun.
Wake up mama, wake up mama, oh, wake up mama, mama.....

Seems I could feel Mama so close this morning and perhaps she was proud of me for standing up for our truth, or thanking me for not giving that fake-Jehovah copperhead the other side of my mind that would have me in jail!! Yet I could compare the yonder fields in my mind to my Kentucky dew-field that Mama was now sleeping beneath. Mama was the kind that if anyone showed up to her door looking for a place to sleep, she would take you in and feed you a full course meal, give you the best bed and play her guitar to you! Even if you HAD been an outlaw! "I'm not the JUDGE," she'd say, "He lives is Heaven". Mama never locked her doors in her dwelling or her heart but would knife you if you spoke untruth!

Ironically, within a mile I came upon a Church and a beautiful graveyard! There was a tall stone fence in the front that leveled even with the graves therefore making a perfect seat rest. Saw the old-time famous outhouse! Great!! Later I brushed my teeth with that expensive K&M medicine-water! Then enjoyed a healthy breakfast of an apple and the left over supper the elderly couple had given me yesterday! Spoke my Prayers as I walked about the graveyard.

From the looks of my map, it shows that most all those big mountains were behind me! Looked toward McMinnville and started with a S-k-i-p! Kept seeing these tree nurseries. They were so well kept and neat. And this went on for miles!

Getting hot and the sky was partly cloudy. Decided to take a break. This neat little church on the right side of the road just seemed to welcome me! Heard someone working inside so I spoke loudly and asked this handsome young man if I could rest outside on his work-bench?

I like to interview everybody I meet so I asked if he went to Church there? He answered that he didn't go to Church because he had this problem about the story of the Virgin Mary. I spoke that I didn't go to any certain Church myself but his reason was an origional because I had never come across that answer before, but I believed in the Great Spirit and Virgin Mary too! He kept on dry-walling and I went on to ramble that my Mama's name was Mary! No reply! "Thank you sir!" and I just sent my butt out the door! Laid this old tired body down on his boards and blocks, dozing off, thinking about the Virgin Mary and Mama and "What is religion?

The twenty minute nap left me feeling so badly. I was all confused as I awakened. Took several minutes to get my bearings! I didn't know if I was to go to the left or right! Finally get in gear and turn right heading West. Didn't get more than three miles and was about to fall asleep in my tracks. Saw an old deserted country Church and hid behind it. Laid my rain-poncho down using my pack for a pillow and found sweet-sleep for an hour. The humming mosquitos didn't even take a bite!

Back to the road feeling much better. The clouds gave warning of rain. This quickened my steps! Met a nice State-Patrolman. He asked if I was alright or if I needed anything? I thanked him and spoke about the only thing I would ask of him was to arrest every fake-Jehovah that he came across!

We both laughed!

Then I meet these road-workers on this long concrete bridge. When this big truck thunders across the bridge shakes! I become very much nervous and the boss-man chuckles! "The bridge is built to give some sway to the pressure or else it would break and fall!"

"Oh, thank you sir. That's real education but I must be going!" I made double time getting off that shaking bridge!

Then I see a sign. SCOTTISH INN, CLEAN ROOMS, LOW PRICE. "Just what I need! My left leg is hurting and my lungs are raspy. Perhaps I'm getting a cold. Why am I so sleepy? I'll be alright. Going to check into that clean motel and call my Mr. Bill and all will be fine! Think positive Alethea!"

This foreign Lady that could have been a model in Vogue magazine just looked at me with these dark and beautiful, but distant eyes. First she hands me a card to fill out. I fill each line until I come to the vehicle department! Time for communication problems! "You must fill out here, right here." pointing her finger at the blank.

"Lady, I'm walking the Trail Of Tears and you may or may not know just what this Trail is that I speak of. You see, I have no car!" pointing behind me toward their empty parking lot.

"No, no, you must fill out this!" persistant and pointing again!

I'm going to do this one more time I thought! "Lady, do you see this pack on my back? Well, that means I'm walking!" And I begin to illustrate, allowing my fingers to walk across her counter! "NO", she begins again. I stop her immediately. "Shit, woman, I'm tired and I'm getting sickly and we ain't getting anywhere so scrap or get somebody that knows just what the hell walking means!"

Just then her Handsome husband-man comes from the back. He has a big grin and speaks their language to her. She disappears and he speaks better English than I do! "No problem, miss, here is your room key!"

I mumble a "thank you" as I fumble with the door. "Having these women problems will be the death of me. I'm so glad that I'm not the typical woman!" growling all the way to the door of my room.

Clean room? Wrong! But I'm too tired to care. Ditch my pack and hide my gun and off to eat. The restaurant is excellent! The owner is Cherokee and the food most good!

Back to my room bathe three times, have my clothes soaking in the tub. Make some telephone calls then climb in bed by five P.M. but I can feel that Message in the Wind......

---

*Its 8:00 p.m. Have message from Princess. She had to stay with some Copperhead-Jehovah last night. She is sick and in McMinnville. Tennessee. Must rest. Said she would call Happys.*

---

# McMINNVILLE, TENNESSEE

McMinn Village was the origin of McMinnville, Tennessee. In 1811, Captain William White built the Courthouse. The village was made up of sixty eight lots and these lots were surveyed by a Dr. Wilson. In 1811, on February 6, the first lot was sold. The price ranges of the lots were low as twenty dollars and to a high price of two hundred fifty seven dollars! This progressive lot sale turned the quaint village into an incorporated town in 1826. With this incorporation came more decisions and the need for a suitable dwelling for the Governor of Tennessee, the well known Joseph McMinn.

Ol' Hickory asked Governor McMinn to be one of his main agents in helping to start the Cherokee Removal. Hickory wanted McMinn to speak untruth about the Cherokees and say that many Cherokee Leaders had made threats upon his life. McMinn followed through with his promise. He requested Government Troops to be sent at his side when he held councils. McMinn went on to speak that he was most afraid of Major Ridge, John Hicks and Little John Scot. They had threatened his life many times. Plus, all white settlers were afraid that these three half-breeds were bound to cause an uprising.

McMinn was watched over by the guards but saw no present danger. So they just laid back and enjoyed their tobacco with the beautiful Cherokee Women that were in the area at the time!

Since this maneuver by McMinn failed, Ol' Hickory still wasn't giving up on the Cherokee Removal. Congress had set aside this Removal Fund to the worth of eighty thousand dollars. Some time had passed now and the Government, mainly including The Secretary of War, Mr. Calhoune, was promised by Governor McMinn that he and Agent Sam Houston had gotten the required 15 percent of the Cherokees to agree to a voluntary removal and all was set!

But this was another one of McMinn's untruths! Along with other Agents, Sam (Raven) Houston and McMinn went on a wild drunken spree and cavorted with loose Wahington women and spent all of the eighty thousand dollars! This ordeal angered Mr. Calhoune so that he didn't invite McMinn to the final Council with Cherokee Leaders in Washington. Later, Old Hickory gave his opinion of the following; The Raven was nothing but a Tennessee Cherokee sonofabitch that was teaching the Cherokees all the legal traits and telling the United States Government what to do! And he spoke that Major Ridge reminded him of a Red-Bull behind a picket fence when Ridge wore his fancy attire, dancing with Amdassadors' wives in Washington! Pertaining to all others, including McMinn, they were all drunken bastards! Seems Jackson surmized a good picture of himself!!

I felt about as lost in McMinnville as the Cherokee and the Black Slaves that were driven through here in 1838. The motel didn't have a safety lock on the door but I slept with Bonnie close at hand and my Buck knife in the door during the night. The parking lot was filled with loud parties and screeching tires. This was no ease to my coming flu.

Mr. and Mrs. Hiwassee came to help me repack and organize. They took me out to dinner but I couldn't enjoy mine due to an anxiety attack and the flu. Whenever I'm scared, too overjoyed, angry, or becoming sickly, I have these attacks. The severe chest pains and sticky-sweats become unbearable. I've had to deal with this all my life. Seizures used to accompany these attacks but about three years ago the seizures just went away. I would have anywhere from one to five seizures a week. Many different Doctors could never give a real reason for them. They usually blamed it all to having polio and this could be true. But when I start to get a bad cold or flu I panic, afraid I'll go into a seizure. I'm sure I got this cold from invading Odudu Walosi (Grandfather- Frog's) private spring-house!

Little Sparrow (Usdi Jisgwa), my eldest sister, brought my mail and reassurance that I would be alright. Mr. Bill brought the warmth and strength of his love and gave me all the news of his account of his lingering divorce. All spent a couple of days at my side and prayed I'd be able to make my journey. When all departed, I cried much and ached with a heavy-heart.

---

*Called Princess at 9:00 a.m. I had to go to court about this divorce. Princess and Happys went out to dinner. She got sick at the V.F.W. due to her anxieties and flu.*

---

*Went to logging show today. Then to Woodson Bend to check on Princess' cabin and start her truck (White-Horse) up. Also Bluebird, her car. Then went on to McMinnville to see Princess. Happys and Sparrow were there. Didn't like her hotel room. She's real sick*

---

*Sunday, September 20, 1992 - Still in McMinnville. We got up around 10:00 a.m. ate and we all talked to Princess to encourage her. I left for Morehead at 4:00 p.m. Got home at 10:15 p.m. It's 668 miles down and back.*

---

But with new inserts in my moccasins and medicine to fight the cold, I headed through the historical town admiring the old buildings. I could only imagine how it looked before the division and sold into lots, then becoming a town named after Governor McMinn, the drinking Quaker. When I think of a Quaker, I can only see the happy smiling face upon that Quaker Oats box! I bid wudeliga (go out of sight) to the town of history, clutched my chest to shield the cool air and prayed I could make many miles today.

Within a few miles my fever returned even more hot!

This nice gentleman saw me. He left his garage and crossed the road to speak how proud he was of me to attempt such a journey and that he read many books about the Cherokee! This did lift my spirits a bit, hoping someday he would be able to read mine.

Started getting real sleepy! What must I do? Just at that time, Leather-Jacket and some shaved-headed white man from Montana, both dressed in black, pulls over. "This is all I need!" thinking to myself. Too weak to stand, we went into a nearby resturant to have coffee.

"Alethea," Leather-Jacket started her campaign again with a big grin! "I figured that you've had some time to think about that offer I spoke to you about back in Dayton. And my boyfriend here is so willing to take many pictures of you. Just think, this would be an asset to your study!"

"Leather-Jacket, if you remember what I told you back in Dayton, then why must I repeat myself? I'm sickly, the clouds are speaking a promise of rain and the last thing I need is you and this bald-in-black to keep pissing me off!" Without another word, I left the restaurant, stomping and swearing and growling ...

"Oh, Great Spirit, help me! I'm only trying to get to the next destination, Woodbury, Tennessee!" Here I am in a sick-sleep-walk and now beginning to doze-off as the traffic flys by! It feels the same as when you are driving and you see things cross the road but you know they're not there. The most intelligent thing to do is look for a barn to sleep in.

Then I see a country store just ahead. Perhaps I'll have some luck! I really liked that old deserted house I just passed. Perhaps I can get reservations there! Wonder if this is where Dottie West lived?

The store lady is nice! We talk quite a while. Spoke to her that I couldn't walk anymore today; too sick and too many delays. Then comes her closing time so she makes a few calls to find me a barn, but all speak, "No!"

Then this sandy haired young man of about seventeen and this woman about my age walk into the store. I'm so weak by now but I do my own talking, "Sir, do you think that you could take me back to the town I just walked through? But not to this one motel where a woman didn't understand what "Walking" meant! I'm walking the Trail of Tears and it's dark now and nobody seems to want to share their barn! So, will you help me? Please?"

His smooth friendly face just lit up and he never gave it a second thought! "You better believe that I'll give you a ride into town! But first allow me to make a few calls to try and find you a place." He tried earnestly but no barns. So back to town I go! They took me to "SHONEYS INN", really a nice place! Then he gave me his phone number, "Anytime you are ready to go back on the Trail just call me and I'll take you back to that old store! Oh, do you mind if I tell my favorite Aunt about you?"

"No, honey, I don't mind. You go right ahead!" It was past nine P.M. now and all I wanted to do was take my cold medicine, a hot bath, and call my Mr. Bill. Ask for a wake-up call at seven A.M. and sick, restless sleep finally came.

---

*Princess called at 4:30 this morning. Started her walk again. Leather-Jacket called me at work. Want to find princess again. (Jacket better watch herself because*

*Princess is ready to tear her up) Got home around 6:30 p.m. Answering machine was on. Very strange message. Princess is trying to talk to an operator. Princess doesn't sound right. Its 8:30 and haven't heard nothing from her yet. Princess I love you. Please be alright.*

---

The phone ringing awakens me, I'd overslept! The desk-person spoke that a Jonathan was downstairs. We spoke over the phone and looking out the window, I could see that the streets were in flood! He asked if he could bring his Aunt Robbie by this evening since I wouldn't be walking.

"Yes. I was looking forward to meeting her but be sure to let her know that I have a cold!" I made two pots of coffee and bathed more and slept, waking just long enough to hear the sweet sound of rain.

Shoneys manager brought me hot soup for my cold. I really appreciated this. Since the hotel didn't have room-service, they called Shoneys Restaurant and spoke of my cold. These people are really nice and I would gamble to speak that long ago, during the removal, people like these handed food out to the starving Cherokee.

More sleep and sugar coffee! I was beginning to feel a little better when the Aunt arrived. This woman, near my age, was so friendly her body seemed to have an aura of gold! We talked of many things, and she asked to take my dirty clothes home with her and would have Jonathan to return them tomorrow; also invited me to stay at her house. I thanked her kindly but I had already paid for the room and had more calls to make! What touched me the most, Robbie even brought me a dinner of potatoes, greens, corn and cornbread. Tears came into my eyes as I felt the heart that she seemed to wear outside for all to see!

We bid goodnight and I sat for a long while wondering

why more people aren't as Miss Robbie is. "Great Spirit, please allow me to meet this woman again and remain friends throughout our lives!"

Next day rain has passed and I've the Walking-fever again! Jonathan brings my clean clothes and we go to Robbie's house. She lives in a brick country-estate and has a beauty-parlor adjacent to her home. There she lives with her Husband-man. She and I had so much in common and to talk about that the day was nearly gone.

Then she invited her Newspaper friend over and this nice and gentle-speaking woman named Frances does an interview. This woman is full of much knowledge and loves life and her work to the fullest.

After the long day of excitement, that evening, I met Robbie's Husband-man and Frances brought her's for me to meet! We all dined upon venison steaks and much laughter! Soon I had to rest. Robbie showed me her guest bedroom that looked like a picture from Better Homes and Gardens then gave me more medicine. I found sleep, knowing that I had found new friends as well!

Next morning finds me back at the country store. There, back on my trail and feeling better, I head for Woodbury, Tennessee! Enroute, White-Arrow finds me! She's with some friends that had to go to Murfeesboro. We had a picnic beside the road. A little gila had started following me earlier and there was enough for him too! I promised White-Arrow I would always keep in touch with her! We both cried upon departure.

Stopped at this feed-store and met most of the family that owned it. Had a good chat and me and little gila moved on! Came upon this roadside table rest and I was just too tired to go any further. Noticed a sign that it was only four more miles to Woodbury. There were many Cattle-Selling barns everywhere!

Two men pulled up, we made our introductions then the older one said "You can spend the night at me and my woman's house, but you will have to help cook supper and sweep the floor!" So proudly he spoke these words, I thought for a second and fought to keep my temper under control.

"Mister, I ain't no damn Betty-Crocker or Susie-Homemaker and after I've walked all day, I'll be damned if I clean your house!" That quickly ended the conversation and they sped away without even a Goodbye!

Next, these two women pull over. The one younger woman has her daughter with her. We introduced ourselves and had a pleasant conversation! The eldest woman spoke that she knew the Cattle-Selling man and they drove me over to one of the big barns so I could ask permission to sleep in one. He told me to make my own choice! My little gila went to play with his dog, so I thank the nice ladies and suggest to the daughter to read the books; Trail of Tears, by John Ehle, and the one, Walking The Trail, by Jerry Ellis. The daughter, Melissa, was much elated and so intelligent to be so young.

They drove away as I searched for the right barn door to enter. There were just too many doors. Asked permission to make a telephone call before bedding down. "Granted!"

---

*Message on recorder. Princess hasn't made it to Woodbury yet. Still has a cold and staying in a barn. I went to doctor for check-up. I think I'm getting bad?*

---

As the nvda (sun) set, I cleaned a place in the loft to lay my sleeping-bag upon. I dined on K&M and dry cereal; said my prayers and waited for sleep.

Now the many cows and calves begin crying. They knew

that something was wrong in their life, just as my People did. These cattle were being hauled in and hauled out. The big trucks went all night long. The cattle were losing their loved ones just as my People lost loved ones along this Trail. Shallow graves were made for the lost as they dropped dead while trying to walk. Mamas carried babes in their arms that had been dead for many days before. Stillborn babies dropped from the women as they walked. All this kept going through my mind as I heard the cattle cries. The barn doves even joined in to share their grief.

Then I got mad at myself for being hooked on cheeseburgers, knowing they come from this kind of cattle stockade, just like my People were driven from stockades just like cattle. The anger in me turned in to tears. The Spirits, the cattle, the doves and myself, all cried together.......

This brought to my mind a poem I wrote when I was in my teens. I would always ask Mama to leave the kerosene-lamp on because I kept hearing night cries. I felt it was the cries that echoed in the mountains and that they came from a little gila or a child (ayohli). Or if we could leave just a lantern burning, then these lost cries could find their way to our shack. Mama understood. Now through my sobbing, I started to recite NIGHT CRIES loudly!

I keep hearing a little dog
Whining at my door.
But when I go to let it in,
Don't hear it whine no more.

And I keep hearing a little child
Crying in the night.
But when I step out to hear,

It all just gets real quiet.
Perhaps I should bake some bread
For the little dog to eat.
Or hang my lantern on the porch,
So the little child can see.

But I know the bread would mold,
The lantern wick would burn, I fear.
'Cause I been hearing night cries,
For nigh on forty years.

Seems the Hand of the Great Spirit calmed all for a bit, then He gave me peacful sleep upon my pallet in the wailing barn.

## "SOME HISTORY OF WOODBURY"

Woodbury descendants are mostly of Scotch-Irish, English and German. In 1806 the Federal Government built a road from Rattlesnake Springs to Murfeesboro, Tennessee following the "Old Black Fox Trail". John Sageley was the first white man to settle in this area and build his log cabin in the 1780's, though no documentation can be confirmed.

Also spoken, was another 1780's white settler; a widow named Mary Todd along with her two brothers. History speaks that she attended Cherokee Indian Dances and lost five of her brothers in fights with the Cherokee. Three brothers were killed in Kentucky and the other two at Fort Nash. Mary lived to see the age of 104. Perhaps its because our Cherokee people liked her and she understood them as well.

In 1805, George M. Deaderick was the president of the only bank in Middle Tennessee and in 1814 he had a large gala in Nashville for Old Hickory when he returned from the South defeating the Seminole Indians.

The Rucker family was interesting, four brothers and two sisters. They came here from Virginia through Knoxville, Tennessee. The brothers, James, Thomas, Gideon and Bennett all claimed to be preachers. This was in 1790's. They couldn't agree an the same denomination but they agreed on women. All four brothers married sisters! Later all became buddies to the famous Donelsons and Old Hickory Jackson. As time passed, the eldest brother James and his wife Nancy had a daughter named Betsy. She grew up and married Mrs. Andrew "Hickory" Jackson's brother Severn Donelson. Betsy and Severn had a son and shortly after his birth they adopted him to Rachel and Old HIckory because Rachel was childless. Hickory named the child Andrew Jackson, Junior!

The first brick home built in this area was by Charles Ready. That was his third house and the year was 1829. Today this house still remains.

One of the best true romances comes from Woodbury, Tennessee. Tina Weedon and Yankee Captain Smith.

Woodbury people have remained close to their ties of brotherhood and this small town has provided men for every war that has been fought. Therefore, I would describe these men as Great Warriors and the women of much Strength and Knowledge.

Another person of great interest is Dr. J.F. Adams. He was born October 19, 1881. My interest is that my last name is Adams, too and I was born October 20, 1951!! My first dream was to be a Doctor-woman! In short, he married Laura Elizabeth Hudson who was from Texas. He finished Medical school in 1911 from Vanderbilt in Nashville, Tennessee. This man did much for Woodbury; farming, banking, real estate and the county government. He built the first ice factory and cheese plant. In the 1930's he built the Good Samaritan Hospital. They raised their children and they all did well for themselves from being raised with busy hands and minds. His missus worked much hard as well. She served as well as cooked the meals for the hospital, plus doing the hospital laundry in her home. Dr. Adams made it happen for the ADAMS MEMORIAL LIBRARY where I was able to purchase a book of knowledge about Woodbury. Though Dr. Adams and his missus have passed on now, I thank "Our Great Spirit" for his generosity and especially to Mr. Robert L. Mason who worked I'm sure, endless hours on his "HISTORY OF CANNON COUNTY, TENNESSEE".

As I was doing research for my own "Message In The Wind", I became so interested in his book, I set my own manuscript aside just to concentrate on his book. Mr. Mason's is a MUST READ book. He speaks it best about history: quote "History, it is US". Thank you Mr. Mason and I would feel honored to meet you. Wada!

## WOODBURY, TENNESSEE

Dying for a cup of coffee! Soon I came upon the little main-street. Just off the path, a bit to my right, I see a place called Joe's! "Thank you Great Spirit. I have a bad headache and need coffee!" Chilled a little, I find a seat over in a corner so I can see the entrance well. Yes, I'm one of those! I never sit with my back to the door!

This high-school age waitress tends to me. She's most pleasant and wants to know were I am going with that big back-pack? I tell her and this brings such warmth to her eyes! She and this other girl make sure that I have plenty of coffee and find me some Advil because I'm out. These headaches have plagued me for so long. Been to Doctors, but its the same old story, "Alethea, you are just a nervous type of person and they will probably never go away. You will just have to learn to live with them!" I'm not speaking that all doctors are bad, I just feel that the majority are lazy and treat you like a cattle-call!

After a pot of coffee and I've washed up a little; at least I got all the hay out of my hair, I left a message on Mr. Bill's machine. Now the road beckons for my return! "So long Joe! You sure do serve good coffee! Just keep the pot warm and I'll be back!"

---

*Getting colder here. I pray for you woman. Have message on recorder. Princess leaving Woodbury. She's at Joe's Restaurant heading for Murfeesbourogh (I'll see you tonight woman.) Princess is waiting for me.*

---

As I am making my exit of the town, these two old-timers holler across the road to me! "Hey girl, why don't you have somebody to walk with you?" laughing, awaiting my answer!

"Well fellers, another woman would be whining and if I had a man with me, he would have something else on his mind instead of walking!" They doubled over laughing to my answer and shook their heads in agreement! We traded waves, I walked on...

Just climbed another mountain and my polio-leg started giving me pain. As I found the bottom land, I see this big oak shade tree. It looks so inviting! Its on private property but at the edge of their garden. Surely they won't mind. The energies coming from the big white house feel warm so I'll take my chance! Just got settled under the old oak tree and it hit me! WOW, what an aroma to pass by me now!! I do love TUYA (beans)!! I felt like Yogi Bear following a picnic basket!

Then this fragil little lady in her autumn years comes around the house with a big warm smile on her face! We introduce ourselves and she invites me in. To a sweet surprise, her whole house in decorated in Indian style! I'm really impressed!

"It has taken me a long time to do all this." She points to her walls with pride as she decribes where and when her treasures had been collected!

I show my warm interest and give her an interview of me that someone had given me in passing! She asked me to sign it for her as she went about her home in search of a frame! Then she invited me to enjoy tuya with her! Oh, so much I wanted to dig into those beans and I was about to say "YES" when her husband-man wheeled into the room. Suddenly I felt a wave of discomfort. Spoke a quick introduction, thanked the sweet lady, didn't smell the tuya anymore, and found my way back to the road.

Making my way slowly toward Murfeesboro, still trying

to shake that cold feeling I got from that sweet husbandman. Pondering wasn't the solution. I think I figured it out! He probably felt since his house was overrun with Indian Treasures, the last thing he wanted to see, since he had just awakened from a nap, was a live Indian! Now I'm satisfied!

The Christian Woman with the intelligent Missy, finds me again. It's growing late in the day, so they suggest that I allow them to take me on into town since it's only about eight miles. With my leg in pain there was no way that I could make the walk before dark. Plus, after a short rest in the town I could return and make up the milage. I agreed.

There had been a heavy feeling in my chest for two days now. There was something, and I knew I was receiving A Message in the Wind ...

## MURFEESBORO, TENNESSEE

Much was going on in the town! There was a balloon race and a horse show. Therefore, we had a problem finding a room. Missy suggested The Gardens Hotel. After hearing, "Sorry, we have no rooms available," we took Missy's advice.

"Yes, Ma'am, we have only one room available!"

As I went back to their car to retrieve my pack, I thanked Missy! "The joke is on me and your Mama, honey. You are the wise one! Keep reading, we will meet again someday soon!"

They prayed for my walk to be safe and I stood at the big lounge doors and watched them drive out of sight. I think of Missy as she waves the book, "The Trail Of Tears" at me with a big smile. She will probably become a professor one day and I hope that I have inspired her by recommending that first book about Indians. Better yet, I give the credit to John Ehle! He wrote about the rise and fall of our Cherokee Nation and I thank him dearly. I've had Mr. Bill and all I meet to real Mr. Ehle's book.

The clerks are friendly as I check in and are much interested in my Journey! That gives my heavy heart a boost as I find my way to the room. "Yes. Just what the doctor ordered!" The first thing I do is call my Mr. Bill! He promises to leave within the hour and I detect a nervous sound in his voice. "Please Great Spirit, let everything be alright. I need and love Mr. Bill".

In 1811, a Revolutionary War soldier, Col. William Lytle, donated this tract of land to Tennessee. Then a few years later he had the town named after a dear friend of his; another Colonel whose name was Hardy Murfee. Cherokee Indians fought in the Revolutionary War beside his Yonega

Udo (White Man Brother) and were promised a penison from the Government once the Cherokee found their new homeland in the West, which was denied upon the Removal.

Murfeesboro was also the battle ground for one of the most bloody battles of the Civil War. Its known as the Stones River Battle. The South, under Gen. Bragg, had had thirty eight thosand men to fight Gen. Rosecran's forty five thousand that served the North. The battle was only three days long. Both sides were in despair. The Northern General was just on the edge of giving up. Then at the last minute he changed his mind. This decision forced the Southern General's hand to defeat. Within this short period of a few days, both sides had lost many soldiers. The South lost eleven thousand and seven hundred men and the North lost twelve thousand and nine hundred men.

I stood for a long time and studied this Monument, wondering the names of the forgotten Cherokee soldiers that were in this war as well. If I could change or make something happen, I would research every name of the soldiers, have a stone wall erected and every soldier's name would be there for the people to respect.

I don't intend to sound biased but all soldiers should have their names placed, especially the Cherokee here. In 1838, some driven through this town like pups sent to a dog-pen, later returned, only to fight in another Yonega-war. Just like a man's best friend, a dog gets kicked in the ass by its master on Earth, then the gila will lick his master's hand. When our people were first discovered, the white man said we were like "Children" always giving and sharing.

Mr. Bill arrives around eleven p.m. and I'm so excited to see him but this worried look on his face, took some of the spark out of our embrace.

"0K" I began slowly, "Let's have Council and get this

darkness off your chest!"

As usual, it takes him awhile to get into a motive gear, then he finally let it out. "Princess, my soon to be ex. won't leave me alone. She talked me into coming down to her house and she just dogged you down as usual. She paid a man that lives at Woodson Bend to tell her a lot of gossip! And I didn't want to upset you while you're trying to make this Trail of Tears happen. Guess I'm just depressed about the whole thing, because I knew that you would be able to know that something is bothering me."

I thought for a minute and tried to sooth him. "Honey, it's all just a bunch of bullshit and envy anyway. Let's put it behind us and enjoy our time together!" Trying to keep his spirits up, I suggested we call the Hiwassees. They would enjoy the time to get away. Mr. Bill agreed. Still, my heart wasn't satisified. There was something more. Well, I'll leave things as they are for now. Soon I will know,I thought.

---

*Got up around 8:am at Plaza Hotel. Happy's came to visit. Mr. Happy and I went for horse feed. Princess and Mrs. Happy walked 5 miles when the rain stopped them. We all ate at Red Lobster Sat. night - Sunday Happy's left around 2:30. I left about 3:30 pm. Got home around 9:pm*

---

Hiwassees arrived the next day. The men went for a drive and me and the Missus had them to drop us off back down the road. Therefore, I could make up some of the miles from where the Christian Woman had brought me into town. Mrs. Hiwassee was all for walking with me! We enjoyed five miles of walk until the rain put us on an old deserted house porch! The Men found us then we went for dinner.

That night Mr. Bill went to bed early. I really knew that something more was wrong. My heart went out for him. "If only he would communicate more with me, I could maybe help him," I thought. "Ayv dadlohyiha (I weep) for you, Mr. Bill."

Hiwassees asked if I would like to watch a movie called Star Wars? I was all for it because I had never seen this kind of movie before! Perhaps this is out of character for a forty year old woman not to have seen it by now but I'm not the Science Fiction kind. I have always invested my time in watching a movie of truth or reading a book of truth. Fiction to me is a waste of time. I recall once, when I was coming home on leave from the Airforce, all the stewardesses were wearing these odd shirts that had the word "MASH" on them. Well, when I got to Mama's, I ask just what that meant? Mama laughed and said, "Honey, that's a Military Sitcom on television that is being taken off and the public wants it to remain. It's really a good comical show!"

"Well Mama, If it's so good and all the people like it so much, why would they want to take it away?" earnestly asking.

"Honey, you wouldn't understand. Just like you don't know about the Star Trek shows I watch. If we all left on a spaceship tomorrow, you would be the only one left behind, waving at us from the back of a horse!"

So I ask the Hiwassees if this was like Star Trek, that my Mama used to watch. They spoke that it was! Fine! I joined in!! "Mama, if you could see your Little Bead-Eyes now, you'd be proud because I've just left Earth for my first time and taken a journey into space!

The next morning I ask Mr. Bill for Council again. This time I must get through!

"Ok Princess, I'll tell you. Next Tuesday I must see the Doctor again and this time I have a biopsy done on my prostate. They are checking for cancer. Really, honey, the fact is, I will know Tuesday whether or not it is cancer. I just didn't want to worry you while you are trying to walk this Trail!" We embraced as if there was no tomorrow.

"I love you Mr. Bill and we shall pray much that it won't be cancer. And I will end my walk now, if you want me to," pleading to him.

"No Princess, this has been your life-long dream and I intend to do everything I can just to see that you make it happen. We will make it. Don't worry honey." His deep and soothing voice went all through me and he tried to calm my trembling body but I knew that he was just as scared about these results as I was. We both held our silence for as long as we could as we held each other...

The Hiwassees knocked on our door, indicating it was time to depart. We four talked about Mr. Bill's dilemma and all had a prayer before they had to leave again. We walked outside with them. and waved to our friends as they drove from the parking lot! And I held on to Mr. Bill's hand as long as I could as he slowly had to drive away. Then I rushed back to my room, threw myself across the bed, and cried and prayed.

Sometime in the night I awakened to find that exhaustion had brought me sleep. To look at myself in the mirror was not a sight to behold. My eyes were fully swollen and red. It was two o'clock in the morning but I knew that no more sleep would come to me. I walked the hotel room like a caged cat, trying to get ahold of myself, knowing that tomorrow I needed to find a Doctor myself. I was in bad need of an estrogen shot. My nerves were slipping out of my control.

Daylight found me still restless and battered looking. I called my sister, Sparrow, to see if perhaps she could consol me. Told the news about Mr. Bill and she cried with me on the telephone.

Then I called one of my younger sisters, Two-Fist, and her calm voice did seem to take a grasp. "Hey girl!" speaking a voice of strength, "Everything will be just fine, you wait and see! And Blue wants you to know that he keeps a copy of your journey-map up at the barn and we're all keeping up with you on the Trail. The ladies I work with here at the office are praying for you and we will pray for Mr. Bill too. So hang in there. Be strong like we were taught to be! Now my name isn't Two-Fist for nothing!" This helped me. Soon I gave into a half-laugh!

"Thanks sissy, I needed this support." But the dead sound of a dial-tone allowed an empty feeling to try to get back inside me. I felt like these poor soldiers must have felt when they fought upon this very land.

Started gathering my pack when I thought of that Nurse that I met back on Spencer Mountain! Finally found her number in my bag. My doctor, Crazy-Horse, had written on his medicine pad what kind of estrogen I needed and for any Doctor to call him if they should have any questions. "Thank you, Crazy-Horse! I promise not to fire you like I do many others!"

After I called the Nurse-Lady, I was getting control of myself. She promised to be there soon and she knew a Doctor to give me an estrogen shot. "Keep yourself together Alethea, don't lose it now!" I kept repeating to myself like a broken record.

Within an hour, her smiling face had me enjoying the beautiful day Our Great Spirit had given us! She gave me a tour of the town. We had a nice lunch and she had found a Doctor for my MUCH needed shot! Then we headed to the small and quaint little town that she lived in. Smithville, Tennessee gave smiling faces of little children and warm hellos from all the people that she introduced me to! Her home was filled with warmth and the smell of down home-cooking! Her Husband-man was kind and jolly and her son was most respectful, unlike most teenagers of today's society.

Before sundown she took me to this Park. So many energies could be felt all around us. We stood there in silence and felt the Spirits as the nvda (sun) slowly found a hiding place for rest over the Western ridge.

Back at their home, her husband-man had already started preparing this fine feast! "We, and the whole world, may be on a diet but, Alethea, you are a special guest and we are fixing a full course meal for you tonight! Just make yourself comfortable there at our kitchen table and plan to eat!"

This I did! The fried chicken melted in my mouth. Perhaps this would make me want to get off hamburgers I thought as I passed my plate for a third helping! We enjoyed much laughter as well as fine conversation! They showed me to my private room that allowed me to have the privacy of their balcony that was nestled near the majestic mountain that overlooked a mountain stream.

Then I called Mr. Bill to speak where I was and how much I loved him.

---

*Princess called around 8:pm She had gotten an estrogen shot and is spending the night with a nurse that she had met. Going to start walking again in the morning. Good night, Princess and don't worry.*

---

After everyone had gone to bed, I stepped out onto the balcony and looked up at the silver moon. "Great Spirit, thank you for my path crossing with these fine folks. And watch over Mr. Bill. Whisper to him my love and adoration.

Please let him live. I will never hurt him and I promise care for him always. If you choose that it be cancer, I won't question because I have no right. Just show us a way to handle it. I will obey you. And let me have safeness upon this Trail of Tears. Wada, Great Spirit, goodnight."

Early morning sun (nvda) guided me and Nurse Galinda through the winding Cumberland Mountains to our destination, the Veteren's Hospital. There I met her co-workers and her best friend! Since Galinda had to commence work, her friend that was just getting off work spoke that she would be glad to drop me off at the point where me and Mrs. Hiwassee had gotten rained out.

At this market I grabbed a cup of coffee (kahwi)! Needed to jump start this body engine and get the ESTROGEN quick to flow! Nvda was warm upon my face but the air was a bit frisky. Traffic was much heavy. Coal trucks were flying as if they were on a big road. There was no shoulder for me to walk upon, just the backditch for retreat.

When I heard the squealing brakes of an eighteen-wheeler just fixing to give a good morning kiss (atawedo?vsga) to a compact car that had only a prayer for a chance, I hunkered into the back-ditch as quickly as a rabbit (jisdu)! Well, the gun (galogwe) didn't go off but there was left much smoke from the tires!!! Now that was a close one!

Came upon these city workers that saw the whole thing and were laughing! "This is an everyday event. Why, it's a wonder we haven't been killed yet. Guess we've just gotten used to it!" This gentle, weathered looking man speaks all this with much ease.

Then I started laughing! He spoke how much he admired me for walking the Trail Of Tears and I in turn admired him for having the nerve to work daily on this dangerous narrow road!

Coming now to a "Y", I pondered for a second to figure the best way to get across town. Spotted another market just ahead "Yeah, they will know!" Having the miles caught up on now, I will take a break and really enjoy some good hot and strong kahwi!

Tugged at the door, wiggling my back-pack through, following the heat that was beckoning me. There two smiling women greeted and welcomed me in! The younger one just stared at the sight of me for a second then offered me kahwi. "How do you like your coffee, Ma'am?"

Smiling back at her with my Mama's favorite kahwi answer, "I like my kahwi like I do my men, HOT and STRONG!" We all three roared with laughter!

Then we settled into speaking of my attire and the reason for my journey. Keeping my cup filled, I listened to the younger one casually speak that she had just gotten married the night before and her new husband-man was presently home sleeping!

"Well," I laughed my reply! "That's one way to start a day. Be an original!" She agreed!

The elder Lady remarked with a grin that her parents didn't even know yet and teased her about calling them to inform! "You better not!" The little blonde yelled as she was now busy at the telephone. I heard her ask someone, "Would you come over here right now?" Evidently the person agreed. Then she hands me the telephone. Surprised, but I took the call, thinking it was probably her new husband-man. But it was an interview-man instead.

"Yes sir, I would like much to give an interview. Yes I'll be right here. Thank you Sir!" We Ladies talked more and I met the Pop Machine Man that came to deliver. Then I spoke to the Ladies just what a soothing as well as handsome voice the Interview Man had.

"Oh, wait till you see him. His voice matches his face too!" Shortly he wheels slowly into the parking lot. "There he is!" they gasped with more laughter!

This handsome man walked toward me with his hand oustreached introducing himself. I knew I could be arrested for the thoughts of my mind! Plus the Great Spirit doesn't allow SUCH to leech (dlanusi) in an usti (little) mind such as me!!! With the light behind him, this enhanced the graceful move as if he were a Hè-Lion. I could see the warmth in his eyes and feel the energies from his stature even more of warmth. "Great Spirit" forgive me?!" I admit to this sin of thought as well as the first chance I get I'll tell Mr. Bill on myself! In my mind I whispered "Uganawa Hlvdaji Aktoli" meaning Warm Lion Eyes!!!

Much was going on in the store so he spoke that we walk outside so he could take some pictures of me for the newspaper. Being a bit nervous, I kept rambling as he kept making pictures! We talked about the Trail Of Tears much and he asked my opinion of the Old Hickory-Magician opinion though not in those exact words! But I spoke that if I could see Jackson right now I would flat out ask,"WHY?"

Soon the interview was over and I stood in the doorway watching as he drove out of sight. "I pray we meet again, Uganawa Hlvdaji Aktoli."

Time for me to move on! Time for the "Quick to marry in the night" Lady to get off work! "Why don't I walk a way's with you through town?" she quickly asked! "I live right on the route that you must walk and I would just love to talk with you more, okay?"

"Sure, as I am ready." answering with a big grin! I bid the nice Boss-Woman farewell as we made our way out the door and I was adjusting my pack. Then we stopped for just a minute so I could meet her new Husband-man. I found him most nice but his energies I found so much in a jumble.

Afterwards, we walked until we came to this Chinese Resturant. My low blood sugar was screaming, "I need something, don't care what it is Alethea!" So I undid my pack and hid my Bonnie inside it. The establishment was most pretty! Being choicy, I selected the table of my choosing not the one the hostess had selected. Now me and Quick-Wed are continuing our life stories when I notice the Instrumental Music. Of all songs and all places to eat who would think that one would hear an instrumental country song in a Chinese restaurant? Oh, but I do!!!

Tears welled into my eyes as the music played, "Lord I'm Five Hundred Miles Away From Home". Bringing this song to her attention, she too agreed, "This is unreal!" The wonton soup was probably great but I lost my appetite. We departed. She walked a few more blocks with me, wished me a safe journey and spoke that she would pray for me. I thanked her much as I waved Osda Dichvsdi (Good Marriage) and wada!

Walking past many stately mansions made this old heart beat fast and made me uhnalvha (angry) both. Admiring the structure and art of these homes was one thing but to feel the cold (kanawoga) feelings they gave made me more appreciate the mountain-way that I was raised. Seemed there was no adageyhdi (love) that surrounded these mansions, just a house without any daksvsdiha (smoke). There's no people about or food on their table.......

Finding my way through the town's court-yard, there was a back street that led me to a much busy intersection. Turning right to find West, heavy traffic and many gas fumes gave me my famous headache. There was no sign that spoke, "Walk or don't think about walk!" and left me scared to make a move. Drivers just looked at me but none seemed to care if I made it across the busy big road or not. I felt I'd been patient long enough so I just threw my hand up to the many cars and walked across the three lane street as if I where a Queen! "Take that! And Wada too!" I mumbled.

After my fight with the traffic the headache returned and I'm looking for a place to take a rest. Seeing a graveyard to my left I choose a big ancient oak tree. The wind was picking up from the West so I wrapped my rain-slicker close as I prepared to enjoy my jola (Virginia Slim). This old familiar feeling came back into my body. "It's the flu," I thought as I started praying. Then I diverted my attention to the beauty around me. Yes, I find a kind of peace in a graveyard.

I noticed these four usdi (little) graves all in a row, side by side all by themselves. Walked over to the usdi graves and allowed my mind to wonder of the many reasons these usdis were here. "Was it a fire? Maybe small pox?" Whatever it had been that took their lives, I felt much sad for them.

I recall my Grandfather Sherman telling me once his and Grandmother's first born were twins. The day after she gave birth, she just up and decided to visit her sister that lived about twenty miles away. "There I stood in the doorway of our log cabin and watched her stride out of sight. The last thing I saw was this tall Cherokee Grandmother of yours, and her long black braids flow in spring wind. I had much to do. The corn needed chopping and I just stood there holding these two babies. What was a young man to do? Didn't have no cow yet. All I could find was some red canned tomatoes. So I just put that down them so they would hush and go on back to sleep. Well, they cried much more hard and then they just was real quiet. Then I seen they was of death child. I wrapped them with all I could find. Just sat there. Well, two days, here she comes all hollerin' and a cussin', "Them damn youngun's still cryin'?"

"No," I said, as quiet as one would speak when they are around the dead. "They have passed on, 'Rinde, and you don't have to worry about these babies." She screamed at me to fetch a quilt so we could go and bury them right then. Well I did. And there in the night we buried our first two little babies. Not a word came out of her and I reckon I never did forgive her but when you bed a woman before you marry her, I been told you stay with her till you die. I can't read or write so I just have to go by what I hear folks a readin' from the Good-Book."

I cried for Pa that day but had to ask just one more question."Did she ever mourn for the babies, Pa?"

"Not that one could tell. All she said was "Me and my Sister was over in Huntington-Town and we saw Jesse James rob a store and I would have liked to went with him!"

Still standing there for quite a long time, I wondered if maybe these usdi had been deserted by their Mama? "No," I convinced myself, "It was probably a house fire." A chill was setting in on me much fast now. I took one last look at the little graves and went on.

The flu always makes me angry. I was coming upon these tall evergreens that seemed to be dancing with the sound of whispering and singing winds. Admiring them, all was interrupted by the roar of machines. "Shit, they are building another big road. Like we need one." The workers waved, I didn't. Then I realized "It's not their fault. They are just working to feed their families." Then I turned around and waved back.

Then it dawns on me. This is Tuesday, I think, and I must call my Mr. Bill today. Yeah, it's today that we know what the Doctor-Man speaks about Mr. Bill! I pray a million times that it isn't of cancer. No, I can't handle that, usdi graves still lingering.

Still fighting this headache, swelling stomach and another flu. Damn car fumes were just as bad. Saw this market ahead. Went in to ask about a place to sleep. This stretch of road doesn't have any barns, just many places of business. This nice lady spoke that up the road about half a mile, I would find this little motel on the right mostly transient workers rent. "You will be lucky if there is a room!" Getting late. I'm getting sicker so I buy me a forbidden sweet-ama (Pepsi) and make my legs find the motel.

I could see that at one time it must have been most pretty! Now it looked more deserted. A cow-bell rings as I fight the knob that doesn't want to turn. Small musty office. I ring the little brass-butler bell and the ding-ding was getting to me big! Then a humble little Lady appears. Must have been well into her winter years and gives me this warm smile!

"Ma'am," I plead with little patience, "Do you have a sleeping room left?"

"Honey," she slowly answers me, "I don't know. I've been cooking and I can't remember if I rented the last room or not." the whole time searching her key board. "Yes!" she squeals, "Here's just one and I'll walk to the room with you. My husband-man died some years ago and I'm here all by myself. It's a lot of work for one person to keep this up. Oh, this used to be so pretty. He gave this to me as a Wedding gift!"

By now we have found the room. As she opened the door, the stench of sweat, dirty clothes and a filthy toilet hit my nostrils. "Isn't this just so nice?" asking with a smile! "It will be fine, Ma'am," replying with a lie and praying for our Great Spirit to forgive me. I couldn't hurt her feelings, I was thinking to myself.

Dumped my back-pack, unstrapped my gun, then ran to throw up! My head was much too cloudy (ulogila). Searching for a telephone, damn, there isn't one! "What do I do?" Went back to the little office and the woman pointed towards the wall near the door as she was eating her cornbread. I just sat there for a minute trying to steady my trembling voice and show Mr. Bill that I had control no matter what the answer he had waiting for me.

The operator made the call happen. "Yes Ma'am, I accept the collect call!" His voice was as nervous as my sickly body.

"Mr. Bill, what did the Doctor-Man speak? Are you going to be alright? I love you and you know that don't you?" rambling and babbling with a loaded question.

"Princess, don't start crying on me now," trying to sooth me.Yet it seemed that both of us were failing the test. "Princess, I have prostate cancer..." There was a time of no-speaking on either side of the line.

"When must you have the operation?" losing complete control.

"My Princess, I can wait until your journey is finished. Okay? I will be alright. Now calm down. Is there a telephone in your room or nearby?"

I just answered, "No", because the woman could hear every word I spoke. I wanted to scream that there was no telephone and I was sick again plus the bed was dirty. "Are you really going to live Mr. Bill?"

"Yes, Princess, I will live. I live just for you. Now go back to your room. You sound much tired. Please don't cry. Go on now and call me again as soon as you can, okay?"

"Yes, Mr. Bill but I will leave the Trail and come home!"

"Oh, no you won't! Now go on, and Princess, I love you.

Just give me a kiss on the telephone and get on back to your room."

"Yes, Mr. Bill. I will go now. Goodnight my soon to be Husband-man and I'll hurry (nula) home to you!

I thanked the kindly woman then left the office with a heavy heart (adanhdo). I couldn't sleep on the dirty (agadahaʔi) bed. Nor could I bath in the dirty water-hole, so I just wrapped myself in my Indian (Ayvwiyaʔi) blanket (unegvhaʔi) and found a spot in front of the baseboard heater. Used my pack for a pillow (akwsdo) and cried myself to sleep (gahliha), shaking from chills and thinking of death (ayohuhisdi).

---

*Princess called from an office in a bad smelling motel. Told her the news about my cancer. She cried. I did too. I love you woman. Don't leave the Trail.*

---

Loud mufflers on the transient worker's cars brought me from my sleep! Wonder what time it is? Well, I figured they were going to work. So I used my bandana to wash my face. Thought maybe I just dreamed that Mr. Bill had cancer. "No," answering myself. He is much sickly, so I must speed my steps. I've lost much weight now, so there's no excuse for me to walk slow, except for this cold I keep getting.

Across the road before good daylight in hopes to make many miles today. Came into a connecting-town which was north of Murfeesboro and South of Nashville. These two preachers wheeled in beside me in one of these business parking lots and begin to speak that the End of Time was very near! I was too tired to argue the point; hadn't had a cup of kahwi (coffee) all day nor any tobacco (jola). "Pour your preaching (Ahljadohvsga) on me!"

THEY DID! After much talk one speaks, "I know math

really well so I have it figured to the exact date!"

"Ok, Mister," firmly inquiring. "What is the date?"

He pauses for a second, "Well, it will be on October the 20th!" keeping a big smile on his face!

I thought for a minute while my mind was flashing, "Many deaths upon the Trail of Tears, the four usdi graves, Mr. Bills cancer, my many colds and the fact that my birthday would be soon on October 20." While lost somewhere in my thoughts, I heard them speak that it was time they go do more preaching and handed me a twenty dollar bill!

"Mister, if the end of time is that close what good is this money going to do me?" asking with a confused look on my face.

He paused and just looked at me as he was getting in the car, looking as serious as the day. "Buy you something to eat because the money won't do us any good either." I just stood there dumbfounded as the wind tugged at the money!

Walked a couple more miles. Couldn't get Mr. Bill off my mind. Needed to take some more cold medicine. My feet started dragging and I kept thinking about those two preachers. If I recall right, from reading the Good-Book, I don't think anyone knows when the end of time will come! But one thing I knew for sure! I see a Big-Mac place right across the busy road and I'm going to get all I can with this twenty dollar bill!

"Yes, you can help me! I'll have two double cheeseburgers, three large fries and two large cokes!"

Right behind the McDonalds was a Days Inn motel and this is what I need to finish my day. I'll call Mr. Bill, while I am eating. This young woman makes comment that the food smelled good and was I alone? Just looking toward my pack gave her the answer.

Then I spoke of my Mission. Went on to my room and the phone rings! She speaks that the owner-Man from India wants to give me a discount because I am walking the Trail of Tears!

I thank them most kindly and ask if they would like to share my food. She speaks, "No!" but appreciated it just the same. The room (kanvsulvʔi) was most clean and perfect! It had a desk, two telephones and a King-Size bed! Oh, if only my Mr. Bill could be here! First I grab the telephone and open my food (alsdayhdi) because a chill should be upon it by now. I detest hot food!

Just hearing Mr. Bill's voice made me feel better. We laughed at the amount of food that I had ordered! Told him about the Preachers and their speaking about the end of time and since I have this fear of hunger and cold (uyosiha ale kanawoga), we agreed for me to eat all the food my belly could hold! We didn't speak of his sickness, only of things to laugh (uyetsga) about! He insisted that I take cold medicine and a hot bath then call him back and he would tuck me in bed (ganihli).

Felt clean (ganvgaliha) next morning but still sickly. Back to Route 41 again, dodging traffic and many dead wasa (cats) at the same time. Then these two men kept following me. I ignored them, yet they continued then came to a stop in front of me not more than ten feet.

One demanded, "Get in the car bitch!" as he was getting out of the passenger side. I gave him my famous fight look and spit at him, hissing, "YOU better get in the car, son of a bitch because I ain't in no mood for this crap. I'm sickly, my Mr. Bill is sick, I gotta cold and I'm sick of looking at dead cats and trash like YOU!" At the same time I swung Ol' Bonnie around.

His face grew much white as he was rushing back to his

seated position and he spoke to the driver, "Did you hear her? Hell, she's plum crazy!"

Gravels hit the back of my pack as they sped away. I just grinned (ujetsdi)! So, I thought, at times it helps to be CRAZY!!!

Walked a few more miles in this busy 41 business district when this little red truck pulls up. "Is he going to steal me too?" I thought.

This one is right beside me and he's alone. "Good morning baby. Help me get this thing off. Will you baby?" There he was, having his privates out.

And really serious, "I sure will," I'm answering with a smile but at the same time bringing Ol' Bonnie to pull me out of this one! "I'll get you off a lot sooner than you expected relief!" When he saw Bonnie, that was it! He left me in a cloud of dust! I prayed, cursed and cried for at least a mile...

As the day wore on, so did my body. Then I see this sign that speaks Nashville isn't far away. Figure I should make it by dark time. Stopped in this little market to ask permission to use the toilet. This nice owner-man spoke that I could and if I needed anything? "Yeah, a hot toddie for my cold!"

When I returned, there was a hot cup of kahwi! Waited for it to cool down a bit then when I sipped, I was surprised! "A woman walking the Trail of Tears in this day and time, you need that coffee!" he chuckled!

"Amen to that!" I agreed! Afterwards, I thought I would have to name that a "Crown-Royal-Toddie"!!

Later, a barber invited me in and wanted me to meet his missus. They were most nice and gave me a precious stone to carry along the Trail! They offered me to rest the remainder of the day (iga). Thanked them but I wanted to be in Nashville by night time.

Saw many crosses along the road. Wonder if this is where people have lost their lives? I would stop and study each one just to see if I could perhaps feel the energies in search of an answer.

I kept looking for The Dancing Wolves. Mr. Bill spoke that Mrs. Dancing Wolf was to visit her brother in Nashville, so they would drive farther South on 41 to see me and lift my spirits. I felt sad that we didn't cross paths as the day wore on.

This car stops and I'm of caution! Instead, blessed. It was three teens. They had read about me in the "Warm Lion Eyes" interview and just wanted to talk. This gave me a chance to take more Advil with the K&M medicine water and rest awhile. One of the gents was studying to become a State Patrolman. I praised him for this but insisted he remain a good one and don't let the Badge go to his head. Let it remain upon your chest (Ganejiʔi). He admired my advice and promised.

His sister (Udo) was going to become a reporter! I told her about "Warm Lion Eyes" and her brother about "Flame", a State patrolman back home in Kentucky. We all embrace as they departed, heading the way that I had just come from.

Mr. Bill said when I got to Nashville that he would meet me there. I was to get a room downtown then call him on his traveling phone to let him know where I was. These thoughts lifted my spirits as I imagined just how much fun we would have! I promise to myself that I would not speak of his sickness. "I PROMISE!" AYV ATUʔISDIHA!!!

Saw this historical looking deserted house to the right side of the 41 route. Thought for a minute maybe I should spend the rest of the day here. It's only about ten miles from Nashville City Limits but if I had a good long rest I would be able to make fast time in the morning. But the Message

In The Wind spoke not to so I prodded on. Would probably get arrested anyway for breaking into it!

Hope I can find a fancy style hotel in Nashville! Maybe I'll get to see HAT-MAN! He's a great singer and songwriter. At the Gathering that I had before my Trail of Tears departure, I invited some friends from Nashville to sing. Hat-Man brought his most beautiful wife. I remember her hair (ustihgv?i) was of brilliant black and shone as if there where sparkles all through it! Her smile was never ending! Song-writer, Vernon and his Missus came too! She had much long hair and we both agreed that a woman's hair is her Glory. Their two sweet and well behaved children stole everyone's heart (adanhdo!) They handed out the Trail of Tears maps to everyone! The Gathering was most full with warm energy But I think the floor was stolen by the handsome couple, The Dancing Wolves!!! They were like Fred and Ginger of the nineties.

"Come on Dancing Wolves and find me!" ...The nvda is growing tired too. It's on the low side of the sky now.

I SEE IT, I REALLY SEE IT!!! The sign speaks NASHVILLE!!! I'm much happy (aliheliga!!) but why do I feel this BAD MESSAGE IN THE WIND?

## NASHVILLE-DAVIDSON

We all know that Nashville is worldly known for its many Music Companies! But many moons ago, a Man named Richard Henderson from North Carolina made the first living place here and settlements far and wide in many directions! The way he made this happen was in 1775. The historical term of his barter was called "The Transylvania Purchase". This included the majority of Middle Tennessee and Kentucky. One would find it hard to believe that he got this vastness of territory from the Cherokee! Now 63 years later the former proud owners are being driven through the same land they once dwelled and hunted upon. By 1780 along came the Donelsons!

This was early families of Andrew Jackson's wife, Rachel. A Revolutionary War General named Frances Nash still has his name borne upon the French Lick Fort Nashborough. These new settlers needed a Self Government so a man named Henderson wrote the Cumberland Compact. Then in 1784 this area was incorporated as the Town of Nashville. Later, in 1806, it became a city. In 1862 the city was occupied by Federal troops and in 1864 the last Civil War battle took place just outside of town. This is when Gen. Thomas defeated Gen. Hood. But in April moon of 1963, the city of Nashville and Davidson county became as ONE. Really the true title of this city is Nashville-Davidson City! But you hardly hear this name. When someone speaks they are going to Nashville, thats all you hear. The Davidson part is rarely spoken.

Nashville-Davidson isn't just a city of music that holds the title for starting the Grand Ole Opry in 1925. It's also the center for many denominations of Religion headquarters. The Methodist Publishing House is the largest in the World pertaining to it's kind. The Vanderbilt University and Tennessee State University are here. I personally enjoy the Lowes Vanderbilt Hotel when I visit for a time of gala!

Beneath the grounds of the 1897 Centennial Park lies President James K. Polk. He was the eleventh President of the United States and was dubbed as "Young Hickory!" His position that led him to the White House was due to the fact that he was the elected Speaker of the House the last two years that Jackson was in office and the first two years of Van Buren's term, therefore becoming the only Speaker of the House to ever be President. Polk was of Straight-Walk type and of Methodist Belief. He wouldn't allow drinking, dancing or any poker playing in the White House. Its been spoken that Sam "Raven" Houston thought the President just drank too much water! Polk's goal was to expand the United States and offered Spain 100 million dollars for Cuba! Plus, he helped set the Gold Rush into action. Northerners disliked Polk because he was of pro-slave belief and they called him "Napoleon of the Stump"!

Three months after his time was up as President, he died at his home in Nashville. He had cholera. Remember, about twelve miles East of this City is the famous Hermitage Place and there lies beneath it's soil, Ol' Hickory Jackson. It's been spoken and written many times that as the once Proud Cherokee and black slaves were driven right by his fancy home he stood in the shadows and watched, perhaps to hide his shame.....

When you pass the sign that speaks NASHVILLE, forget about the STARS that would normally dance in your head! One has to fight for their life due to dashing cars and follow-you-with-sinful-eye!

Yes I was scared! This one driver in a fancy red sports car kept driving pass me, then waiting for me as I had to cross another busy street. He has the nerve to make licking moves with his tongue! I ignored him but my mind had a grin! I would like to see his tongue (ganhgoʔi) if my BONNIE could have licked (aganadiʔa) IT back!!

Now a new admirer! He is talking on his traveling-telephone as he keeps winking. He would drive a few blocks more and wait for me, just staring yet still talking on his phone.

Hell with all this, I need a break. Kahwi ale jola (coffee and tobạcco)! So I dash into this market! There a Gentleman asks what of my journey? We talk awhile about the Trail of Tears and Poetry! He bought my kahwi for me and I thanked him (wada) kindly. It's growing much late, so I hurried on. Someone had told me about this Holiday Inn that was only a few more blocks away. I planned to spend the night there since too much danger lurked in these city streets after dark! It's bad enough in day time.

I see this Law-Man, ask him how much further I must walk to find this Holiday Inn? This Law (dikanowadvsdi) gives me a look of complete confusion!

"Is that where you are planning on staying Miss?" speaking in a sadlike tone.

"Well, I guess so, unless you know of a better place I can reach before it's plum dark!" I answered with as much strength as I could muster. He looked up toward the sky as if to see if it really was getting dark then rubbed his peaked jaw in a much nervous way.

"No, you better hit it now because in the morning, this part of the road is wild. Hell, they about run over me! Good luck and I hope you make it!"

I thank him as I watch him remove his hat and climb back into his cruiser. Then I got to thinking as I was walking much fast and faced the blinding car lights, "Mister Law, you are supposed to care about a crazy Indian walking through your town. Why didn't you invite me to stay in your home? Okay, I am probably too dirty looking and your woman would get mad! Right?"

There it is! Stumbled in the door and immediately took a seat. Too tired to even speak to the Counter-Woman. On first looks all seems to be fine! The smiling Counter-Woman would take a curious glance at me then take a message for some trucker then look back at me again! I figured this was a trucker motel and a safe place to spend my first night in Nashville! Recharged, I ask for a room. She gives me the oddest look!

"Well, I have only one room and you will have to climb many steps then go over this bank up to this third level. Oh! The door doesn't lock very good. Any questions?"

As she handed me the key, I spoke that I have no question of how to find the room, I just want to know why you look at me with such strangeness! She grabs the ringing telephone and turns away. "You're welcome!" I answer myself, limping out the dirty window door and looking toward those many steps (akihlosvsdiʔi).

Searching for my room, I see many truckers all along the steps and balconies laughing and drinking beer. Many stares and wahya (wolf) howls slobbered from their throats. I was shaken all over by the time I found my room. Dropped my pack in a frantic search for the Advil! Now, I must call my Mr. Bill so he won't worry and speak "I'm finally in NASHVILLE!"

Just hang up the telephone and it rings! "Would that be Mr. Bill calling back that fast?" speaking out loud to myself!

"Hey, baby, saw you walk in your room!" This whining drunk voice half whispered.

"So what, Miller's-breath!" answering with coldness.

"How many do ya have lined up tonight for your bang-party, baby?"

For a minute I thought I would pass out! But I can't keep my mouth shut long enough to pass out! I'm out for blood! "Bang yourself, you bastard!" Then I slammed down the telephone!

RING RING RING RING!

Here we go again, I thought!

"HEEEY BAAABY! Step to ya winder. Look what a big banger I got fer ya. Can't turn it down honey!" laughing loudly!

"Well darlin'!" using my famous Indian-Scarlett voice. "Why don't you just come to my room and I'll show you all about some BANGING! Why, mine's about NINE inches and gives real BLOW-JOBS and it has nine BULLETS! What do ya speak NOW?" In a split second, I get a dial-tone! "You're welcome!" I speak out loud, smiling to the telephone!!

---

*Sept. 30, 1992. Princess called. In the first part of Nashville in a nasty trucker's hotel. She's mad!*

---

Stuck my knife (ahyelsdi) into the door, pressed two chairs against it. Figured I'd rather be dirty (agadahaʔi) than dead, so to hell with the water hole. I just climbed in the smelly bed, dirty and all, with Bonnie beside me. Just catnaps is all I get tonight. Left the lights on and stared at that damn telephone for a much long time, speaking my prayers OUT LOUD!

The nvda streaked through the curtains, which caught me by surprise! How had I slept so late? Rushed to wash up, no water hole time. Just strapped on my gun (galogwe) and backpack, tossing chairs to find the door! Dying for a cup of kahwi, felt it wasn't worth my time.

I'm heading Northwest 'cause I get to see my Mr. Bill this evening!! It just dawns on me! That counter-woman thought I was a "working" girl!

Dodging traffic, thinking this is a whole different style than me and my sister, Little Sparrow, had around this time about a year ago! It was her birthday and we came to Nashville just to have a good time! Rented a long white limo from Uncle Jim and had a night on the town (gaduhvʔi)!! She, the quiet type, rode up front with Uncle Jim! The limo bar was stocked with my favorite requests but I brought along a half gallon of our Kentucky's finest Moonshine for a sure backup! Met Hat-Man, Vernon and Bud as well as Bud's brother Plow-Boy. Had a ball!! Sparrow and Uncle Jim watched us dance the night (usvʔi) away while they sat quietly in each bar's corner table. I lost three pounds; forgot to EAT!!! I think I celebrated her birthday just right!

Darn it's hot this morning and I need some Advil. Here's a filling station! I'll freshen up again and soon feel better. The filling station man looked at me kinda cold like when I asked to use the toilet. Kept watching me like a hawk (tawodi)! "What does he think I'm going to do, steal his toilet-paper?" Sorry buddy, that's just too much more weight to carry!

"Oh, Mr. Bill, I can hardly wait to see (agowhtiha) you!" I feel that Mr. Bill watches out for me, even though we are miles apart because he asked me NOT to interview here in Nashville due to a lot of crazy-folk perverts that would be on the look-out for me only to bring harm. I feel he is of most right. Soon I'll see you TODAY! I can fall into your arms and CRY if I want to, can't I?

In this underpass I meet a group of young punks,

speaking most awful words to me. I try to ignore them, yet they are persistant! I stopped. They stopped. The Leader just grinned as if he had found a Noon-snack! I just pulled back my jacket that I had wrapped around Bonnie and stood there, waiting for his next move. He halted, held up his hands, turned back to join his gang.

"Well that's good thinking!" answering his gesture with a smirk and walking on.

My eyes are searching for those big fancy high rise hotels downtown. It's getting in afternoon time, I'm getting tired and mean! But when I see this tall Stouffer's Inn yet much distance away, my feet become quicker, my pack lighter! "Now here's your plan, Alethea! A fancy room, soak in the water hole for at least an hour, call Mr. Bill on his traveling-phone to let him know where to meet me! No, first I must buy a pretty outfit 'cause tonight we will dine, laugh and Love!!" These pleasant (udanhti) thoughts finally drag my moccasins into downtown just as the sun makes the tall buildings cast long shadows!

"Thank you, my Great Spirit, for the safe long walk across Nashville today!" Before I step into the fancy brass and glass doors of the Stouffer's, I brush off the dirt from my long skirt, readjust my dirty white bandana! That's good enough.

"Hello, my name is Alethea, and I am walking the Trail of Tears. I am much tired and I'm meeting my Mr. Bill here this evening later. Could I have a room PLEASE!?" Presenting a big happy but tired smile! The Agehya (Woman) behind the long desk looked at me as if I was plum crazy! Or perhaps lost in the wrong time zone!

"Well Miss," speaking firmly and holding a cold stare to my eyes "We are having a Convention in town and if you have no reservations, there's NO ROOM for you. Next, please?"

I gently stepped aside to do some thinking. "Now Alethea, you're dirty and sweaty and you know you need a bathing. Just think how you look compared to these pretty panty-hosed woman customers and the fancy pin-striped man-folk?" So, I talked myself out of a WAR-PATH due to my low energy level. "But I'm hungry and tired and Mr. Bill is somewhere en-route! See ya! I'll just find another place!" Got to think positive!

Now there's the Four-Star Holiday-Inn! Got it!! "Hello, my name is Alethea! I'm walking the Trail of Tears. Could I have a room PLEASE?" This handsome Black man gives me at least half of his attention. That puts a bigger smile on my dirty face!

"Ma'am," he speaks with a deep voice of strength, "Do you have reservations?"

I pause for a second, "No sir, it's kinda hard to make those if you're walking the Trail of Tears isn't it?"

"Sorry Ma'am, don't have a room for you. Now will you kindly step aside?" giving me a smirk at the same time.

I stepped back and leaned up against this shiny white column there just a few feet away from the polished counter. I was hoping to rub some of my road dirt onto the damn column! This awesomely dressed woman steps into my tracks! She looked like a Movie-Star! My heart (adanhdo) grew heavy as I watched her receive a room key and a smile, both without any reservations.

"Calm down Alethea. If you lose that temper, you'll end up in jail!" I could see the Nashville Headlines!

INDIAN GOES ON WAR-PATH, WALKING TRAIL OF TEARS NOBODY WOULD GIVE HER A ROOM BECAUSE SHE WAS DIRTY CALL THIS NUMBER TO

FREE HER or $$ FINE HER...

Shook these thoughts and quietly walked out. Looked to my left and spotted the Days Inn! Isn't it always spoken that third time is of CHARM? Just had reached for the door handle when this Man in a suit speaks. "We have no rooms, Miss!" Then stands there as if to attack me if I tried to go any farther!

I stomped my foot then yelled at him "How in the hell did you know I was going to ask for a room? Maybe I just needed a drink of water! Do I look like a kind of woman with a mattress strapped on my back? Maybe a BAG-LADY?" He just strolled back into his building without even an answer! So much for that third time crap! Don't try smoking that jola in your pipe!"

"That's it, no more being a Lady." Then I see this Hotel called the Heritage! "Yeah, they will take me in! It's probably got that name because of us Cherokees anyway!" I stroll into the lobby as if I just may be on the Board of Directors! This Counter-Man gives me a big grin and I quickly return one!

"Sir, I would appreciate a room. Ya see I ..."

He interrupted me in mid air! "We have no rooms. Perhaps you should try another Hotel!" still keeping that warm smile!

I kept my smile too! "Sir, which Hotel do you suggest?"

"Oh, any of them," he said nonchalantly.

"Thank you," I replied with a smile. "May I use your telephone?" He motioned for me to do so.

I called the Stouffer's Inn where I'd first been refused a room. A gentleman answered. "Sir," I politely began, "I'm in town on business this weekend with the Wells Corporation. Would you have a suite available? Preferably a smoking room?"

"Oh, yes Ma'am. Will that be cash or charge?" He seemed eager to please. I paused for a second.

"Oh, that will be cash, I guess, really it doesn't matter!"

"Thank you, Ma'am, will you be here by 6 pm?"

"Yes, sir, I will," I confirmed. I thought to myself, "Honey, I'll be there in three minutes!"

"Okay, Ma'am. Your confirmation number is..." I hurriedly wrote it on my dirty arm.

"Thank you kindly sir!" I hung up and rushed back down the steep grade to the number one joint. I felt no pain. All my tiredness was temporarily gone. I strutted in like a princess and smiled at the counter-woman.

"I told you earlier, Miss. We don't have a room for you," her stern, glaring eyes spoke for her.

I cocked my head sideways and gave her a mischievious smile and spoke softly, "My lady, you're badly mistaken. You see, I have a confirmation number. You just fibbed and I'll have a room key, NOW!"

She'd lost this hand of draw poker because my dirty arm had the ace. She puffed like a blowing viper as she searched for a key. I slapped two one hundred dollar bills down on the counter, grinned enormously and triumphantly strode to the elevator.

Once inside my room, I jumped for the phone to call Mr. Bill. Great! I had so much to tell him. I was excited as well over our floor number, twenty three. Indian numerology you see. Two plus three equals five and five means SURPRISE.

I charged to a mall across the street and asked a security guard there to protect my pack while I was inside. "Please take care of my pack sir," I began talking a mile a minute. "My name is Alethea and I'm walking the Trail of Tears. My gun is in this pack. I must buy a pretty outfit because my

Mr. Bill will be meeting me soon." He joyfully laughed and assured me all would be fine.

I detest shopping. I never try anything on even when I'm clean and have plenty of time. I found a wine colored sweater, off-white skirt and wine shoes. I bought everything in a large and dashed off to find my security guard. I gave him a thank you kiss on the cheek and he wished me safety and happiness as I left.

Oh, my bath felt so good that I took a shower too. I washed my hair three times and got all pretty. I called Mr. Bill again --- he was less than thirty minutes away. I ordered a bottle of wine and sat down in a fancy wing-backed chair to relax before I finished dressing.

Suddenly, the door swung open and there were two couples. "Who are you?" I demanded.

We were all startled, especially me. I was half dressed in just my sweater.

"We were given this key," one of them said.

"Don't move," I instructed them. "Mister, hand me that phone. I am, as you can see, not clothed enough to reach it and be my witnesses." The old counter -woman answered. Thank you, Great Spirit, I was thinking. "Well, are you just passin' my door key out for jokes? Is there a special on them this evenin'? Or do you need me to come down there and straighten your cobweb-ass out! Better yet, I wanna talk to your chief and I mean NOW!"

Quickly the manager was on the phone apologizing in all directions, offering discounts, another room, anything I wanted.

"Thank you kindly, sir, apology accepted. You understand, me and my Mr. Bill could have been makin' love or anything," I told him.

"Yes Ma'am, yes Ma'am," he sadly acknowledged.

"Well, I'll make a deal with you. I'll be here for two sunsets and I don't want that counter-woman in my eye sight. Deal?"

"Yes, Ma'am," he conceded.

The strangers and I talked a minute and we all agreed it could have been a most embarrassing situation. With everything cleared up they thanked me and out they went. I finished dressing.

Finally, Mr. Bill arrived. He laughed as I told him not only how hard it was to get a room but about that loose key deal and temporarily firing the counter-woman.

The surprise was that Mr. and Mrs. Hiwassee were on their way to join us later!

Much welcome to our Hiwassee friends as we each caught up on our news! We dressed for the fancy dinner place downstairs and set out to make the very most of the evening. The Stoffers food and waiters where most nice and I spoke this to them, wishing I could speak the same thing about the counter-woman!

Then right after dinner, we rented the Beautiful White Coach drawn by a more beautiful horse! This elated me! With such a hard time to get in this Hotel, I intended to enjoy this buggy-ride and get some business finished! I informed the handsome driver my plans and he spoke that he was to keep only upon his route!

"The hell with your route tonight darling. You are going on an adventure!" holding a big smile until I received his!

"Got your number!" he speaks with a grin, ready for his first Indian-Adventure!

Our first stop was the Holiday Inn. The Hiwassees, Driver and Buck, the patient sogwili with his arched neck and muscled body, saw the scenes unfold!

"Howdy Mister, remember me?" I firmly addressed the same man that had turned me down earlier.

"Why, no Miss, I do not recall your face," answering with only a half of a look to me.

"Well Jack, I'm the woman you wouldn't let have a room 'cause I looked not to suite you. I was too dirty looking. I'm all fixed up now. Hell, I couldn't change that damn much!" stomping my foot as I tongue-lashed him.

"But Miss, I'm sorry. It must have been one of the other clerks!" speaking to me most gentle, keeping an eye upon Mr. Bill and stepping away from the counter.

"Like hell it was another clerk. It was you! Now who is your Chief around here that I can council with about you?" By now he was much shaken and mumbling but never taking one eye from Mr. Bill!

"Oh, Miss, the Manager is out of town and I'm awfully sorry if someone here in this Hotel insulted you. I er, er.."

Interrupting him, I slammed my fist upon the counter. "See, Mr. Bill, I told you what an ass-hole he was!" Then I grinned real big, took Mr. Bill by the hand and headed for the door. As I turned to get a last glance, the big robust man of Africa-American was wiping the sweat from his face and just staring at the floor.

I gave Buck, the horse a big kiss for being patient as we all rode away laughing, heading for the next Turn-Me-Down-Hotel!! There, same speaking and stomping. Just as they spoke untruth of not knowing me! "This won't be the last you hear of me!" I growled at each one as we departed the entrances, leaving each clerk wiping his sweat (ali) and trying to regain his composure! Kissing Buck again and back onto the coach, we all laughed and spoke of the way many people are treated just because of the way they may look (ni) in appearances sometimes!

But quietly in my mind I thought,"From the three Black clerks and the one Land-of-Sand-Indian, I just couldn't accept the fact that the Black clerks wouldn't know of the Trail of Tears. They work and live right or near upon this Trail! All they would have to do is educate themselves a bit and know that their people too were driven right through this town along with the Cherokees. Sometime or other their Mama had told them the sad story of History. I'm right and I know damn well I'm right!

Mr. Bill finally gets me calmed down, then we take the regular route that Buck is supposed to go upon. Back at the Motel, Mr. Bill pays the nice young Gent and he thanked us for such an interesting evening! I had to give Buck one last kiss right in his big horse-lips, rubbed his forehead and promised to see him again!!!

We made the night (usvʔi) long with laughter and talk! I fell asleep mumbling something about bad Nashville Hotels and bad clerks...

Next morning we found a greasy-spoon cafe to eat in just for an adventure! Walked pass many old but beautiful deserted buildings, wondering what would ever become of them. I feel sad when I see art-structure slowly blow (ajotasga) away in the wind.

Then we went a little ways out of town and shopped. We women bought our Men-Folk cowboy hats and they bought us a dozen red roses but I had to send mine back home with Mr. Bill. He promised to press them in a big book for me! Time came too soon for us to take our different paths again. Mr. Bill spent one extra night with me and I wasn't very strong as I watched him drive away. All I could do was wave and cry. I thought to myself that I may never see him again. He may die of the cancer devil (ásgina). I never thought what may lay ahead in danger for me. I felt whatever it may be I can handle it. But his cancer, we know little of.

Nobody knows when Our Great Spirit may call. These words I could hear ringing in my head. Mama spoke them to me many times. "Try and be good to all you can everyday of your life and help all you can and never judge anyone. Because the next second you may be gone. So what then, would you answer to the Maker Of Breath, if you where so filled with untruth?"

"I can hear you Mama," I spoke out loud as I watched my Heart drive out of view.

---

*Oct. 2 Princess walked to center of Nashville. Holiday Inn, Days and Stoffers wouldn't take her! Tried twice at Stoffers and got in. Happys came and stayed with us. All had a good time. Happys slept on the floor.*

## GOODLETSVILLE

This little wide spot in the middle of the road found me in a cool but light drizzle of rain on a lonely Monday morning. My heart was much heavy with the blues, wishing that I could find someone to talk with and see if the little place was on the map when my People were driven through. One good thought (adanhtehdi) did overcome me! I had lost quiet a few pounds now and the Fifty-two pounds upon my back didn't feel so heavy. Therefore I was surely growing stronger! Had another pair of new inserts in my moccasins! That seemed to give me a bit of a quicker step!

Then in this straight stretch, I could see this little market on the left side of the road. The folks were really nice to me! We talked a lot about the Trail of Tears as I gulped down warm coffee. The gentleman informed me that the Wagon-Train-Master that made the Trail a couple of years back lived just back down the road.

"Oh, do you think that I could meet this person?" showing the admiration that I had for him and all that I had read and heard about him.

"No, lady, I don't think anyone is home. Him and the Missus both work. Oh, how my heart fell just a little lower.

Sipped the last bit of my coffee (kahwi), thanked him much and went on my way, thinking still about the Wagon-Master-Man. If I make this Trail of Tears again perhaps I could at least ride my Nelly Bly and invite other riders along too! I want everyone to know about this lonely and never to be forgotten "Trail of Tears".

Seemed the miles were just slipping beneath my feet when the kahwi asked to be turned loose! Too much traffic to take a quick stand beside the road but in view was a little pumpkin-stand!!!

I'm somewhere between a dance and a walk! Didn't think I would ever reach that little pumpkin (iya) stand!! FINALLY! This nice young lady greets me and asks if I would like to buy anything! I smiled a weak smile and said, "Woman to woman, I need to pee in the worse way of any possibility. Where's the john?" She looked kind of sadly at me saying that she had no toilet. "No problem, I'll just step here behind this big Pumpkin-pile!" I did! We both laughed and she gave me a nice Fall-apple.

Now I've come through Ridgetop and Greenbrier. This is good I thought! Then just near the edge of town, I'm growing much of hunger and I meet these two boy-kids. They pull their bicycles to a halt and just smile at me, then turn loose with many questions!

"Are you a real Indian? Where are you going and where did you come from? You don't live around here, because we haven't seen you before. Have we Bubba?"

The thinner one was quick to agree with his little friend and had a loaded question of his own! "Are you running away? Hey, what's your name? Are you hungry lady?"

I stood there with all the calmness for the children and kept a smile on my face and answered every single question! Then it was my turn! "Hey, young men. Is that place right up there a good place to eat?"

"YEAH!" They both answered at once, telling me that was the best place in town and the hamburgers were THIS big!" indicating with outstretched arms! They went on to tell me that nobody could eat all the French-Fries and the hamburger too. It was just way too much!"

I thanked them for the interview they had taken and the news about the hamburgers!! I stood there as I saw them take the next corner in a perfect slide that only kids seem to be able to do!

The folks were warm to me in the Family-Inn, everyone speaking at once! The Sheriff was admiring my Bonnie! Spoke that he had a good one to trade for mine! I spoke that ten good ones couldn't get Bonnie! The folks teased him since he couldn't make the trade go through. My guess was he usually didn't lose in his deals!

They told me that Springfield was only about seven or eight miles on up the road. After I had eaten my last French Fry I thanked them kindly, gave the Sheriff a wink as I patted my Bonnie, then gently closed the galohisdiˀi (door).

There was much evening traffic, road construction and barely a place to walk upon. Almost got hit a couple of times and I'm getting mad. Then just ahead I saw this confusing sight. Couldn't figure out just what it could be! Finally this comes into focus! I begin to laugh! There sits two beautiful yellow-haired women on a sofa beside of the road! I just had to talk with them.

"My Ladies, what are you doing out here beside the road on this new sofa?"

They both tried to answer me at the same time then we all begin laughing really hard! The older one, maybe in her mid twenties took lead. "Well, we don't need this one, 'cause my Mother gave us her old one. But it's really a new one and me and my Sister In Law, want to go out tonight, so we need to sell this damn sofa so we can have some money!" Then the other lady finished by informing me that their husband-men were working away from home and they weren't about to stay home tonight. They just wanted to enjoy a few beers down at a local bar in Springfield!

I agreed that sounded like a good plan but the nvda (sun) had set and a chance to sell was much narrow! They thought so too so we spent a few minutes talking about the Trail of Tears and I found them to be of much education about the

Trail. Then they loaded up the sofa onto the bed of their truck and waved good-bye to me, heading toward Springfield!

"Its possible they could sell it in a bar," I thought! Me and one of my sisters traded a watch for a bar tab once. So they can surely sell a fancy sofa!

Its long after dark by the time I find the Springfield Inn. The desk clerk first told me there were no rooms available due to the construction workers in town. I felt sad for a second then gave her an idea. "Then call their rooms and tell somebody to double up because I NEED a room." She gave a little smirk then spoke that she had only one room but it was for non-smokers. "What makes you think I smoke?" eyeing her with intentional war. She gave no reply, just a key to the top floor that was the farthest away. I mumbled as I kicked the door to find the far-away room. I was so tired that I could hardly open the door.

Taking off my pack that seemed to be glued to me, I searched the room with my eyes until I found that fire-squawker and ripped it off the wall. Then I gave it a good sailing across the room, lit my Virginia Slim up and smiled as I took my first big puff! Next I call my Mr. Bill. He was proud of the many miles I had gone today, which lifted my feeble spirits. But he was a bit upset with me for walking after the nvda had set. We kissed goodnight by telephone then I hit the ama (water)!

---

*Oct. 5. Awfully tired today. princess called. She's in Springfield, Tennessee. Made a lot of miles today. She's doing good.*

---

Morning came far too quickly but I had to move. This made me know what my people felt like when the dog-soldiers made them go quick and fast each morning. I can just see a woman that may have given birth the night before. No matter, her weakened body had to move on. No time to rest nor wash away the blood. As I stood there looking out the window towards Shoneys place to eat, I grew sick in my stomach. Broke my own silence as I strapped on my pack. Then as I started to empty the makeshift ashtray, which was a plastic glass with ama in it, I threw it toward the bathroom. Don't really know what made me do this, I just did. Then I cried.

Outside, the smell (alsvsdiha) of the food (alsdayhdi) drew me to Shoneys door. The seating-woman greeted me with a goodmorning smile! Thinking to myself, she should be the one that greets you at the sleeping rooms next door! Then she asked about my backpack. I spoke of my journey and one by one the whole staff came to my table to speak how much that they admired me for walking the Trail of Tears! I thanked them with all of my heart and celebrated by eating the forbidden sweets; three pancakes!!

As I prepared to leave, the manager came over to inform me that the food was free. Then they spoke that they would pray for my journey of safeness. Tears filled my eyes so full, I could hardly find the door, This was meant to be I thought. Someday I must come back here and buy them a breakfast, yes I must...

As I was making my way through town this sporty-like and fancy dressed gent pulled up beside me. We bid good-mornings then we talked about the Trail of Tears. Suddenly right in midstream of talk, he asked if I would like to spend the day in a motel with him! I growled like a big yona (bear) at him and rushed off stomping and swearing. First the bad clerk, then the nice folks that give me food, now the ass-hole that wants to bed me. Hot and cold, on and off, that's the way energies seemed to flow around me! What would I be within the next mile, mad or sad?

As I got out of the town, I started crying again and for some odd reason. I wanted to see my Daddy. "Oh Daddy, I pray that you are alright. I pray this is not a bad "Message In The Wind"...

Still a much high nvda (sun) but my body was growing so weak and tired. Why am I so sleepy, I kept asking myself. "Wake up Alethea!" Oh, I now know the problem! Its those sugar-cakes that I ate back in Springfield! Well, no matter, I'm going to have to find a place to sleep. The road was straight and wavy, seeming endless to my sleepy eyes. Then I see this much thickened selu dlogesi (cornfield) and make a quick dash for it just after a batch of cars had passed! Laid my rain (agasga) poncho down, adjusted my pack to make a pillow, curled up and found sleep (gahliah) listening to the sweeping-arms of the selu as it seemed to protect me...

The cry of koga (crows) awakened me. They spoke that it was time to move on! Found my way back to the road, walked just a few yards and saw a State-Law in his driveway preparing for work! Had to laugh! What if he had caught me in the selu dlogesi?! Would he have been nice about this? Or maybe much upset?!

This road (nvnohi) seemed to never have at least an interesting curve or deep banks. Just lonely field after field. Finally a cow (wahga) pasture! I stopped to admire the way those Mamas where tending to their big calves now! There I did my pretension of me being a school teacher as I held a make-believe book and read to them! All large shining watery eyes of their warmth was upon me! "Now class, turn to page seven in you books as we all read aloud together!" I felt that the wahga understood the play but not the people that drove by and stared!!

Cedar Hill and Adams were behind me now but I don't think that I can make the border town of Guthrie before nightfall. I begin to pray for comfort. Then I see this cemetery off to my left! I like grave-yards. They are peaceful and I can feel the sad Spirits that have remained behind. When I was a young girl in my years of ten to twelve, I had this desire to steal a horse every once in awhile! To hide from the owner or my mean Cherokee Grandmother, I would seek the old mountain graveyards because nobody would look for me there! This gave me time to rest the horse (sogwili) and become friends. Therefore, the next time I chose to BORROW it for a night's ride, the sogwili would come to me more easily!

After I become a woman, I still chose these places. I then called them my POUTING PLACE! Not always to pout but to be alone and write poetry and songs. So whenever I was missing for a long while, Mama would just speak, "Leave Alethea alone, she's hid out at a graveyard somewhere and will be home at suppertime!" With all these memories touching my tired mind, I automatically turned into the graveyard! Leaning up against a big oak tree that Mama spoke was our Brother, I closed my eyes for prayer and rest.

The sound of an engine broke my Peace. There smiling at me were two warm-face gentlemen! We traded greetings and I felt no fear. They admired my gun and we talked about the Trail of Tears and stay-behind Spirits. I asked about the graves; as to why the energies felt different. The driver-man spoke that it was an all Black resting place. This made me ask him endless questions! He went on to speak that he owned the Sleeping-Grounds and Black folk came all the way from the deep South to lay their Loved-Ones to rest there. His Father had started this and he kept the tradition going! I admired him for this as well as I understood why the Black-Nation would want their own place of rest.

Then he invited me to spend the night at his home. I thanked (wada) him kindly and took up the offer. There I bathed twice, ate a fine home-cooked meal and found sweet (uganasda) sleep (gahliha)! Next morn he took me back to my brother the Oak tree!! Wada much Mister Keeper of the Sleeping-Grounds! The briskness in the morning air kept me quick upon the flat and winding road.

TRAIL THROUGH TENNESSEE

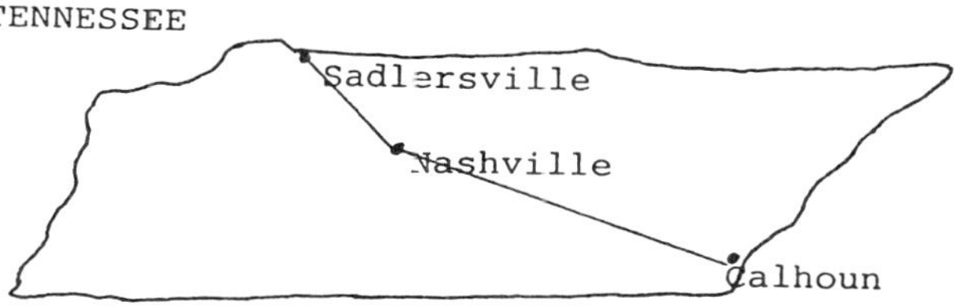


Northern Route

1. Calhoun (Rattlesnake Springs)

   (Departed Setember 3, 1992

2. Dayton
3. Pikeville
4. Spencer
5. McMinnville
6. Woodbury
7. Murfreesboro
8. Hilltop
9. Nashville
10. Goodlettsville
11. Ridgetop
12. Greenbrier
13. Springfield
14. Adams
15. Sadlersville

# KENTUCKY DUST TOWN (GUTHRIE)

"I made it! I made it!!" I'm at the state of my Old Kentucky Home!! I danced into Guthrie! Once this was a big railroad town and I was expecting to see stately homes and well kept lawns. I just stopped and stared. Seemed I was frozen in my moccasins! As I looked around and stumbled as a tourist would do, I begin to feel sad. The wind was literally blowing the town away! I watched the wind whip at the aged bricks of the old and deserted buildings. Each time the unole touched the bricks, another piece was taken. Now I could hear the words of the song "Dust In The Wind". This would forever stay in my mind as the Town of Dust.

Finding my way onward and pausing to look in dirty windows where laughter and life once played, I cried. The town seemed to whisper, "Walk easy my Child and I understand your tears for I saw your People walk and cry through my then muddy streets long, long ago."

Bearing to my left, I come to this sign that speaks TINY TOWN. Well, that it was. There I saw life, lawns and a store with a few people mingling. "Why couldn't they all mingle back down the road a little ways?" Then I see this large (egwa) sign that spoke The Holiday Motel! This thrilled me and I prayed that there may be a sleeping room for me to rest and to call my Mr. Bill. I opened the screeking storm door but saw nobody. Waited to admire the many antiques before I picked up that little brass bell that one jingles for the clerk.

Suddenly this warm beautiful and strong faced Lady appears. she makes the room happen for me and I set in with endless questions. She had come from Germany many moons ago by being married to an American Soldier of the big Two-War. I didn't want to wear my welcome out before

I got in the room, so I thanked her kindly and dismissed myself.

Rested and called Mr. Bill, insisting that I just had to feel his warmth and he had to see this Town of Dust! I spoke of this sign that I had passed back on the Tennessee side that read "The Bell Witch". I wanted to learn if that was of truth or untruth. He promised to meet me the following sunset.

Sleep did not come easy that night; too many energies going through my head (askoli). But I'm in my own home state now, I kept thinking! The long trek through Tennessee was much hard on me but I'm in good condition now, all will be well, hang in there Alethea! I know if Mama was alive right now, she would just give a big laugh and speak of how strong we Cherokee Indians are and how could I find doubt about myself?!" Still something was lingering in the shadows of my thoughts (adanhtehdi). Was this a bad Message In The Wind trying to get through to me???

By the time Mr. Bill arrived, I was a nervous wreck! He tried to soothe and comfort me but the more he tried, the more I wanted to eat. I even ate ketchup! I hate ketchup!

"Maybe you need your estrogen shot," he soothingly spoke to me. I tried to recall when I had that one in Murfreesboro, Tennessee or was it in McMinnville? Darn, I can't remember. Well that's one of the signs, so I must be in need of a shot! Well, until then, I'll just eat! Mr. Bill just looked at me sadly as if I was a little mangy pup that he had found beside of the road. Nobody else would pick it up but he chose to with no regrets ... all he had to do was to figure out where he could get it a mange-shot!

We got to spend two whole days together. I cried even more hard when he pulled out of sight. I crawled into the bed and ate three cheeseburgers then cried some more for my own guilt. Made myself throw up and stayed up all night, reading the story of Bell Witch.

I had about thirty miles from Tiny Town to Hopkinsville, Kentucky. From no sleep and a sickly stomach that I made to give food back up, I really wasn't in any condition to walk. Then I (ayv) grew so uhnalvha (angry) with myself, I stomped my feet and cried! "Alethea, you glutted, you made it come up, you wouldn't let sleep come to you and the children that walked the Trail Of Tears were more strong than you are!"... After this good slap (asihtvniha) to my esteem, I gained enough control to head out. I didn't even have a tobacco before I started.

Sleepwalking, yet admiring the well kept fields and picture book farms, I saw this one mansion that one would have to admire but the energies that touched me were of much cold (kanawoga). I spoke an adadolisdi (prayer) for the sad mansion.

By the time I had stumbled through PEMBROKE, ayv could go no step farther. "Just a little nap!" I thought, when this blue battered pickup truck asks if I want a ride. "No Sir, I want to sleep!" I growled. He took his time thinking about it, then pointed toward a deserted barn off the road. He took a look at my gun; didn't ask any questions and I wasn't in the mood to speak any answers. He drove the opposite direction and I squinched my eyes to find the path to that deserted barn that was about to have a bedfellow!

Old blacksnake (ga?legi) skin-shed and musty dirt was all I needed to rake and make my bed. Thought I would sleep a couple of hours and get into Hopkinsville just after dark (ulsihga). I don't recall my head finding my backpack for a pillow...

Sniff, lick, sniff, lick, was a wake-up call! I could smell the gila before I opened my still sleepy eyes! He can't be a mean dog or he would have awakened me with a loud growl and bark. So I just lay there for a couple of minutes until inspection time was over! I made a whining sound for communication. The gila began to lick me more. Then I opened my eyes and gave a big smile and talked to the little blue colored skinny female and we instantly became friends.

When I started to look about me, darkness was setting in. Then I remembered where, or about where I was. "Who is you master little gila? Or are you all alone like me?" Her answer was many more licks about my face and hands!

Back toward the road, I heard the shutting of a truck door. I waited. Then an engine started. Saw the truck lights come on and the driver was backing out. I figured the man I had growled at earlier had probably seen me sleeping here then decided to leave me be. Perhaps his usdi (little) gila decided to stay and protect me!

My head was coming apart at the seams and I wanted ama (water) to chase my tobacco (jola). The jola was no problem. I found my Virginia Slims, just didn't know where to look for ama. Readjusted myself, loved on my new friend and spoke that I was much sorry that I had no big supper, just one Slim-Jim that we would have to share! Gila spoke that that was just fine! We sat there alone in the darkened barn and listened to the unole sing through the wide cracks and remind a board that it was just loose enough to play the Wind-Dance! After I had a couple of my tobaccos, I begin to sing to the little gila!

"Now usdi gila, I wrote this song many moons ago for some little children that I baby-sat for when I lived back in the woods all by myself for seven years!

Little Black Puppy Dog

Once there was a little girl, lost out in a storm
And on the other side of the mountain, was a little black
puppy dog.
And Jesus sent that puppy dog to keep the little girl warm,
Then show her the way home, show her to her home...

The little black puppy dog found that little child,
He barked and played around her until he made her smile!
Until he made her smile!
Mama was praying and pacing the floor,
Then heard the scratching at her door.
And when she saw her little child she got down on her
knees,
Crying, "Oh, thank you, Lord, for guiding my child to me...

"But Mama," cried the little child, this puppy found me lost!
I was crying, Mama, beside an old damp log.
Can I bring this black puppy in?"
"Oh, yes my child, and I have warm milk for him, for
him..."

Later when she tucked them in to bed,
She prayed again to God and said, "I recall when I was
young,
And I was lost out in a storm, you did the same for me...
I was lying beside a dampened log when a little black puppy
dog
Led me from the storm and showed me the way home.
Yes, it showed me the way home and Mama then prayed to
you,
And let me keep that black puppy too...

Oh, there is a child lost in every storm,
And a little black puppy dog to show it the way home,
Yes, show them the way home...

I was crying by the time I finished the little song and the gila was snuggled up to me as if she was the child and I was the black puppy dog that had found her. I looked toward the clear night and found the Northern star, said my prayers then covered me and the little gila with my Indian blanket to find cool but sweet sleep.

Next morning the little gila was gone; I'm sure back to it's master. I found the road again taking me toward Hopkinsville. Since it was only about seven or eight miles, in no time I found the Main street. When I came to the first motel, I checked in. These people from India were the owners. They seemed nice and I chose a room that had a desk so I could catch up on some writing. Wasn't really at myself yet, wanted to eat but was afraid to from lack of control. Called Mr. Bill instead; bathed taˀli (two) times then crawled into bed.

---

*Princess called. She's in Hopkinsville, KY Slept in a barn last night and sang to a dog! That's princess!*

---

The telephone awakened me at sunset. It was my sister Little Sparrow. Spoke that she would drive to visit me tomorrow and Mr. Bill had told her that I was going to spend a week in Hopkinsville because my birthday was coming up!

"That's great," I assured her of me spending a week or so but not so sure about my birthday! I will be forty-one, won't I?" Sparrow agreed that I was truly going to be forty-one! Later I got to thinking about my birthday. Wow! I never really expected to ever live this long! Four plus one equals Five. hey, Five is Suprise!!

By next morning its time to eat, control or NO CONTROL!! I found this little place toward town and stayed there to eat. Figured if I ate in public I wouldn't glut and sin. It worked!! Picked up a couple of books and a paper to see what was going on in the world today!

The owner-Woman came to make up my room so I helped her! I'm just that way! Plus it helped to calm my nerves and have some one to talk to! Sparrow called, it would be another day later before she could make it down. "No worry, I will just sleep!"

When she did arrive, I was so glad to see her! We caught up on all the news and she spoke that the pretty Lady from Canada and her Husband-man were going to visit me too! They still lived in the old school bus that I had given to them!

Soon they arrived and the Lady gave me a large hand-made-of-pottery unicorn! I thanked her most kindly. They had to return to Somerset by end of the day.

My spirits seemed to be on an upward climb! Sparrow suggested that I get all cleaned up and she would take me down to the Trail of Tears Commemorative Center that was nearby! This had me much excited but I needed another towel. This one was two days old. Still, I jump into the ama-hole and the owner-woman comes. I ask Sparrow to ask the woman if I could please have a clean one because this one was much dirty! The woman spoke that I could NOT and that was their rules. Sparrow relayed the message to me in her normal shy way. I just walked out of the ama-hole with only a towel and a smile!

"My Lady, you must understand that I NO UNDERSTAND why I CAN'T have a clean towel!"

keeping my voice as soft as possible and showing the confusion on my face! Her reply was now more in HER native tongue but clearly and firmly that the only way I was going to get a towel was if I paid extra!

"EXTRA," I yelled, "I give you about a half-minute to get me a damn clean towel or I will call those Health-People on you!" She spoke some words that we couldn't understand but we knew it wasn't of nice! I made a dive for her, losing my towel while she made a dash for the door! Sparrow started pacing because she was nervous and I was trying to find my skirt and sweater. I felt I had some unfinished business with this woman that needed to learn about a better way of health! Sparrow pleaded to just forget it, we would just go to another motel.

"Okay, I give in just so I won't lose my mind and end up in jail (asduhvsga)!! So we gathered my things and were in the car ready to leave when the owner-man appeared speaking most bad words to us! "That does it," I scream as I get out of Sparrow's car heading toward him! When I heard him call us bitches, I grab Bonnie! "I'll show you just what a bitch can DO!" Sparrow runs toward him and speaks that if he should make another step she could not keep me from shooting him! He ran to his office and locked himself behind his glass-office-room. We drove off; Sparrow shaking while trying to drive and me swearing up a storm and stomping the floorboard.

Found another motel about two mile from the Trail of Tears Park. I explained to the new clerk who was much nice and gave us a whole bag full of towels! But the day was ruined for going to the Park; my energies were in disarray. Instead we went to eat and I sinned again right there in public!

Had to report to Mr. Bill. He laughed! I spoke that this

motel, The Travel Inn, was much better and we have many many towels!!

---

*Princess in Hopkinsville. Sharon arrived. Moved to another Motel. Travel Inn.*

---

Then he put someone on the telephone. It was one of his daughters who I call Brewsky. I had never met any of his children but felt I could get along with her if she would allow. He talked most often about her and spoke that she liked to have a few beers now and then, so the name "Brewsky" just came to mind. Her voice was most nice and she was coming to Hopkinsville with her Father and was looking forward to meeting me! I too felt the same!

Within a few days Mr. Bill, Brewsky and the Hiwassees came for the weekend to bring in my birthday! We had all our rooms close and they made a cake happen for me! I sinned again against my low blood-sugar. I ate many pieces of the cake. Next! Pray to the john!

We decided to go out for a prime-rib dinner the next night and we are all in a most joyous mood! This resturant is fancy but rustic. It reminds me of our favorite restaurant in Kentucky, "Hall's on the River". We get a special table in the corner because I have this thing about sitting with my back to the door.

Everything is in order as we ask for some nice burgundy wine to make my birthday toast! The waitress comes and takes our order. We make it easy for her, we just all order a prime-rib! I feel as if I'm in Heaven (Galvladi) because all the energies are just right between everyone! The steaks begin coming and everyone has been served but me! Mr. Bill asks me where my steak is and my reply is that it should be here any minute. So I just sip a little on my wine and wait and wait and WAIT! Now I'm getting edgy because everyone else is like getting finished! So I motion for the waitress.

"Miss, where is my dinner!?" speaking real nice to her.

"Oh, let me check," professionally replying while making her way toward the kitchen. After a few minutes she returns with a bit of a red face!

"Ma'am, I'm so sorry but your order didn't get turned in somehow, I'm really sorry!" speaking just above a whisper to me.

I kind of turn towards her more so to face her well, scoot my chair back and place my hands on my hips! "Woman," I speak firm and slow, "I need some education here. I just want to know how in the hell you can take many orders and they all speak of wanting the same thing, yet you lose mine somewhere from here to the kitchen and its all down on one piece of damn paper! No understand!?"

"I'll be back," that's all she speaks and rushes away! Everyone is holding their breath and I have a feeling I'm going to see that jail-house yet! Next comes the manager-man! Now he gets down on his knees and asks if there is ANYTHING he can do to make up for her mistake?

"Sure," quick to speak! YOU keep that lily-woman away from our table. Don't want any chairty of free dinner and get the hell off your knees and out of my face before I throw you both through the window!" He was gone in a flash. I wanted to cry and laugh at the same time!

Laughter came and we had another toast then left that bad memory behind. Later, back in the motel, Mr. Bill spoke that he was proud of me for not attacking the staff! We played poker to uplift the mood and Brewsky said she needed some of my energies! I reached over and touched her arm, making a prayer that she would win. She did! She won about fifty-dollars!!

Sunday had to be because that's when everyone leaves! Mr. Hiwassee had made some really nice maps for me and had them in plastic so I wouldn't get them wet. Felt depressed yet restless. We just had breakfast. I wasn't forgotten this time; they just didn't bring my food until they brought the check. We all had to laugh!

On Tuesday, October 20, the real day of my birthday, I am more at ease again and I go to the Trail Of Tears Park. This real nice Lady named Cathy D. Cavanah, from the "Kentucky New Era" interviews me! I enjoyed the volunteers that work at the Park. They keep the Trail Of Tears Park in perfect shape and display much Indian History as well as present day art!

Here at the park are two graves. One is of Chief White path and the other is Chief Flysmith. They were of Autumn-moons of age. The journey of tears had become to much of a burden. Here they found peace at last. The park has two larger than life statues of our Chiefs and the graves are covered as stone-box form. You can see how over the years, people have tried to pry into the graves. What are they looking for? Do people that rob Indian graves think our people were laden with silver and gold as they were driven like animals? When I touched the two Chief's statues, I did not find the stone to be cold. They were much warm due to the spirits.

Also during my stay in Hopkinsville, I was able to meet the woman that helped put together the Trail of Tears National Historic Trail Assessment Book. She gave me a copy of the manual which took her long hours and much studies to complete.

*Got to Hopkinsville around 7:00 pm. Brewsky went with me.*

*I think she had a good time. The Happy Hiwassees were there too. Played Poker, had Princess' birthday dinner. They forgot her steak. Late on her breakfast. Sparrow, Brewsky, Hiwassees and I all left around 4:00 pm. Love you Princess.*

---

Leaving Hopkinsville with many moods and my body BEGGING for a shot of ESTROGEN!! But there was nothing I could do right now, I wasn't even sure what Trail-road I was on! Was I supposed to take Route 41 to 109 or route 91 to Marion? Since I'm the only one to ask, I'm the only one to answer! At this point I had no control of my mind and body. All I could see was a big fat Cherokee Woman that just turned forty-one, a raw throat from throwing up too much and a swollen stomach to match these swollen eyes! The only person I love right now is The Great Spirit. I hate everything now including my dog and I don't even have one...

The rain (agasga) set in but I walked all the more hard! Maybe I will get the flu and be in a hospital somewhere, lose fifteen pounds of lard and get an estrogen shot too! Damn me! Damn me!! Finally I see through a blur of tears mixed with agasga this fancy sign. Its pointing to my left speaking Pennyrile Forest State Resort Park! "Ok, Alethea, try this one!" Darkness was coming upon me and left with no choice, I headed down a long winding mountain that didn't seem to end. Why in the hell can't a sign speak how far a place is? The darkness was becoming to the deep forest picture. This I did come to my senses long enough to admire.

"Hey, there's lights!" calling out loud to the scurrying sounds of usdi animals that I could hear in the woods but not see. I began running toward the sign that spoke OFFICE!

My backpack was making a noise that seemed to match the flump-glunk noise that my belly made as well. "Fat-ass," saying to myself as I reached the door!

The place seems to be vacant but the desk has three clerks! Why? I didn't see any cars in the parking lot! I have a big smile on my face to try and hide my misery when I ask the clerk nearest to me if she had a room available? They all three just looked at me as if I had just asked if there was a local moonshine still in the back room! They speak there are NO rooms available when I notice the Lead-Hen nudge the one to her right with her elbow. I tried explaining again who I was and that I was walking the Trail Of Tears.

"Sorry ma'am, we have NO rooms," looking at some papers in her hand as if they where being prepared for the President!

"Lady, where in the hell is the party? There's no cars in the parking lot! And I have no intentions of going back into the rain and darkness so I'll just pile up in front of your warm fire here to sleep until daylight!" jerking my backpack and heading for my destination across the room!

Then in walks the Forest-Law! He smiles at the three-hens as he approaches the desk and they all four look toward me, speaking in a low-council. Personally I feel that is one of the lowest acts, just above molesting an innocent animal, that a human animal can do. They whisper loud enough for you to know its about you but too low to hear just what they speak and do this right in front of you! If that Forest-Law makes me leave, I'll knock him out with my first lick then slap those hens to relax my hands again!

One of the hen's voice interrupts my plans as I try staring into the fire (ajila) to calm myself. "Oh, Ma'am, we DO have just one cabin available. It has two bedrooms with a fireplace but that will be 92 dollars even." she has her eyes on me now, with her eyebrows raised high and mouth gaped half open like our grade school teachers used to do when they asked a question, awaiting your answer and you wasn't at school the day before; she knowing the question pertained to yesterday's lesson.

I slowly get up from my warm seat and walk to face the Principal and three hen-teachers. I stare at only the lead-hen and speak as FIRM as I NEED an estrogen.

"Woman, I don't need a damn full size house, all I need is one, just one damn bed!" holding my finger, feeling she needed sign-language.

"Well, we're sorry, but that's all we have, isn't it ladies?" nodding her head to the other hens for an AMEN!

I just started fumbling through my pack and pulled out a hundred dollar bill that Mr. Bill had given me for my birthday. At the same time she had gotten the key and flipped it on the desk! "Here," I growled, throwing the single bill on the counter.

"Oh," she puckered and snipped, "I'll get you change!" All the rest, including the Forest-Law, moved out of her way as she went for the money-place.

"Forget the change woman, you need that for personality-school!" I snipped back, grabbed my pack and headed for a sign that spoke FOOD!

The Waiter was really of manners. I spoke of my trouble at the desk. He laughed and agreed those hens think they own this place! As I looked at the place-mats, I saw it was a collection of all the resorts in Kentucky. I showed my waiter where I live at the one called Woodson Bend Resort in Bronston, Kentucky! He was as thrilled as I was! Then he asked me to autograph the mat for him. "Sure thing!" Then the Head-Waiter came over to my table. For all I knew he was going to tell me they were out of food! Instead he spoke that I was in the Newspaper that he had read earlier! Also he knew the Newspaper-Delivery Woman and wanted to know if he could invite her down to the Resort to meet me! I spoke, "Yes!"

I was proud of myself. I didn't sin this time when I ate. I had only a baked potato and green beans! The staff wouldn't allow me to pay for my supper!

"It's on the house!" They all spoke, then brought me a single cupcake with one candle! I was thrilled as they sang Happy Birthday to me; truth is I blushed!!

It was getting late and they were closing the restaurant when the Paper-Lady came. I met her in the lobby where there could have been a BATTLE earlier! I ignored the desk-hens as I sat with the soft-speaking woman and her lovely, well mannered children! As we all parted I caught the lead-hen looking at me then looking back to a Newspaper!! I accepted the one that the Newspaper-Woman gave me and went out the door in search of the HOUSE I had rented for the cold, rainy but forest-beautiful night!

The cottage looked just as they do at Woodson Bend and my friends there came to my mind most strong. I smiled when I thought of how nice the Guards are to me and that they where feeding my pet Montana, a wild raccoon! I bathed taʔli (two) times and walked about the spacious cabin feeling a lot of homesickness (uhisohdaneha).

My nerves had calmed a bit, hunger gone and I had made some new friends! I erased the desk-hens from my mind, called Mr. Bill, then I spoke my prayers (adadolisdi) then found long awaited sleep!

---

*Princess called from Pennyrile resort. Charged her $92. She's mad!*

Found myself at Dawson Springs but there was a bad Message In The Wind. I felt that I was off course. Though I was weak and sickly, I couldn't feel the energies of any Spirits! Just a little, here and there but not enough to make me want to stay on this route.

The long winding mountain ways were of most beauty and I came to visit several White-Mans-Resting-Places but I would have to make another turn somewhere.

Found a Bed and Breakfast to sleep. I met the owner-woman's Mama. We sat on the veranda and she told me of the days when she was young and courting her husband-man that had now been laid to rest in a nearby grave. I thought to myself, "I was probably standing at his tombstone sometime earlier."

She went on to describe how handsome her beau's carriage and horses were. I lost myself in the midst of her stories and rode in that fine carriage, smelling the honeysuckle, laughing at the gala's that where held at the fancy Kentucky estates and could see her on her wedding day!"

In the daughter's living room was a photograph of the little woman just before she was to marry. The daughter called to her Mama to speak that it's Church time! This broke our journey of the past but she embraced me farewell and spoke that I would probably be asleep when they returned. "May God bless you upon your walk child and I will Pray for you daily," she whispered in my ear so sweet but fragily...

"I Pray I live to be your sweet age of ninety and be so beautiful," whispering back to her and gently squeezing her thin arms.

I waited for sleep that night and looked about the fancy antique room. I wondered what I would have been like if I had been born wealthy in this part of Kentucky instead of the mountains and poverty? Probably like that pretty lady; in good health and winter years but nobody that would listen to my courting and gala days of long ago...Still I like how the Great Spirit chose for me to be Cherokee and Irish; poor with little of a warm fire but with a loving Mama and a moonshine still up a mountain crevice and stealing horses for a thrill!!

---

*Nothing from Princess tonight. Its 9 pm. I'm so tired I'm weak.*

---

Heavy eyes overtook my rushing memories and what-might-have-beens!!! Still remaining on this route but "Why?" I decided it was to be. I would follow the Message In The Wind and question no more. The traffic was much heavy with trucks flying past me and not taking much care to a crazy woman walking! Some weight was leaving my body again from the hard walking. I pushed to every limit that I could withstand. The most I would rest was to admire a beautiful Appaloosa horse!

"Don't get any ideas, Alethea!" My body was so in need of estrogen that it felt like shock waves where having a pow-wow! Every mile would bring a different mood. I sweated more than I should, my stomach would swell so bad I couldn't snap the pack buckle tight enough so my shoulders wouldn't be carrying all the weight. I would find a pretty stone and add it to the unneeded collection. I had found a pretty box made of wood. Carried it for miles before I looked inside. When I did it was a box of .22 hollow-points! Now this I can use!! Still I couldn't remember just what route I was on now. It didn't matter, something was driving me this way, so I must go...

When I could walk no more and I didn't care that it was long after dark, whoever should try to attack me right now would end up calling the LAW on ME, because my body and mind felt like some animal that has been in a cage for a long time with people throwing rocks at it. Then it see's that the cage-door is about to come loose! I have spoken to many doctors about the way I feel when I need an estrogen shot. They just laugh! Only Dr. Crazy Horse and Dr. Lewis understood. Well maybe I shouldn't be too hard on them. I don't think a man could ever understand this. As Mama spoke to her Doctor-Man, "What the hell do you mean it doesn't hurt to give a baby birth? When was the last time you had one ol' corn-cob!" I loved hearing Mama tell that story!

There in front of me are real lights...I think! Out in distance and much darkness I find a sign that speaks HUDSON MOTEL!!! After a few knocks upon the door, this woman comes to the door. She looks just like Mama did; black hair and dark skin with a big smile! Mama had to be walking this Trail with me because her face shows up in many people.

I spoke that I was walking the Trail Of Tears just once to this dark, warm faced woman and she didn't put me through hell (jvsgino). She knew exactly what I was doing and knew what the Trail Of Tears was all about.

"Yes honey, I have a room for you. Just follow me." There was this big bed and the room was all done in blue (sakonige?i); this being one of my favorite colors!

"Oh, Ma'am, I do thank you with all of my heart. You don't know just how much this means to me to meet someone with so much kindness and not turn me away." I know I was rambling but I couldn't help myself.

"You just get some rest and I will see you in the

morning. How do you like your coffee, honey?" her deep but soft voice asked with no rush for an answer.

"Black, Ma'am, just black. And I really do thank you!"

"You are welcome and I will have you black coffee first thing in the morning and you are safe here,' then silent as a shadow the door was locked and closed as she gave me a goodnight smile! My body was trembling from being sick and excited! I turned my face toward the ceiling right then and thanked the Great Spirit for such a person...

---

*Princess called. Says she is off the Trail. She's in Sullivan, Kentucky. Needs to be south of there. Must go see my princess and help her. She's bad off needing estrogen.*

---

Don't remember getting in bed. It seemed as if I had only closed my eyes for just a minute (iyatahwostanvʔi) when a gentle knock at the door and a familiar voice spoke, "Are you ready for your coffee?" I didn't know where I was for a second. Then I made it quick to the door to greet the smiling face and the morning sun! I thanked her a dozen times!

"My name is Gladys, honey and as soon as you are awake and have your coffee just come on to the office."

"Oh, yes Ma'am, I will be right there!" Then I started to recall the long walk and the darkness. Flashes came and went as I searched for my toothbrush. I have to brush my teeth before I can really taste this Glad-Woman-I-Am-To-See's coffee!! I was trying to rush. I didn't dare try to brush my hair for it was much too windswept from the coal trucks! Am I really at a place so good or is this a dream?

We talked and we laughed and we talked some more! Gladys showed me her fine collection of Indian pictures and clippings from papers. We had so much in interest.

I asked her about a Doctor. In no time she had me in

town at a Doctor-Man that had been giving shots for centuries! I have never had a shot in my butt so fast in all my estrogen-years!! There was no thinking about it on his behalf; he knew what I needed just by looking at me. He did it then spoke, "Pay out front honey!" It only cost $10 dollars. Now this included office and shot! All this went so fast I didn't even need to rub my behind!

After two sunsets here it was amazing to see the change in my face and body! I had lost weight. Good color returned to my skin and Gladys had me in an interview with this nice man from The Sturgis News, plus all the homemade green beans that I could eat! I loved the whole world again including the gila that I didn't have!! Then I called Mr., Bill and he was so happy with my progress and was coming to take me back to the right route!

"Oh, thank you Great Spirit. Now I know why you sent me in this direction and I will always follow your Message In The Wind!"

When Mr. Bill showed up to point me in another direction, I had a heavy heart (gageda adanhdo) when I had to wave farewell to the Angel Gladys.

"I will see you again and I shall never forget the kindness you have shown!" I begin to cry as we were going to another route. Mr. Bill soothed me and spoke that everything will be alright, that I had come a long ways and soon our journeys would come together and life would be good to us.

---

*Got Princess to Marion, Kentucky. We had a great time. Helped her repack. Left for home around 1 pm. I love you Princess. We will make it.*

---

After more research I find that I must cross the Big River

at Cave In Rock, Illinois. Back on the track. I walk from Shady Grove, Kentucky, through Marion that leads me to the Ohio River!Felt much good to have all my mind back! With spirits even higher to guide me with care...

I found Marion, Kentucky to be a sleepy and quiet little town. No stray gilas or stray children running about! The only person that I found to talk with was this nice Gentleman and his Missus just on the outskirts of Marion, toward the Big-Ama side! He had some treasures for sale.

I nearly lost my breath when I saw these fine Kentucky Ivories! In other words, they are known as the private part of the male raccoon! One can make fancy necklace and earrings to match! When I was in my coon hunting days I used it all. One should never waste. I would prepare the raccoon (kvhli) for a good meal that I shared with my gilas. Then of each male I had caught, I would save this private bone to clean, polish and make into my adornments! My Grandfather made a nice toothpick that he would always have at hand when needed and Grandmother would file this ivory down to use for her handstiching needles!

Once in my modeling days, I was attending this fancy gala in New York. This lady kept admiring my jewelry! Finally she musters the nerve to ask. "Oh where did you find this unique jewelry? Where can I find such art?"

I smiled an ornery grin and spoke in the finest Kentucky accent that I could draw, "Why Ma'am, this is IVORY, Kentucky Ivory that is found between every male raccoon's legs that one can find!" This woman jumped like she had been shot, then looked down at her hands as if they were dirty because she had touched my necklace! My escort came over to me and asked why I did such?! "She asked a question and I just educated her!" holding my grin as I sipped the wine, my eyes following her as she made way to the PUFF room!

This cool October (Duninhdi) morning finds me with songs in my head and I joined in with the Fall-Birds as they make a greeting to me! I waved at this woman that was sweeping her porch. She made a rush inside her home; took a peek through her window then opened the door just enough to grab her broom! I just stand there in new shock! "Damn, I've been known to steal horses woman but not brooms! But the way you are acting I believe you may NEED that broom!" In one way I felt hurt, in another I laughed!

Came to this sign that spoke it was fourteen miles to the big-ferry! This elated me! Already I had many miles beneath my moccasins and still was full of energy! The scene was awesome! The high Sun (nvda) shown upon the golden and red trees! Leaves would fall and twirl around me. Then just when my body seemed to become heated with the walk, wind (unole) wisps would touch just long enough to cool me! This part of my journey felt much spiritual. The warm eyes (akta) of two does and their handsome buck watched with ease as I passed them in one of their favorite eating places! All the farm animals came to share a fenceside chat! One mama cow (wahga) even allowed me to rub her forehead!! I thought, if all people could be as these animals and nature are today; filled with such harmony...there would be no need for a woman or any person to walk this far to remind one of the dark (ulsinga) clouds that were made to happen many moons ago by Man himself against his Brother. Why can't we live and blossom and grow into full bloom with warm thoughts. Then when it comes to our time to fall as the full grown leaf does, go peacefully and gracefully, whomever or wherever we are destined to fall upon and around. I do not see the mama cow thrust her horns toward a falling golden leaf. I do see her eyes give it warm attention only...

This Trail I now walk (a?i) upon should never have cried the first time. Just before me hovered this dark and metal contraption that did no justice for beauty upon the Ohio River. But its called a Ferry and one will never cross the big ama without it!

In 1818 there was a ferry, though they were log ferries and not as strong. The rough currents ripped and swallowed some of the ferries. The proud Cherokee could only stand along the banks and shiver with fear and coldness as they watched loved ones being taken beneath the frigid waters. Which was better? Die here in still known territory or live and be driven onward? Even then Mother Nature and The Great Spirit were giving rein to lash and seemed to make war upon the dog-soldiers.

First she baked their heads with her scorching sun and made their boots sweat much in her powdered earth. Then she drove the soldiers nearly blind with her hard heavy rains that pulled their very coats and threw the fancy Army Hats into unreachable distances. This being a picture of history to fit the words that were taught to the Cherokee with a whip. "And the rains shall fall upon the JUST and UNJUST."

We can never know the thoughts that went through the weary minds of our Cherokee People. I cannot speak that a certain phrase or line was whispered aloud. Nor can any other writer, poet or speaker. We may think what they may have felt or thought but never really can we know verbatim.

Yet as I stand here upon this machine and cross peaceful waters, I have my own wonders! If I had been a Mama watching my Child being drawn into the water. I would have torn myself loose to save her or just join her. Maybe I would have been shot in the back by the dog-soldier. That

would have been alright too. At least I would have no more to suffer. Perhaps I may be the life of a new bride and I stand crying as I see them make my Husbandman board the rickety ferry. I would fight like an animal to join my love in waters that are deep and rough but when I found him, we would be peacefully together in the Spirit World. I would have even tried to help another person that maybe I was not so fond of. Yes, if I had been here in the Removal and had made this far into the journey of hell, this is where I would have ended my pain. Perhaps some of my People had peace come into their minds despite the badness that surrounded them, just as I found peace and beauty in the last fourteen miles. This would have been as far as I go. Who is to speak yes or no that upon these deep waters and upon the cold and filthy banks that many that stood there had a special Message In The Wind?"

TRAIL THROUGH KENTUCKY

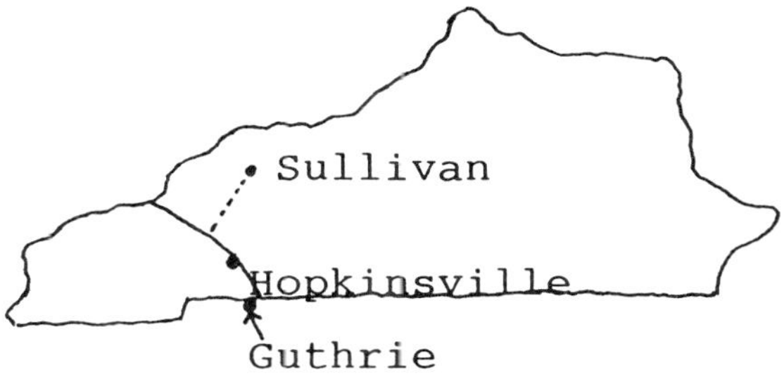


Northern Route

1. Guthrie
2. Tiny Town
3. Trenton
4. Hopkinsville
5. Pennyrile State Resort Park
6. Macedonia
7. Dawson Springs (Off Trail, but found Medicine!)
8. Sullivan (Medicine and Rest!)
9. Marion (Back on Trail)
10. Ferry (Ohio River)

# ILLINOIS

I'm into my third State now! The men on that metal of cold was most nice to me. They refused to take the fare money! I was alone on the ride; not one person or machine was in view as I easy-stepped upon the metal that made me a bit uneasy! The wind cooled my face as we crossed in silence. Just the roar of the engine and the flapping of the ama were the only sounds...

Cave In Rock is nestled with warmth and smiling faces as I bend forward to climb the steep bank from the ferry-edge. The first to welcome me are two gentlemen in their Winter-Years! They wave warm weathered hands to me as they bask in the afternoon sun. I puff, smile, puff some more and return my wave! This is good I feel. This town will be most kind to me.

Found a little restaurant on the right side of Main Street, smelled supper on the table!! Met two little Ladies in their eighties that shared stories of their younger days when they slipped down by the river to meet their sweethearts! The steak dinner tasted so much good (osda)! I didn't even sin! Just met many of the locals and wished the Owner-Man good luck because he was running in an election to become the County Coroner! Personally I don't vote but that doesn't make me not voice my opinions! I enjoyed the fine company and food; even lingered a little longer than I expected!

The clouds where growing dark with a promise of rain as I headed out of town to a little motel the locals spoke to me about. I was more tired that I realized when I couldn't push my steps any further. This nice man stopped to ask if I wanted a ride. "No, but how far do I have before I reach this motel?"

He spoke that I was going off my path about two miles. I might reach it before dark or the rains came. He still offered me a ride. I thanked him again and felt some rain touch my face! It felt good! I smiled and spoke prayers as I saw just ahead the faded light of a motel sign!I had bathed and called to check in with Mr. Bill and felt safe and warm as I rested upon the old fashioned bed (ganihli).

The one television station that I got was dogging down some man from Texas that was running for President! I feel I'm right after all about politics! They all stand in front of National television and insult each other! Why don't they just speak to the people what they believe in and their intentions instead of looking like a child in kindergarten fighting on the playground just to see who gets to sit close to the Teacher! But for some reason when I saw this little-rooster man tell this interview woman that what ever she had asked him, "It wasn't any of her damn business!" right on little rooster!!

Knocking upon my door startled me with confusion! "Who knows me here?" Well, it was the nice man that offered me a ride earlier and he had brought his missus to visit and brought me food as well! They even offered me their home the following night! I accepted!!

---

*Princess called from Cave In Rock Motel. Had a lot to tell me. Says its raining there and she met some nice people.*

---

The next three days were filled with meeting lots of nice people and warm hospitality! We went sight seeing and I gave all my attention to the children as they chose Halloween costumes for school (junadehlohgwasdi?i)!

"Did you go trick or treating when you was a little girl?" the youngest of their children asked with big curious eyes!

"No sweetheart, we don't believe in this Holiday and even if we had, there was nobody in the mountains to find treats from! The nearest neighbor was about seven miles away and we really didn't know when it arrived unless our mailman told us and he rode a mule!"

Returning my smile and rolling his handsome eyes, he grabs me by the hand in the middle of the aisle squealing, "Mama, Mama, guess what Alethea knows about Halloween?"

I had to walk to Elizabethtown, Illinois, blending my onward journey with the pleasure of being with a family. There I stayed at the Rose Inn. The Owner Lady was from Canada and she reminded me of a rose. Her complexion was of perfection; manners like a true southern belle and was devoted to her husband-man! We talked of our life and loves as we admired the sunset from her veranda. I noticed, as the sun became stronger with rays slowly sinking behind this delicate woman, with hair vivid as natural henna, that there before me this woman seemed to be a portrait of some famous artist from long ago as the rays of gold touched her deep red thickened hair. I keep this scene in my mind for the day that time allows for me to take my paint brush in hand and bear her portrait as a gift.

She gifted me with fine food and a clean bed, a warm fire and prayers that I make my journey. The husband-man with the family took me to Golconda when it was of too much rain to walk each day. There I met a Newspaper man and his missus. We enjoyed a long lunch and I gathered much History about the Removal. One of the legends goes this way...

"During the Removal, two Cherokee had slipped away from the dog-soldiers and came upon this White Woman cooking as usual. They being of much hunger were trying to let her know that they brought no harm, just wanted food. She in turn couldn't understand Cherokee and was much confused! Turns out, she never got hurt and feeds them. They thank her for the food and remain behind and hide well from the dog-soldiers! As time passes they become much of friends and end up tending to the woman's farm, doing chores for food and lodging. She never turns them in and they protect her until the time her husband-man returns from a far away journey."

I get to visit the Cave In Rock Lodge Resort! The Manager and his missus are most kind to me and we feast upon fine meals that the Family Man prepares there! We took many photographs and promised to meet again in the future.

One afternoon I was invited to speak at this School! I found the system quite of good nature. In this large building were all the twelve grades! This is better for all the Children in many ways. For one reason, the Mama doesn't have to go to several locations to make sure the kids are in school on time. Also this does allow the older siblings to keep an eye out for younger. I spoke this to one of the Teachers; about what a great arrangement I felt they had!

In the class as I was speaking to the students about my journey and how much education was so important for their futures, no matter what they chose to become, I spoke of Sequoyah and how he had invented the Cherokee Alphabet. They found this of much interest!

Then this one young boy asked. "Miss, what kind of weapon do you carry?" waiting patiently for an answer. I was sort of beside myself! If he had asked do I carry a gun, I would not have been so shocked! But he used the term WEAPON! Trying to recompose myself, I answered by looking him straight into his eyes!

"Yes, I carry a J.C. Higgens model 90 with interchange cylinders, double nine blue steel with double-action and no safety .22 long!"

He waited for a minute looking at his hands then looking at my hands paused, cocked his head sideways with a big grin and spoke, "I would say that you have chosen the right weapon to fit you your hand!" Then the whole room and myself give loud laughter! The rest of the time was spent on who was going to get the biggest BUCK come deer season!

---

*Princess left for Vienna, Ill. Me, Sparrow and Brewsky will meet her there.*

---

As I passed the many farms and fields en route to Vienna, many hands would wave as I passed them by! Saw a little hollow and slipped up there for an hour's nap! This little ground squirrel gave me a friendly wake-up call by running past the speed limit across my ankles!

Feeling great! I hadn't gained any weight and I was thrilled with making new friends. The new November (Nvdadegwa) air was brisk to the right degree for walking! I felt light on my feet and even waved at the many blowing horns that sped by!

Then a pick-up truck makes a U-turn and stops just in front of me! The Father steps out with a big grin speaking something about me needing a pony to carry my pack! Well, I just kind of laugh about it, speaking that it would be nice but probably hard to find a place for him at all when I am invited into homes, especially if they should have no barn! He refused that answer and insisted that I take a look at this fine paint pony that he has to sell me. I love on the pony and talk with it for a minute as I'm listening to his speech. He speaks that all he is asking for would be $500 dollars!

"Mister, are you crazy? Where I come from $500 dollars will buy a fine mare that's full grown, like in a style of a horse and that's with a baby in her belly!" My voice was a bit raised but so were my nerves!

He and his son both spoke that ponies were a big selling thing in this land and he must stand firm to his words! I quickly informed him to stand anywhere he pleased but just get away from me! "Hell, we give ponies away in Kentucky," I mumbled as I walked away, shaking my head in "no understand!"

The rain had set in I was soaked to the thighs. Darkness had come and it must be ten at night. Soon I should be coming into Vienna...

This fancy white car pulls up beside me. It's a man in his winter moons of age. He slowly rolls down his window, seeming unaware of the pouring rain! "Hey baby, would you like to go out with me tonight and let me buy you a big ol' steak dinner? My wife died and I'm awfully lonely. We could spend a little time together and I'll pay you a fresh twenty dollar bill after a little talkin'!"

I was well aware that I looked like a wet, stray gila that was in much need of a warm aganawhdiha place but I damn sure didn't feel like a dumb stray gila! As his words rang back through my wet head, I clenched teeth and narrowed my eyes as I snarled to this loose-brain! "Mister, can't you see that I'm enjoying this rainy night? Why, I thought I'd just style my hair and polish my toenails since it's so nice out here!"

His mouth just dropped open! The strong smell could have given me a cheap high. He didn't even flinch to the cold rain that poured into his warm car. Then he barked back, "You're crazy woman and I was gonna give you a big twenty dollars!" Then he started rolling his window much fast and sped quickly out of sight! I just stood there in the heavy downpour and laughed as I watched his tail lights disappear around a stiff curve!

By the time I found a motel, the rain agasga had put me through the water-mill! The motel clerk just looked at me as if to try and figure just what I was; a gila or a woman! I gave a pitiful "Thank you," as I reached for the room-key then spoke that I was sorry for all the ama that I had left in many puddles upon his shiny floor!

Bathed for an hour to rewarm my chilled bones. Called my Mr. Bill and he promised to meet me for a couple of days! This lifted my dampened spirits and allowed me to find sound sleep as I still laughed to the earlier scene of the man wanting to give me a BIG steak dinner and a BIG twenty dollar bill!!!

---

*Brewsky and I went to find princess in Vienna, Ill. Had dinner then played poker until 3:am Princess won, as usual.*

---

When Mr. Bill arrived, he brought Brewsky to visit! I was much glad to visit with her again and appreciated this spray-mist she gave me for my hair! Since the wind unole whipped and dried my hair so badly, she spoke that I really needed this Perma-soft spray in conditioner! She was right! Plus she had me a pair of sun glasses! I had bought some candy at this Candy-Factory that I had passed. Some were in the shape of poker cards! Gave those to Brewsky and a big chocolate fish to Mr. Bill!

To our surprise, Little Sparrow shows up the next day! We all go toward Cape Girardeau, Missouri since this was my future destination. There we found a great place to eat and enjoy some spirits along the Mississippi!! The Manager gave us a tour of the place when I noticed the beautiful deer hide upon the wall. I spoke of the more beauty it could show if he turned the hairbrushing in the correct position! He did!!

We accepted the words that their prime rib was the best. They even suggested that we choose our own from the see-into-cooler. They spoke the truth, one could cut the prime, with a fork!

Late at night en route to the motel, I listened closely to Brewsky singing! Her voice was so smooth and with heart. "That I hardly ever do in front of someone," she spoke with a true blush about her face.

Little Sparrow's car broke down, so we put it in the nearby shop to be fixed. Then, back to the Cape to find this well known Park that was built for memory of the Trail of Tears. There, just to the north of Cape Girardeau about seven miles, we find this true commemorative Park.

This was on the Northern Route which I am presently on. The women showed us all the displays and a video of a reenactment of the removal...

As we studied the three routes, I decided to connect the Northern Route to the Central Route; this being what was called the Benge's Route. Since this would put me upon two of the Trails, I could maybe drop on down to the Southern Route that was known as Bell's Route. This would allow me to cover all three land routes and feel the Spirits that still lingered along this hardly marked Trail of Tears...

Sunday brings a cold rain as I watch everyone drive out of view. Mr. Bill spoke that he was feeling a lot better yet I know that is to just make me feel less worry about him as I struggle on this Trail.

---

*Sparrow shows up. We four had a nice dinner in cape Gerardue. Visited Trail of Tears Park in Missouri. Princess liked the nice maps and education they had. Still raining.*

---

The housekeeper sneaks and does my laundry. Have nothing on but the television when the door swings wide open! There stands the Owner-Man with two visitors! I give a big scream as they all back out the door like crayfish (jisdvna)!! Can't help but wonder why I have all these unwelcome guests in my room when I always have the "Do not Disturb" sign on the door?! Damn that makes me mad!

Now the 6th day of November and I'm in Anna, Illinois lame again. I have to fight the damn devil (asgina); referring to Mama's numerology the date speaks for itself.

The walk from Vienna was most beautiful! I met fire-wire workers along the way and they took a break to talk with me! Many knew all about the Trail of Tears and admired me for wanting this sad event NOT to be forgotten. One gentleman spoke that if he had already enough money saved up to keep his Family going, he would be grateful to finish the journey with me. I thanked him for his heart of warm thoughts for our Cherokee People.

Don't know why my left foot went out on me! Perhaps I did walk a bit too fast on it. Then it could be the rain (agasga). I know it kept wanting to draw up when I put my moccasins on back in Vienna.

Took only one rest and that was just for about ten minutes. I had found this deserted drive to my left. The nvda was still much high when my body called for a usdi gahliha (little sleep). Then I noticed far across the field, folks sitting on their front porch since the rain had passed and brought some warmth in the Fall noon time. Just as I got comfortable this man started walking toward me! My foot was drawing even more but I just got up and explained to him that I was walking the Trail of Tears and just needed to rest a little. He just stared at me! Didn't speak to me a yes or no! Not being sure of his language, I pushed my self onward.

Then when the cold (kanawoga) evening came, I knocked upon three doors only to be turned away! So I kept pushing on! Darkness had long been around me when I found this little family-owned motel!

I stayed in bed for one and a half days before asking the owner-woman to please get me pain pills, red vinegar and jola...

Twenty four hours had passed since I had eaten. I called for a pizza. Though hungry, I didn't eat but one piece! "Thank you Great Spirit for taking away that sinful eating habit that I had."

When I called Mr. Bill, he felt so sorry for me because the most far that I could walk was to the bathroom. He promised to have his cancer surgery on the date that the Doctor-Man had scheduled for him if I would quite crying and carry a tent! I had to stop giving them away! I spoke that I just misplaced them, that's all!

---

*Princess in Jonesboro. Hurt foot again. keeps giving her tents away. Says she is afraid of them, plus they smother her!*

---

"Princess, if you keep your tent, you would not have to walk so far to find a sleeping place when night comes," he gently pleads to me. I listen and half promise! Those damn tents scare me too much! I would rather be chilled than in a piece of canvas or what ever they are made of, lying there fighting the fear of not being able to breath or seeing my enemy! Plus, if I could make myself use a tent, this might slow my journey down and not allow me to be home at the end of January for his operation.

Brewsky comes with him again! She helps me to walk and put more weight on my foot, a little at a time! Mr. Bill informs me that little-rooster-man lost the election! Some man named Bill Clinton was to be the new White-Chief in the Big-White-House "Does he like Indians?" was my first question!

After nursing me for a few days, they depart. Tears come to my eyes and the rain falls. "Will I make this long journey to Oklahoma?

I can do better! I MUST! January Moon has to find me beside my Mr. Bill and thanking The Great Spirit for allowing me to see, walk and feel the land that so many people died upon.

More lard has left my body! Have just a trace of a limp and I am much determined to make the twenty-some miles on to Cape Girardeau!

Anna and Jonesboro, Illinois are separated only by the railroad tracks! I found this interesting as I found my way through town. Right outside of Jonesboro, I find a sign dedicated to the Trail of Tears! This brings warmth and a smile to my face. I don't feel the misty rain falling upon my face. All I could think of was "Many Thanks" to the people that made that sign happen.

Seeing fields and fields of peppers just laying there and rotting, I get my bristles high! Then many trucks and workers show up. My curious tongue would wait no more! "Hey Mister, why do you come now to gather the peppers? Just a bit late aren't you? Why do you let them lay there and rot when there are so many people hungry?" I stand asking firmly with my hands on my hips, not moving until I am pleased with an answer!

"Well Ma'am," he stammers, "I just work as a foreman for this man. I've never really seen him because he lives somewhere in Chicago and gives me orders! The price of peppers don't suit him this year, so we just redo the ground and grow them next year. If the price comes up, then we harvest them! Simple as that," shrugging his shoulders, finishing his speaking with all honesty.

"Well I DON'T find it SIMPLE as THAT! I'd like to give your boss-man a good talking to! Plus, he shouldn't be living in Chicago. He should be here and telling you all to give many baskets of these peppers to every poor person in the State! Now, do you agree with me?"

"Ah, Yes Ma'am, I do," answering politely and putting his truck in gear at the same time! As I walked on, I couldn't help but give my opinion to that Chicago-Pepper-Man!!!

I enjoyed the vast fields and the rain eased up for awhile. Then I see some strange figure laying in the middle of a well-mowed field. Walking up to this sad sight I almost become sick. There lays a beautiful ahawi (deer), a doe at that! She had been shot with a bow, but the hunter hadn't been a good one. I could see how she had struggled for her life a long while. The peppers are dead and now a doe! I'm mad at two strangers now!

Getting tired and its getting late. I never like walking into a tavern but I don't have a choice right now! The agasga is pouring from the sky and this is the only shelter that I can find! Many men are playing pool ball and all faces appear to be of warmth!

I settle in near the door and just check the energies that are about the room, Then I walk up to the barman and ask for a double of his brown liquor, Jim Beam Boy! This brings a chuckle as he fills it to the rim! This smooth but biting taste brings quick warm blood (giga) to the point of removing the chills in my bones! Thought I better have another one to make sure I don't get a cold!

This man asks me if I would like to play pool ball? I speak that I don't know how and really have no interest in the game, I prefer playing poker for a sport! Since he felt like a nice man, I ask about the nearest place to lodge. He points to his friend that just put one of those balls in a hole and waves him over to my table. The man speaks that he owns a hunting lodge and I was much welcome to stay the night there! He tells his son to take me to his nearby establishment and of no charge! I thank him kindly as I pay my tab and get some potato (nuna) chips to go.

---

*She is staying in a hunter's cabin. Called from a phone booth. mad about dead peppers and a dead deer. That's Princess. More rain.*

---

The rain comes much harder by the time the sixteen year old boy gets me to the lodge. This place has like ten small bedrooms and he speaks that it used to be a Church and many other businesses over time. I can have the room of my choice! I take the nearest one to the kitchen and the ama-hole!

The bed is so clean and fresh! The kitchen is every Betty Crocker's dream! There is so much food to choose from that I'm not sure what to eat first! Good thing I don't sin anymore when I eat! This would be the place that I would probably end up eating until I passed on!!

The young man speaks for me to wash my clothes, enjoy the food and watch the television when it works, then he leaves. "I'll be here tomorrow to check on you," shyly smiling and locking the door as he leaves.

I enjoyed the much hot ama then curled into the small bunk bed. I listened to the rain as it pounded hard against the window. I wanted Mr. Bill to be there with me; besides, he would like this place! But I still couldn't get those dead peppers out of my mind nor the sad little doe that was now being rained upon and never even got a decent burial.

Still agasga all the next day and the radio gives two more days before it may quit. Well, I was lucky enough to call Mr. Bill the night before and let him know where I was. I made some cooking; not my calling in life, but this cow meat is good! Washed what few clothes I had dirty and read many hunting articles. The young man comes to check on me and suggests that I forget about walking, due to high ama everywhere. I take his advice and try to sleep my blues away.

By the next day; still no let up from the rain as I insist on leaving! Some Man that is a friend to the Family stops by and offers to take me back to the Trail then on to Cape. "You can get a ride back to this point and make your Trail up," he speaks with a big grin and prides me for my journey! I agree, then we almost can't make it through the deep waters that have overcome the road!

Once in Cape Girardeau, he takes me to this Thrifty Motel that's a couple miles out of the way but he speaks that it will be less money and the people are nice! He gives me his telephone number just in case that I should need a ride back to my starting point. I thank him so kindly and go dashing through the rain like a fleeing fox!

---

*She's in Cape Gerardeau at Thrifty Motel. Sparrow and High-Cheeks supposed to go and see her. I am too sick to go.*

---

TRAIL THROUGH SOUTHERN ILLINOIS

1. Cave In Rock
2. Elizabethtown
3. Rosiclare
4. Golconda
5. Grantsburg
6. Vienna
7. Mt. Pleasant
8. Anna-Jonesboro
9. Ware
10. Reynoldsville
11. Mc Clure
12. Mississippi River

## MISSOURI

Got to call my Mr. Bill! He was much glad to hear that I was safe and in Missouri! Little Sparrow called. Spoke that she and her beau, High-Cheeks, would come and visit me! Plus the beautiful Dancing-Wolves called to speak that they had me in their daily prayers and I would make this journey. This gave me a lift but was saddened that Mr. Bill couldn't come, due to work and heavy rains.

For two more days I looked out my window and stared into the rain that I felt was a Blessing even if it prevented me walking...

Finally Little Sparrow and High-Cheeks come to visit and tell me all the news of home! They brought Sweet-William, my guitar, and I gave them a concert!! We went back to my drop-off point so I could make the Trail beneath my feet. They took me out to dinner and bought me a new skirt and sweater! High-Cheeks even allowed me to drive his limited-edition Cadillac!! This really felt much strange since it was my first time to drive in such a long time! We even drove ahead so I could spot a barn and see what my next part of the journey looked to be!

My heart was heavy as they left the parking lot but I was restless to continue my walk! Across the Mississippi now, I felt as though Jackson would be proud of me! I was now where he wanted all Cherokee Indians to be; West of the mighty Grandfather Longarms!

Fighting my way through the Cape Girardeau traffic was not an easy battle, so I kept thinking about the good luck to have met the nice people at the Cherokee Park that gave me more knowledge that allowed me to connect my journey from here to the Benge's Route!

Finally as I make my way into the more open road, I felt

a bit more at ease. Took a couple of breaks near the big road and nobody stopped to bother me.

Studied my map, finding that I must turn to my left (aksgani) at route 34. There was a roadside market and gas-up place, so I decided to have an early supper and call Mr. Bill to let him know that I was heading into the deep country again and I wasn't sure when I could call again. I also called Kay. She had been acting as my Indian-Affairs Coordinator from Xenia Ohio. She felt that I had been making much good time! I felt that I could do better!

Resting and enjoying talk with the market-owners, I made a supper of three hot-dogs and two colas; my favorite, R.C.!! Then bid them farewell as I watched the nvda slowly find it's way to the down-side of the sky. This is when my heart (adanhdo) starts to beat much fast because its near time to knock upon doors and pray that I'm gifted with lodging in their barn!

My prayers where answered! Fighting the traffic on this smaller road is a mystery but I see a barn!! After about three knocks upon this door, an elderly man comes to my call with a smile on his face! "Mister, my name is Alethea and I'm walking the Trail of Tears! You have a nice looking barn behind your house, can I sleep the night here? I won't be any problem to you," pleading like a child wanting candy!

He paused for a second but never took away his smile. Then scratching his head, he slowly answered me, "Well, I don't see no harm in it. But its calling for cold weather tonight! Well, I'll be right here if you need anything 'cause my Missus is sickly."

My heart felt like a proud trophy-owner of a Kentucky Derby winner! Quickly I danced toward the barn to prepare my pallet!!

Unrolled my sleeping bag, got out the National Historic Trail Book that I had received from the wisdom-woman in Hopkinsville, Kentucky and made my little space for the night! Flipped the barn light on and off a couple of times, excited that it worked! I must call this the Holiday Inn Barn!

Found the perfect spot in the barn corner to avoid the cold breeze that was picking up. Was all cuddled in and read for awhile and made the light go out to just enjoy the silence that was taking Place. Traffic had died down and I listened to the deserted old barn as it spoke the stories of it's days gone by! Guess I have a certain respect and love (adageyhdi) for old barns where once they watched the children play, young lovers meet, protect the cattle or witness the birth of a newborn foal. The modern times leave it without a child to tend to; no more hide and seek plays. But tonight this old friend has some company!

My ode to the barn was interrupted by truck lights and voices! Now what? Suddenly the lights are on and this man comes to my pallet-place, followed by another man and a kind-face woman. "What are you doing here and who in the hell are you?" this lean boned man speaks just short of a yell!

"Well. the Owner-man of this barn spoke that I could spend the night here and I'm walking the Trail of Tears!" speaking back to him, looking upward as you do when the Law stops you!

"Well, I DON'T want you here. YOU may hurt MY Dad. That's who owns this barn! So I suggest that YOU get your stuff together and leave now!" pointing his finger in the road direction!

Immediately, I stand up, placing my hands on my hips and meeting him eye to eye!

"You Mister, just wait an all-fired minute! Your Papa

spoke that I could spend the night in his barn and I damn sure intend to! If you have a problem, call the Law! I ain't going any damn where. If maybe you had come before dark, we could have had council but I'll be damned if I'm going to go out into this cold night and GOD only knows what could happen to me. So just get the hell out of here and leave ME ALONE!" keeping my stance and stare!

That was it! He just backed off and left! The nice woman was his missus and lingered as he stomped toward his truck."I'm glad you did that!" softly whispering to me.

"Yeah, and one more thing!" I yelled toward him, stepping out of the loft, "If I was a bad woman, do you think I would be carrying this heavy backpack? Where's your damn brains!?" My answer from old-lean-head was the slamming of his truck door! I watched him back out of the driveway and he never even went into the house to check on his sickly Mama! "Ass-hole!" I growled as I found my once peaceful pallet where I was busy giving this Barn-Ode! !

Later as I prayed for sleep, I had the honor of listening to the barn mice do their dances and slides across the weathered boards close to my pallet. I expected to awaken with the whole troop sleeping with me! My last thoughts were, "Mice are more friendly than most men in Missouri!"

Prepared to leave by dawn. Didn't find much shoulder to walk upon and I wanted a cup of kahwi, NOW! Forget that. Kept walking all the more hard! Passed a big barn that held a whole stack of hides of deer! I just stood there in awe! The busy men never did see me.

Thought I would take a short break and have my first jola for the day, listening to the little creek fighting with the many stones! That's when it comes to mind just what the words mean, "Babbling-Brook!" I'm admiring the beauty of the naked trees due to the winter and find beauty of nature all around me when this truck slides in for a landing beside the little bridge that I had found to rest on.

"Get that white bandana off girl. Don't you know its deer season 'round here?" The yellow-haired women screams to me!

I just sit there like I hadn't really heard her then met her painted eyes with a cold stare. "Woman, if the damn fools around here shoot this close to the road then its time to die. Now get on down the road and leave me alone because I'm already pissed off!" She took a quick glance at Bonnie and tore out spinning her new truck tires! I figured the way she was all painted and her hair looked as if she had just come from the beauty parlor, her time wasn't to drive the road just to speak of hunters. I think she was out hunting her husband-man to make sure that he was HUNTING!!

My next rest time was upon this warm-feeling Country-Jubilee porch. Sitting there on a log trying to rub this new soreness that was coming into my legs and hip when this friendly man drives up! He speaks that he owns the establishment and I ask that when I return this way could I sing there!? "You will be most welcome to sing," was a soft, deep country reply with a warm smile!

Then as we keep talking, I speak of the nice elderly man that gave me his barn last night when this ass-hole come in to run me away. He stood there and listened patiently as I rattled on then with his way of speaking, I find that was his brother!! We both laugh! "Now, you can find a good cup of coffee at the crossroads just down the road a ways and I'll see if I can't come up with you a place to lodge for the night!" was his departing words. As I repacked, he drove away!

True enough, I come to the Cross-Road Market! Couldn't help but think that I wear my moccasins in my mouth more that on my feet! He took my tongue-lashing that I gave his brother with a smile!

This friendly woman takes my order of a double cheeseburger with extra cheese! True to order! I hadn't seen one this big since I was in Morehead, Kentucky at "Jim-Bo-Thackers!" I was about halfway through my Cheeseburger-Heaven when these two deer hunters (ahaw ganohalidohi) came to my table (gasgilo)! "Miss, we understand you are walking the Trail of Tears!" both handsome men smiled down at me!

"Yes I am!" trying to swallow a big bite and keep my smile too!

"Well, there will be many people that will think you are crazy and discourage you. Just ignore them and keep your Faith and walk on! We admire you and best of luck lady!" giving me a thumbs up as they grabbed some snacks to go.

I just sat and studied for a minute. "Why can't other people see me as these two Gentlemen just did?"

I had finished eating when the Nice-Brother came back into my life. "Here's you a telephone number that might have a room for you tonight. Might be best if you call it now, never can tell."

This surprised me! "Oh, thank you Sir, I will ask this woman if I can use her telephone! This is good and again Sir, thank you!" He was working so he departed much fast and the woman smiled because she had heard the conversation and spoke that I could use her telephone!

This husky but warm voice answered me on the other end. "Yes Miss, I have one room available. When do you think you will be here?"

"Well, that I don't know exactly. I'm walking the Trail of Tears and I'm not sure how far away I am!" giving a serious laugh!

"Oh, you should make it by dark. Just be careful and the room is waiting for you!" As she hangs up I thanked the good cooking woman and offered to pay for the call.

"No, there's no charge just make this journey! I have Cherokee Blood in me too!

"Thanks again Lady!" giving her a big smile and hoping I have plenty to give her a fine tip!

Back on the NO SHOULDER ROAD and even harder to handle the traffic. Something keeps coming to my mind. I have this good "Message In The Wind!"

There's a strange sound in the air all around me! No understand. Never heard anything like this before! The cattle and horses didn't seem to care yet they didn't seem to notice me either! I kept waiting for something to land or a U.F.0. to appear over the treetops but nothing shows up!

Starting to wear down a bit, wondering how much farther I have to Marble Hill? Now coming into this grove of fine kept homes this couple are just pulling into their drive. They greet me at the edge of their yard and we speak much about the Trail Of Tears! The Missus spoke that during the removal that passed this way in 1838 she knew for a fact that she was part Cherokee because her Grandfather (Ududu) of many moons ago made an even trade with the dog-soldiers! Seems they needed a wheel for a wagon and him being a young man, needed a wife! There a good deal took place! They got the much needed wagon wheel and he received a beautiful wife! I found this of great interest. Then her husband-man made the remark that he too knew that she was Cherokee just by her temper!

We had a good laugh and learned much from each other! They spoke I would be in their prayers and I pushed on. Finally the sound is no more a mystery! Came to this big gas factory!

Don't know just how it works and this scares me much but the sign speaks GAS! Now I know too, where all the traffic is coming from. Found myself walking lighter and faster as I pass this modern monster!

Crossing this old fashioned bridge, the rain comes again as I seek shelter at a closed filling station. Sitting there chilling and burning up too when the owner pulls up. "Mister," unable to control the quiver and weakness in my voice, "Is there a place to eat around here?"

He smiles at me as if not to build my hopes up, rubs his chin and gives more thought then points toward this small hill! "Well, up there they have either Church going on or serving food! Today is Sunday (Dodagwasgvʔi) but they might be having something to eat. Just give it a try!" Taking my time to remove myself from his porch, I feebly thanked him and went on the route to the Church-Food place.

Felt bad due to sickness and worse due to my appearance! Seeing everybody in their Sunday best raised my temperature, not sure if I should ask for food or a corner to sleep in! Then this smiling face that just glowed and showed years of wisdom behind it beckoned for me to come on in! "Come in! Please come in. Sorry you missed our Sunday Service. But we always have room for one more! Now grab a plate and fill it high!"

I obeyed! Then this young attractive girl that was a senior in high school begin telling me many history stories of the Trail of Tears! This lifted my spirits and for a minute my fever seemed to rest. I asked if she intended to study History in College and she assured me that she was! Though I couldn't eat but very little, I filled up on kahwi and juice! I thanked them all kindly as they prayed for my safe journey. Hoping the juice and warm environment would have made me feel better, I was wrong. Growing more sick by the step and getting mean and moody! "What's wrong with me?" Then the worse comes to mind! I'm in need of an estrogen shot. Can't recall when I had the last one but it must be near time for another (soʔi)!

Darkness was falling by the time I find this motel. All the strength had left my body but when I see the smiling face of the motel-owner, somehow I feel like someone in this world really does still have a heart! Then she shows me a warm and extra clean room at the end of the hall. Ditched my pack so fast and threw myself across the bed. "I must call my Mr. Bill,"I thought, "Before I get more sleepy!"

Since there was no telephone in the room, I had to walk back to the office. He tried lifting my spirits by speaking that I was still making good (osda) progress and we would surely be together in Popular Bluff to celebrate Gvna-Iga!!

---

*Princess left message on recorder. Now in deep country. I pray for you princess... She calls from a country motel. i think she needs a shot of estrogen! raining again. She sounds depressed.*

---

Agasga held me indoors for three days and I felt so far behind in everything! The motel-owner tried so much to ease my pain and worry. She took me to the Mail-Office to send my Treasures home to Little Sparrow to keep for me. There were many bones from possums, birds and turtles, not counting the pretty pieces of wood that I just had to have at the time! My pack seemed to have hardly any weight. She also gave me a tour of her home that was finely adorned with expensive collecting plates of many subjects! I adored the Native American collection the best!

Couldn't hold out any longer! I spoke that I needed an estrogen shot!

"Why, that's no problem. I'll take you to my Doctor!" smiling and heading me out the back door!

Walked into this small office trying to be as polite as this mean mood would allow when this young Nurse asked me with a smirk, "What makes you think that YOU need an estrogen shot?"

I stand for a second praying for composure then my teeth clench, eyes narrow and the growl sets in, 'Woman, I don't allow that tone of speaking and WHAT makes YOU think I DON'T need an ESTROGEN SHOT?"

She removed herself much quick and this more wise Nurse comes forward, "Follow me honey," as she opens the door, "to my Magic-Room." Up goes my skirt, in goes the shot and the whole world is much safer for another Moon!

As we sat at her kitchen table and spoke many stories of our life. Staring at the rain, she taught me the true words of "Thou Shall Not Covet." I really didn't know that this meant NOT to want what someone else has. Giving me an example, she spoke about this man that wanted his friend's horse. The friend kept speaking that he didn't want to sell his horse (sogwili) but the man just couldn't take NO for an answer. Finally, he even hocked his home to buy the sogwili. The friend gave into the sale but before the man could get his horse home, there was a wreck and the horse was destroyed! The man was in hock two times now. No horse and no home. I felt so sorry for this man yet from this story that had taken place nearby, I learned a valuable lesson! I thanked her most kindly.

The time had come for me to move on. Feeling some better and wanting to see my Mr. Bill, she helped me read my map and pointed me in the right position (aktisi). Still the agasga was of heavy mist as I found my way over a mountain (odalv?i), searching for route 51. I see this sihgwa (pig) farm and talk to the little babies. The mama's weren't so friendly but I spoke to them anyway. Off to a field by itself, I see this many-moons pig that had a sunk-in back! Broken, I guess, but it was happy and seemed to be the boss!!

Back on the road, leaving the sihgwa smell behind, I kept hearing sounds of whispers in the wind! I wonder just what the Unole speaks?

I felt a child holding onto my leg! I stop to look in all direction...nothing. I begin to pray! When this Message comes that this is a child-spirit that died along this stretch of the Crying-Trail and she wanted to go on to join her Mama! I then spoke out loud with much gentleness, "Come my usdi, I will show you the way to Oklahoma."

Didn't make many miles this day. The rain kept coming and going. I would be too hot then chill; feeling that I had no time for another cold! I needed to be in Poplar Bluff in a couple of days.

Saw hunters all about the fields but cared less of getting shot! All I wanted right now was a place to lay my fevered head and get out of the rain.

To my left (aksgani) was a building that gave warm energy! I must give a try. This husband-man and his missus were most kind. We talked to know each other better when he spoke that his little camper-trailer in the yard wasn't much but I could stay the night there! Being so thankful and needing another shirt anyway, I bought one from them. Their work of clothes making was of beauty. They even gave me a discount!

"Allow me first to tell you a little about the trailer! I got it from a feller at a sale! Well, I parked it right where it is and locked it up. You know those padlocks?" I shook my weary head to a yes-nod! "Well," he goes on, "Next morning me and the missus come to work and the lock is unlocked and the door is open! I just lock it back, thinking maybe some kids did it, but the next time same thing! It won't stay locked. Its a mystery to us!"

I just stood there for a second before I spoke, "Well, if there is a spirit there, maybe it will visit me and I will council with it!" Darkness was setting in and I was too. The missus had gone home and returned with supper, plus a kerosene lamp! I thanked her kindly as I lit the lamp that brought back many memories, then asked her where they got that little black dog?

"Oh, it just came here to the store one day and never did leave and nobody ever claimed it!

As I set there eating and thinking of the mystery door and the black puppy dog, I decided to play five card draw poker as I listened to the agasga pound upon the tin trailer roof! In my hand I had an ace, king, jack and ten all of clubs! I'll go for it, knowing the odds were much against me. But I drew ONE card and it was a QUEEN of CLUBS!!! This gave me a Royal Straight Flush that who would believe!! With a smile on my face, I made my pallet on the floor listening to the hard rain and figured the spirit that lived in this little camper was at one time a GAMBLER!!

The cool morning found my fever high again and tried to rush my steps! My hip was now hurting. The right joint didn't want to work! Tried to keep my mind off this by admiring this Duck Creek Wildlife area! I would stand for a long while at a time to admire them in take offs, flight and landings!! How can anyone kill the Sky-Babies? They mate for life.

Came upon more pretty rocks (dahlihgeha) and had to load up again! This truck slides to a halt as I was making my selection of stones and speaks, "I thought you was a Man and was going to offer you a ride!" Then he just tore out before I could give my opinion! But I hollered at him anyway! "Didn't want a damn ride!"

Hadn't reached the distance my mind spoke to! But my hip wouldn't make it happen. By now I was reaching down, taking my two hands and moving my right leg! Then in a short distance I see a market across the road! Move myself into the back where I find a chair and am at the mercy to ask the store lady to find me lodging for the night! Just down the road about a mile was a place to rest!

This seemed to be another hunter (ganohalidohi) lodge but smaller than the one in Illinois. I called Mr. Bill from the office and stayed a long time in the ama-hole to soak my hip. In no time sleep overtook me! I was thinking about the Sky-Babies and the spirit of that little child.

---

*No call tonight. She left marble Hill this morning ... She called from another hunter lodge. Spoke about some Spirits and poker cards, she's sickly again.*

---

Still had the flu but my hip was in forward gear again! Got to Puxico and ate. The waitress there spoke that I could find a place to rest near the Wappapello Lake. This lifted my spirits. I am just one more day from Poplar Bluff and Mr. Bill!! These many treasures were getting heavy but I was gonna keep them! I'd take a break, puff my jola, take another Advil and move on!

Now darkness and coldness were setting in. I felt so bad I just started crying. Then I prayed that someone would take me in and doctor me when exactly then a truck stops and this man in his Winter-Moons speaks that he had seen me all day walking! So he takes me to this fancy motel by the lake. First the Woman spoke that she didn't have a room! But when he spoke to her, she found a key!!!

"God bless you Child and be careful." he softly spoke as he got back into his truck.

Called Mr. Bill and he could tell that I was much sick but spoke that if I could make it on to Poplar Bluff by sundown (nvda eladi) tomorrow, he would spend a few days with me and he had a surprise for me!

"This made me happy but I was really too sick to care. Went to sleep crying because I didn't even have enough fire (ajila) in me to challenge the desk-woman about the room when there wasn't even a car in the parking lot!

---

*She's at a lake motel. Had a hard time getting the room. She is happy about me meeting her when she gets to poplar Bluff. I promised her a suprise!*

---

I didn't turn in the room key or speak bye, I just headed out!

Misty rain was still falling but I had miles to put beneath my moccasins. Fever back again! At least twenty miles lay before me and I was going to make this no matter what! But I had to keep seeking shelter from the agasga! People (yvwi) would stop from time to time and ask if I needed anything then wish me the best and safeness upon my journey! I could only mumble a Thank-You and stumble on.

As usual it seems, the skies were dark as I found a cheap motel. The traffic was heavy and I had never been to Poplar Bluff and didn't really know what to expect! But the twenty three dollars in my pack spoke that one thing for sure I wouldn't be in the fancy side of town! Didn't care, couldn't get past the first dive I came to due to money (adela) and this cold (kanawoga)!

Had two dollars left after I got the room only to find no hot (udihlehga) water (ama)! This starts me to growling but that takes too much energy. Instead I call my Mr. Bill and he speaks that he will be at my side sometime before midnight (svnoyi)!! I just crawl into the smelly bed waiting for my hero.

---

*Princess called from smelling motel. She is real sick, going to meet her... Moved her to Holiday Inn. I fix her favorite food, elk and deer meat. made her toddies. She slept a lot under five blankets. Got her supplies, she hates the new boots and sweats! Likes the hair conditioner. Had a nice dinner.*

---

Mr. Bill knows how much I love elk-meat and that was my gift for the next morning which was Gvna-Iga!! So he backs Ol' Blue up to the door and I prepare it on the camper stove that he brought!

Needed to go back to bed but he wasn't so liking the motel that I had chosen, so he moves me to the Holiday Inn! Once there, he tucks me in and gets me flu medicine and room service for many juices to drink (aditasdi)! Then he prepares me venison and tries to get some hot-toddies in me! After about the third one, I'm finding that I really am alive.

The five blankets he had kept me covered with sweated and purified me once more! The next evening we had a fine crab leg dinner in the hotel and enjoyed some spirits from their tavern!!!

The last day together, we pack more road-treasures into Ol' Blue and Mr. Bill walks until he finds me that Pantene Hair Conditioner Mist! He then suggests that I wear sweats and winter boots. I start to buck on this. I hate britches and my moccasins are perfect! Plus, how am I to be able to pee standing up!? In the end, I LOSE!!

New sweats and moon boots are upon me. I'm bound to smother to death! The first thing I do is use my Buck-knife and cut the front of the sweatshirt to my liking!

We were watching the News and see about thirty Cherokee Indians leaving from around Cleveland, Tennessee to walk the Trail of Tears. This made my heart heavy when we saw that they didn't have warm winter coats on and only tennis shoes!

"Oh, Mr. Bill, will you send somebody to help them and take a message from me about what all they will have to encounter?" half in a cry as I pleaded to him!

"Yes, Princess, I will see what I can do!"

The next day was sad for us. He took me back to the Trail. We figured that I had about twenty miles to the Arkansas border. There I stood with tears in my eyes and feeling like some kind of Moon-Walking-Woman from the way that he now had me dressed! We waved at each other until we could see no more.

---

*Took princess back to the Trail. Wants me to help some other Cherokee that she saw on TV. Guess I'll have to make some phone calls. Its so cold. She was better, but heading for Doniphan and hating the new clothes! can't pee standing up! Poor little wild Princess.*

---

Turning to face the wind and cold, I figured the tears would make me be of sickness again. This stretch of road had no shoulder to walk upon and I could see for miles ahead of me! Walked twelve miles before I took a break. Saw this little country store just ahead on my right! "Howdy, my name is Alethea and I'm walking the Trail of Tears! Could I rest here for a bit and maybe get a bologna sandwich?" smiling to the owner woman behind the counter!

"You sure can honey. Now tell us about your journey so far! Where all have you been?" Our talking and me meeting her sisters and children took the rest of the afternoon! Then Pat speaks that she will bring my pack and for me to walk on the four miles to her house! Just to go in and make myself comfortable! In no time at all, I had the four miles beneath my feet and found her warm home.

The gilas greeted me in the yard. I patted each one and they allowed my intrusion!! Soon Pat and many of her family members came to visit and meet me.

We talked of everything and I showed them my poker cards that my Mama showed me how they speak! The way I do this is, the person that wants a reading must shuffle the cards for seven times! This allows their energy to come into the cards. Then I speak my prayer out loud as I lay them in the order that Mama taught me to. I read each family member their cards that night and spoke to this one young man that his cards spoke that he would receive a large amount of money within a day or so! I didn't feel offended when he didn't believe me.

This family made me feel so welcome and they cooked much good food and gave me the best bed! The ama-hole felt great and I was praying that my flu didn't return due to little rest! The worse thing that happened to me was a BIG blister on my heel-side from those damn moon-boots! This put me in a rough mood and limping. Later that day, Pat took me on to Doniphan. There I called Mr. Bill to speak how much I hated those boots! But I got some medicine, rested then made up the eleven miles the next day.

Then the following day I pass Doniphan and make a sharp turn to my left. Stopped in this home-type restaurant for kahwi. The two women of Autumn- moons were very wise about the Trail of Tears and gave their strong opinion of the forced journey! They wouldn't charge for the coffee and B.L.T., instead they embraced me and spoke a prayer that I would be safe.

Another stretch of land that had miles of neatly groomed farms! I had to admire the work that went into these. My energy was high and I kept thinking about the young man that the Talking-Cards spoke would receive money. The day after I had called from the motel to speak farewell and he spoke that he had received a check in the mail that was many dollars! "Good for you. Now you can build that little cabin on the river bank you so much want!" showing my delight as much as he was!!

Feeling lean, stronger of mind and far lighter on my feet. Dark (ulsihga) was coming sooner than I expected! I was nearing the State Line and would have liked to go on. But many steps without a farm in sight was no wise decision!

Then to my left I see this country bar that speaks LAST CHANCE BAR --- LEAVE YOUR GUN OUTSIDE! Well! This could mean that one would not have to make any decisions!! But I'm not leaving my Bonnie outside! Instead I shove it inside my pack as I pull at the sturdy door!

Took a minute to adjust my eyes, then I find a seat with my back to the wall. Shortly this lady, a few years past my age comes to my table with a big grin and takes a beer order! I ask if she has any brown liquor; the answer is no! That leaves me to order a Coors Light! Its hard to get down and I already feel my eyes swelling, so off to the john to be sick, then back to order another!

The owner and the waitress are most nice to me and tell me of the time that they were all snowed in at the bar! We traded many stories and laughs. Then a local comes over and he swells out like a fighting-rooster just to speak that he didn't think that I was walking the Trail of Tears because my face wasn't wind-burned to suit him!

"I don't give a damn if you believe it or not and my mission in life is far from suiting YOU!" They all laughed at him as he found his barstool again!

About three-lost-beers later, the waitress speaks that I can stay at her house tonight. She gives me her house key and directions! I was much thankful and headed out into the darkness to make the mile and a half quick as possible!

Once inside, I felt so comfortable! I stocked her stove real good and refilled it with more logs. Now, she did ask me to have her some coffee made! I took a good look at that coffee maker and just couldn't figure out how to make it happen! The first pot runs all over the counter but the second batch went where it was supposed to!! Another learning in life!

Then I jumped in that hot-ama-hole, put on clean sweats, rolled up in her blanket and my Indian blanket (unegvhaˀi) to find warm, sweet sleep as I listened to the hickory log sing to me!

---

*Haven't heard anything. She may call after while. Talked to my Doctor. Brother called from London, KY. Goodnight Princess.*

---

# TRAIL THROUGH SOUTHERN MISSOURI

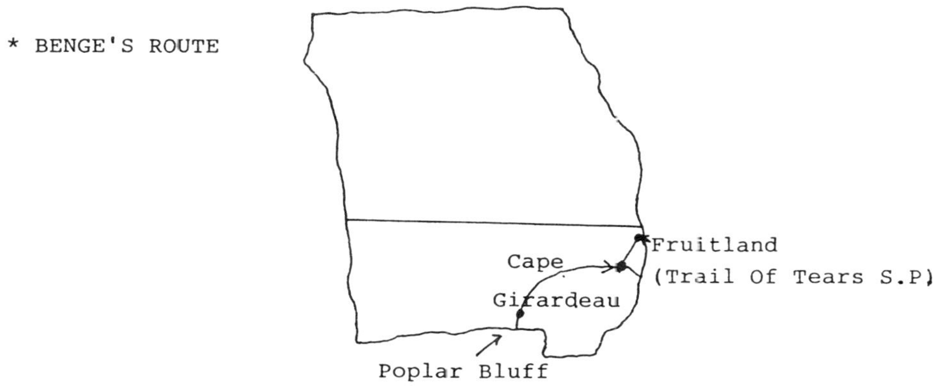


1. Cape Girardeau
2. Jackson
3. Burfordville
4. Marble Hill
5. Dongola
6. Zalma
7. Arab
8. Idlewild
9. Puxico
10. Wappapello
11. Hendrickson
12. Poplar Bluff
13. Fairdealing
14. Doniphan
15. Naylor
16. Neelyville

## ARKANSAS

Winding narrow roads, several little towns and much traffic later I come to POCAHONTAS! Weary and dirty, I find this little dive at the edge of town. Its getting dark again and I'm too tired to care about anything to eat.

The young man that checks me in asks if I needed anything? I speak that I would be grateful if he would wash all my clothes! He did! Within two hours he delivered them to my room, asked if I needed anything more? Would I like a good hit of speed!? NO, I was quick to answer but do you maybe have, whatcha call, a half pint of fire-water?

"Oh, no Ma'am, this is a dry county and the Law is real mean if they catch you with whiskey!" answering with all seriousness and his eyes widened to show!

"You mean to tell me that I can get drugs from you in this town but no fire-water! Mister I think you have it backwards!" widening my eyes back to him! All he spoke was "Sorry, and there's no charge for your clothes." This quick conversation left me feeling confused!

The door facing had been busted, so I stick my Buck Knife in and brace a chair against it as well; another time that I will have to sleep with one eye open!

I had left a message on Mr. Bill's answering machine, so when the telephone rings, I'm much happy!

"Princess, you are going to be mad at me but I have to get this off my chest! I sent my ex some flowers for her birthday! I'm now sorry but its done and over with, ok?" holding his gentle but unsteady voice.

First I was sitting on the bed just shaking then I stand up holding the telephone in my hand as I start pacing, which I tend to do when I become nervous. "Mr. Bill, you did WHAT? You mean to speak these words to me that you know drives me to not a healthy place inside my head! FLOWERS! Hell, you've NEVER sent me FLOWERS!" By now I'm making a turn from pacing, step upon the bed, across it, step off the other side, turn around and backtrack! "WHY?" But I don't wait for an answer. "Have you become an old fashioned certified Mormon that has to have many women? Are you finding out that death is upon you and you now want us BOTH? OK, this is all a big joke to test my love isn't it!?" back across the bed! "How could You do this to ME? What did I do wrong?"

"Princess, please calm down, I didn't mean anything by it. Its you that I love. I just did it that's all. Please understand."

"Oh, I understand what you speak alright! I wish I HAD an "X" Beau that I could send FLOWERS to! I would send him a hundred dollars worth! NO. It would be five hundred dollars worth!" back across the bed, making a turn. Hell I DON"T even have $500 dollars! I'm on the WAR-PATH BIG! "Mr. Bill, you understand what I speak!?" make a step up on the bed - too much work so I throw the telephone and the cord pulls out!

RING. I pick it up and put it down!

RING, RING, RING ... I pick it up and put it down.

RING. "WHAT?"

"Princess, please don't hang up again, let's talk about this," his words so deep, soft and pleasant. Silence on my end. " Princess, have you had anything to eat? You know how you are when you have those low blood sugar attacks."

"LOW BLOOD my ass! I am having a HIGH-BLOOD-WAR-ATTACK!"

"Princess, let's not quarrel, its not worth it."

"FINE!" I'm trying to soften a bit 'cause I've run out of gas. We bid goodnight as the telephone goes across the room again!

"You don't sleep by me, your RING makes BAD news!"

---

*Princess called from Pocahontas, Arkansas. She is on the warpath! I sent my ex flowers for her birthday, had to tell her. She always seems to know these things. She threw the phone and hung up on me. I'm in trouble! Love you Princess.*

---

Next morning I was as mean as a copperhead (juktajisdahli) crossbred with a rattlesnake (ujonati) just looking for someone to strike!

As I was finding my way through town, heading toward Cherokee Village, I noticed these two men following closely in a pickup truck! Thought I would let them do their cheap thrill for awhile but they followed to the outskirts now. I stop, turn slowly, squint my bead-eyes and give Ol' Bonnie a pat! They take a look of shock at each other and make a quick turnaround!

Found myself crying, kicking rocks and praying! But I have to get my mind together! I'm not watching the cars for my safety. I MUST put this flower arrangement behind me!

A small mule tied to the back of a truck caught my attention! As I walked up to the pretty critter, the owner was coming out of the restaurant."Ain't she a beauty? Do you think I made a good deal for a few hundred dollars?" the country man half hollered!

"Well, if a feller can hunt with her, you've made a good trade!" giving my opinion as I rubbed her long nose.

"The ol' boy said a kid could hunt from her!"

"GOOD!" smiling to his little girl now,"You did alright!" Gave the sogwili another pat and waved as I headed into the restaurant!

Ordered kahwi and took my time sipping and puffing my favorite jola! This will give me some time to rest and think about things, but with last night's anger in me, I'm going to have to fight the damn devil (asgina) all day!

So this is the new White-Chief's State huh!? So far I have seen more well kept farms and fancy homes! Darkness caught me before I could reach IMBODEN. I had a misstep when some car lights blinded me and stepped into a back ditch! Not knowing if there were lodgings ahead, I hobbled until I saw many lights! Came to the Main street and made a choice to the left, off the Trail a ways, but old asgina didn't win today! I have found a place to sleep!

Checked into the room and there were nothing but Indian pictures all over the walls! These folks have my vote! They like Indians!!

Didn't call my Mr. Bill, just soaked my sore and swollen ankle in the ama-hole then fell asleep listening to The Great Spirit's soothing agasga!

Couldn't start until late in the morning due to the heavy downpour. Took my time as I had a country breakfast and talked to the Owner-Woman of the motel. I called the police station in Cherokee Village to make sure that I was on the right track! He called his missus and assured me that I was. After the agasga let up some, I headed for Cherokee!

Strange, I keep seeing dead baby owls (wahuhi). Did someone kill them by accident, maybe by a car? Yet there was no blood (giga), just sad eyes staring up at me. I spoke a prayer to each one...

The rain had turned to sleet now. Kept seeing this sign advertising a roadside restaurant. Maybe I'll have luck there, I prayed. The little town of WILLIFORD comes into sight but I must cross this long, icy, cement bridge first! I skid and slide the whole way right up to the little cafe!!

Begin talking to this nice local woman. She invited me to her home that was far up on a ridge. She took me to the very springs that our Cherokee People drank from during the Removal. We both got out in the sleet and drank from it too! This we felt was in honor for the Cherokee! Spent the rest of the stormy afternoon meeting her family and all the animals! Adored her mountain home. All about the yard she had a fine collection of rocks! One idea she had I find so intelligent. As you walk into her doorway, there was a coffee-sack full of walnuts! As you wiped your feet free of the clay, you were removing the hulls from the walnuts (sedi) as well!

Though invited to spend the night, I appreciated the offer but didn't want to put anyone out of their bed (ganihli). instead Ayv took the offer to be taken back to the Trail. The lady took me to this little family owned place. We shopped for food since the rain had set in for a few days, then bid our farewells!

In CHEROKEE VILLAGE, I called Mr. Bill. All was forgotten about the flowers. I was now on a mission to find another Indian that must live around here! I was so sure that Cherokee Village would have many Cherokee dwelling here was only in my mind! This turned out to be a White-Mans-Reservation-Resort!!! But not one to give up, I made many calls from a Doctor's office to the local Historian. They all spoke that there weren't any Indians.

Then I think more deep! Who would know everybody in a community for some special reason? Why an animal Doctor-man!! I call the first Veterinarian in the telephone book and the lady that answers has a boyfriend that is of the Creek Tribe!

I invite them over to my little motel room and we cross many fields and streams of talk! Everyone calls him Two-

Dogs! I even got Mr. Bill on the telephone to talk with Two-Dogs! They spoke of fishing and business! Two-Dogs also spoke to Mr. Bill that he believed that I would finish the Trail just fine because my energies were strong and spirits much high! Two-Dogs spoke that I was right on the course of the Trail and we compared maps and knowledge. He pointed out places of interest that I would come upon as well as the places to be aware of! I listened to him with much care...

---

*Princess met another Indian in Cherokee Village. He is Creek. We talked about fishing and her journey. So at least she is talking to me again. She said that it only cost a dime to make a phone call in Arkansas. I told her the new president liked Indians! She needs a shot, pray she finds a doctor.*

---

Another day of freezing rain held me indoors but I wasted no time. Washed clothes, wrote letters and bought me a glass coffee cup. That foam cup can go to hell for the amount that I care for them! I feel this world is poison enough without adding more to your mouth! My backpack needed mending, had to make those repairs.

The agasga kept falling, though lighter now but I started to pace the floor and get redneck at myself! Saw this little gila outside that someone had just dropped off beside the road. Grew much angry and wondered what the world would feel like if it was attacked by all the stray dogs that people discarded because they were too cheap to invest thirty dollars to spade for unwanted puppies?

When I first moved back to the mountains for seven years, five gilas came to my porch! I spoke to each one and fed them soup beans! The next day a local farmer asked if I had seen a pack of wild-dogs? "No," I speak, "But I fed five friendly dogs!" He grew much upset, speaking that they were wild killer dogs and ate two of his calves! I was quick to defend the pack and spoke they should have attacked all the former Masters that had dropped them aside! So don't even think about shooting them, 'cause I would buckshot his hind end!

Think I need an estrogen shot! The following morning as I headed into a light drizzle, I looked for this Doctor's office that Two-Dog's woman spoke of. I was all ready to warpath as I had to do the miles behind me when just the opposite took place!

"Nurse, I'm walking the Trail of Tears and I need an estrogen shot much bad. I have the necessary papers to show this!" keeping warmth in my voice!

"No problem, Miss. Just step back here and we will take care of you right away!" she spoke bubbly!!

The Woman-Doctor talked much about the Trail of Tears as she weighed me and gave the magic shot! I was down to 123 pounds!! This was a thrill since I was in the 140's at the start of my journey. I spoke a long time to the nice staff and the Nurse gave me a Christmas Pin to wear upon my coat! Thanked her kindly as I walked out into the strong wind.

The agasga had now stopped! Took a break at this Dairy Freeze to have hot kahwi and Virginia Slims! Nodded to this Lady State Patrolman, then on my way! The endless narrow road has a slant in it therefore making my right hip hurt again.

Darkness caught me again as I came into the little town of ASH FLAT. Needing lodging for the night, I walked into this Wal-Mart where I see this Lady State Patrolman again! She speaks that she will drop me off at a place called Horseshoe Bend! I'm having to go off the trail some ways but this is alright!

We talk about her job and her children; how men can be so jealous and ect. When we come to this turnoff, she just pulls over and speaks, "This is as far as I can go, good luck. The High Hill Lodge is that way," pointing to the left and giving a wave bye as she drove off!

I find myself in the middle of nowhere but thinking that the lodge is just around the curve! I then see a sign that speaks "Horseshoe Bend 6 Miles." First I stomp my foot, then let out a few words that aren't too becoming to a lady such as myself! But try to figure this out!

What calms me down is the Full of the Moon (Nvda)! I stand there moonstruck! The dark sky is so clear and the winds have calmed.. There is a reason for this I speak out loud! But I have this bad Message in the Wind!

The road was much winding and hills took me up and down. Gilas bark as I pass each country home! I speak to them gently and they welcome my passing! I see the white tails of the deer (ahawi) as they dash into the brittle bushes and dry leaves! This brings a warmth to my heart (adanhdo)! I speak to them as well. I then find myself wondering what the bad MESSAGE is when I'm in the midst (kanuyoladiˀa) of beauty and nature!? But I remind myself this is not good thinking to ask such questions to Our Great Spirit!

Onward I trod...

Many cars pass, including the sheriff car. Why doesn't he stop and ask if I'm alright? Then I see this long final mountain plainly showing in the moonlight!! So tired by now, I don't know if I am happy or mad! Readjust my pack for this steep climb and attack!

See lights! This must be the place! Make a turn to the left when this big truck pulls over. "Where are you going little woman?" this husky voiced man asks.

"Well I sure ain't out for a midnight stroll!"

He chuckles loudly and speaks to hop in!

"Sir, I'm only going to this place called the High Hill Lodge. I think I can make it from here. Can't be too far, can it?"

"No, its not too far, just about another mile on the other side of town but they close early in the Winter time so you better hop in! My name is Bill and I won't harm you!" chuckling again!

"Oh, I'm not afraid of you. I carry a gun. I just want to sleep. Mister, my beau's name is Bill too but I call him Mr. Bill!"

"Why's that?" raising his eye brows to show question!

"Well, my Cherokee Mama always spoke that when you address someone that means much to you, then address them as Mr. or MISS!"

Another laugh, but more serious this time. "Well, I wish I was addressed as Mr. Bill! Here you are little woman. Now hurry on in there before they shut it down!"

"Thank you Mr. Bill Number Two and goodnight!" finding my pack and half flopping onto the hard ground!

The three woman desk clerks were most friendly and within a few minutes I had a room key and they were locking the doors! Had to walk clear to the back of all the rooms. There were but two cars in the lot and this was a big place but I was thankful that I had made it and I'm heading for the ama-hole to warm up and call my Mr. Bill!!!

This room is freezing! Start to turn on the wall-log! NO HEAT! I can tough it out, I'll just take a hot wash! NO HOT AMA! I'm going to make a call, DEAD TELEPHONE! The hell with this! I stomp my feet only to hurt myself! Tear out a few words but there's nobody to hear me! Just shut up

Alethea and pretend you are in a rock cliff! Well, come to think of it, this is a fancy rock cliff.

I take all the covers from both beds and lay them on one, carefully over the top of my sleeping bag! Crawl in clothes and all, keep fully covered except for my mouth and nose. I go to sleep seeing my breath as I speak my prayers...

---

*No word from princess. Went to see my doctor in Lexington. I'll dream of you Princess.*

---

Takes just a few minutes to retie my sleeping bag onto my pack at good day-light! The sky is still clear and the sun seems to promise warmth! But I have some business to tend to!

"Good Morning, ladies, do you all have a boss man or one of you the Leader?"

"Oh, no Miss, the boss man should be here anytime. Is something wrong?"

"No, if the room didn't include a dead telephone, cold water only and no such a thing called HEAT!"

"We're so sorry. What can we do?"

"Get that damn boss man on the line!"

"YES MA'AM!"

I'm just sitting there waiting and intend to until he shows! I noticed the woman on the telephone but she turned her back as she spoke to someone.

"Oh, Miss, the boss will be late. I'm sorry!"

"I don't give a damn how late he is, he's going to face me sometime today. So I just suggest you call his ass back and tell him to come and face the fiddler!"

"Yes Ma'am, I will." She does! Within ten minutes he comes through the door as if he's this new White-Chief that's just been elected.

"Ma'am, do you have a problem?" he spoke so like a President!

I wait a minute, thinking how to speak my problem and at this point I don't care if I see JAIL!

"Sir, does forty dollars include a telephone, hot water and heat?"

"Of course it does, what kind of motel do you think this is?" rearing his head back and sticking out his chest!

I give my famous mean smile as I speak, "I think you have a whore house going on here and the only time the damn things work in this joint is when you're making money on women! Plus I've never asked for money in return in my life but I'm telling YOU! Plus I speak its best to call the Law Man!"

His whole body language changes then he dashes behind the desk and gets me forty dollars!

"Thank you kindly," I speak as I head toward the door.

When he thinks I'm out of hearing range, he mumbles, "Her people didn't even have a motel to stay in when they walked the Trail!"

I STOP, walk right back up to his face, ready to knock him into the next century! "Asshole, you have a point there. But if it hadn't been for pale-face, low-life, maggot thieves crawling behind my Cherokee People with guns and the clap, I wouldn't be walking this damned Trail so my People won't be forgotten!"

He immediately removed himself to a door that had no sign upon it!

Walked out into the warm sun and spoke a morning prayer! Found a filling station to have kahwi and calm down. The lady asks if I want a large or small cup? "Neither, I want my glass cup filled. Keep your poison cups!"

"Miss, help yourself at no charge and I agree with you about the foam ones!" smiling, then asked if I wanted anything to eat!

"No, but what do you think about that damn motel called the High Hill?" waiting a reply.

She made a bad-face look and shook her head "No"!

"I feel the same way and its a place of disgrace to this quiet, beautiful mountain town!"

She shook her head, "Yes!"

Walked hard until noon! The Sun became much hot! Took off my coat and was calmer now and even got a bit of a tan. Came to this road side cafe. The people were much nice! I just had to speak of the High Hill Motel Man! They all knew him and laughed as they agreed with my opinion. Not only was the company great but the food and service was too!

Two-Dogs had given me a name of a man that lived in Violet Hill that he spoke would be glad to put me up for the night and share many stories about the Trail of Tears!

Came upon this little country store and as I was walking in, this man that drew my attention for some reason was walking out. I spoke to the lady store-owner about this man. She looked at me a bit oddly and spoke that the man I was speaking of had just left the store as I was coming in!

I asked her to call him but she spoke that she couldn't because she didn't know his telephone number or if he even had one!

"Forget it, I'm too tired to fool with this!" I bluntly answered. I ordered a double bologna sandwich and she spoke that a single one was $2.50! "Lady just give me a double!"

Sitting there at the store window watching the nvda slowly set behind the tree tops, I wondered where I would spend this night? Supper over, I paid and was out the door when she called to me! "Miss here are some brownies that I made at home to sell in the store. They are stale but you can have them!" handing them to me gently but without a smile. I didn't think anything about them, just thanked her and walked on, heading up this steep hill.

Once on top I take a break and the stale brownies come to mind! "Well if she couldn't sell them in her store, are they good enough for me?" My answer was a wave of my hand as I tossed them into the woods!

As the evening sky was turning purple and gold, I stopped to admire the beauty and saw many mountains in the distance. Yes, I would be crossing them too!

Met a cattle man feeding his herd. Spoke for a minute. By the time full darkness had fallen upon me, I was so tired I could hardly feel my feet. The blister that I had to keep bursting was even numb!

Now the land was becoming different! Kept seeing many chicken feathers beside the road! It dawns on me that these are the ones that go to market somewhere! Felt sad for the jitaga...

Felt I could walk no more. The passing lights blinded me and this blister was becoming unnumb! Saw this little house upon a bank, thought I would try anyway! Knocked several times before this little woman in her winter-moons came to the door. "Ma'am, I'm walking the Trail of Tears and I need to sleep in your barn or that shed over there!" keeping this smile about me!

"No honey, you can't sleep in them but you know its not safe to walk after dark. Now be careful. Goodnight!" smiles and shuts the door in my face! I just laugh and walk back to the road. I think her and the brownie woman could be a great comedy act!!!

There's another mountain to climb! Trying to keep my senses together, I sing a song that I had written when I was in the Air Force and had this prisoner that was my custodian! I couldn't type so I traded him jobs! I mopped the floor and he did my typing!!!

WHEN I WAS A PRISONER (but you was pulling time)

Well I was sitting here thinking about an' old pal of mine
When I was a prisoner but he was pulling time.
Well I met him in a little dusty town,
I'd buy a bottle of whiskey, and we'd pass our dreams around.
I'd hear his dreams an' he'd hear to mine,
When I was a prisoner, but he was pulling time.

He'd robbed some old bank
And lived at the F.C.I.
Me a restless woman,
Trying to play the game G.I.
But I'd hear his dreams and he'd hear to mine,
When I was a prisoner and he was pulling time.

Oh Pal of mine, I'll never reveal you name,
Society would take you and drive you insane.
So here's to you ol' pal of mine,
Here's to you I toast this 'shine,
When I was a prisoner, but you was pulling time!

By the time I had finished my song, I was setting in somebody's driveway! Forgot all about how steep that mountain was. Two things concerned me now; a place to sleep and not to find the bottom of this bag that I was eating peanuts from!

About then a truck comes from the driveway and this man speaks that he had seen me walking most all day! I ask how far it is into the next town? "Just a mile but come with me and my daughter to feed the horses and I'll run you on in!"

Threw my pack into the bed and hopped in! Their horses were so beautiful and warm! His daughter was so grown up and had much wisdom to only be of ten years! I helped them feed the barn wasa and thanked them with all my heart! I knew that I could make that mile up before breakfast in the morning!

The motel-woman was most nice as she rented the room but spoke that there wasn't any telephone! I cared less, all I wanted was to burst this blister and get clean! Looked out the window, I couldn't find the moon but I had never seen such a little town so into Christmas lights!!!

Had to walk a mile the next morning to find a place to eat! But I enjoyed the buildings that beckoned to tell all their history! At the restaurant I left Mr. Bill a message on his machine to speak after a long day's walk I would be in MOUNTAIN HOME!

---

*Made more copies of her interviews. Got a message on the machine, she had to walk a lot after dark. Petted some horses and cats in a barn somewhere! headed for Mountain Home, Ark.*

---

Passed many little towns before my destination. I thought PINEVILLE was an artist-looking town! There were deep woods to admire and some beautiful horses! Had only one bad encounter.

This one THING; could not call him a man, spoke that he

was the devil! "I dress in black and believe in the dark," smiling as he stared into my eyes not three feet in front of me!

I just laughed at him, "Well, if you are the asgina, show me your strength! You look like a pup's piss water to me. So I suggest you get off my side of the road before I knock you off!" hands on my hip with a smirking smile! He looked shocked, crossing the road mumbling something about me being a crazy woman! As I went on, I do recall that someone spoke that I may run into some devil-worshippers but I didn't feel evil from this young man, just ideas in his head that he was trying to practice a way to scare people, then HE met ME!

My faithful sunset was with me again to show red skies! In the distance I could see many lights and a promised-rest when suddenly this bad Message came in the unole. I do a little twirl around the sigh I had just met!!!

## MOUNTAIN HOME

Never expected this to be so big! I kept reading signs until I got to a motel that was on the Trail of Tears. This Manager-Woman was so kind. The room was so nice and clean. There was a telephone and she allowed me to do my laundry in the maid's washroom! I even got a discount because I was walking the Trail of Tears. This woman was pro-Indian much!

Just jumped in the ama-hole and cleaned osda (good)! Put on my clean, warm pajamas and found sweet sleep!

Agasga awakened me beating against the window! I welcome that! Recalling the red sky yesterday always speaks rain and here it is. Spent some time in the lobby, filled my glass kahwi cup many time and talked with the Manager! She showed me a photograph of her beautiful daughter then with a quiver in her voice speaks how she was killed in a car wreck! This made my heart so heavy for her.

Later I went to the Bonanza Restaurant just in front of the motel and brought my friend back something to eat. Seems she was always working!

Found out the date was the twelfth day of December (Vsgihyi) when I started to catch up on some magazines! Felt much good! Had my blister under control and planned to go to the courthouse tomorrow and study the History of the Removal and find Mr. Bill a Christmas gift! Then I called him to speak where I was. This is Sunday (Dodagwasgvʔi), he should be home so I'll just leave a message on his machine!

Must have fallen asleep reading. The loud telephone awakened me! I couldn't wait to talk to my Mr. Bill. There was so much news to catch up on!!!

"Howdy, Princess! I love you and I will be meeting you

in Eureka Springs for Christmas, how's that?" his warm and deep voice just weakened my heart and made it beat fast at the same time!

"Oh, Mr. Bill, I DO love you and I miss you so very much! You will really be there?" excitement would hardly allow me to talk!

"Princess, I'm going to speak something to you. I WAS married to her for almost thirty-eight years and I thought it would be the right thing to do if I sent her flowers for Christmas and after this I will never send her anymore! But I figured if I didn't tell you this, the wind would. Somehow you always seem to know what's on my mind! OK?"

On my end of the telephone wire, silence...but I don't know what to speak! More silence, then...I give him a dial tone! An hour or more goes by. Now I know what the bad MESSAGE in the unole was. "Keep yourself together Alethea, just get much calm."

RING... Hello Princess! Let's talk. Please don't be angry!"

"Mr. Bill, I have no words in Cherokee or English to speak how I am ashamed of what you are doing. I know a maggot wouldn't jack off on your boots right now and I wouldn't let you kiss my pretty little brown ass! Good-bye and don't call me again!" I even place the telephone in it's bed. I didn't throw it, scream, or curse much, well I didn't compared to what I have been known to do! Instead I crawled in bed and slept. That was the only way I knew how to deal with this odd behavior that Mr. Bill was giving to me...

---

*I messed up again. Princess on warpath. I sent ex some more flowers for Christmas. Princess won't answer the phone. Told Doctor to do his operation on me in january. I love you Princess.*

---

Rain still coming down much. Stood at the motel window and prayed for the Great Spirit's rain to wash away all sad thoughts from every mind in this cold and lonely world...

---

*Rained all day here. No word from Princess.*

---

The Courthouse people had a plaque upon the wall that spoke a bit about the Removal. I wasn't satisfied. Finally I meet this woman and she shows me some old readings that spoke the dog-soldiers screamed at the women that were about to give birth that they would have to wait until everyone got to Mountain Home before they could drop their babies! As if those damned soldiers could be in control of Nature or the coming out of a baby. The birthing-dying place was just about ten miles southwest of today's Mountain Home. I couldn't help but wonder how many babies that where made by the Cherokee Womens' Husband-men or the raping by the dog-soldiers. I left the Courthouse crying for them and crying for myself.

Went on about the town to shop. I HATE shopping! I DON'T even believe in CHRISTMAS! It's all bull now. When you get someone a gift, chances are they won't like it. Cards are signed with X-MAS that speaks that Christ has been removed. Why don't people give from their heart all the year, not just at this time of Moon?

I remember when I was about eight years old, these people came up to our mountain home. I was living with my Irish Grandfather and full Cherokee Grandmother. When they offered a basket of much colorful food to us, Grandfather spoke in his soft and weakened voice, "Why do you bring us food at the birth time of the Lord? Why didn't you come last summer when my crop-garden failed and we had no food to can? Just go on now, you made a long walk here to ease your mind. That will not ease your way into Heaven and I can't even read."

Me and Pa went back into the cabin. I watched them go out of sight. They never even spoke a word to Pa. That night I wondered just what all that color food was and what did it taste like?

Walked into a jewelry shop and searched for a gift. There I saw a solid gold piece in the shape of a bass fish. Mr. Bill likes to fish! I will buy this for him! He can take the symbol of this any way that he may choose!!!

Still no telephone conversation that evening and I have all the clothes cleaned and repacked my gear. The cool unole hit my face as I turned toward the West for the next town. If my map speaks the truth I would have only about fifteen miles and I could rest.

---

*Called Mountain Home. Princess has checked out. No word or message on the machine.*

---

Saw many old landmark homes and small businesses. Took an hour's nap beneath an old bridge. Crying cows awakened me! Washing my face in the creek, I took my time getting into the little town of COTTER.

This was a family owned motel on the banks of the scenic White River. There was a restaurant attached to the motel but I was too tired and depressed to eat. Tried to sleep but kept waking up every few hours.

Started early next morning. Met the friendly locals that were much educated about the Trail of Tears. Several invited me back for a summer (gogi) ride down the White

River!

The night air was cold as I found my way through the busy streets of HARRISON. My hopes had been high to find a place in PYATT. I got to witness the last day of a long-time roadside Cafe! Many people gathered around the only three tables left! I met the Mayor. His life was in a wheelchair but his spirits where not dampened by this!

There was no place to rest in YELLVILLE so I had to keep bursting my blister until I found Harrison. The motel women were much friendly and invited me to the lobby to have snacks and cola! Soaked for two (taʔli) hours in the ama-hole then slept like a child.

Misty rain met me at the door as I headed northwest! I felt numb and hollow. Wondered what was going on back in Kentucky! In a way I did; then on the other hand, I cared less. Wonder what day of the Moon it is?

The agasga comes down more hard now! I'm trying to look at the countryside but I must keep my head (askoli) down to watch my steps upon the rough shoulder of the narrow road. Hey, this looks like a busy intersection. Maybe I can find rest here.

"Howdy Mister, is there a room to rent for the night? I am walking the Trail of Tears and I must get in from this rain! I felt if anybody knows the place, a filling station man will!

"Miss, ALPENA has nothing of the sort. You will have to go to a place called Green Forest. That's about nine or ten miles on up the road," then turned back to his customers.

My heart was as heavy as the agasga was wet. Will I make those ten miles? Damned right I will! Felt that I was literally dragging myself when I came into the little windswept town of GREEN FOREST.

*Still no call. Where are you , Princess. I am so sorry and I love you.*

---

Opening the screeking white gate to the cottage motel office, I first had to go through the inspection of an overgrown pup! After a few licks on the face, I was welcomed!

The owner-woman in her late forties was much nice and gave me her best little cottage room! Then she shows me the two rabbits (jisdu) that nobody seemed to want, so she adopted them too! "Now that big rooster (jitaga achvya) over there; I caught some kids being mean to it so I gave that baby a home!" speaking with warmth and glee in her sad eyes as she pointed to each adopted baby!

After I got rid of my pack-burden, I was so tired that I much wanted to cry but hunger drove me back out into the agasga to a small tavern that served food.

---

*I am worried. No calls anymore. I'm sorry, Princess. Please call me. I LOVE you ...*

---

"Make that a double cheeseburger with extra cheese and extra fries!" The bar-woman smiled at me then made a comment that I must be really on hunger! I spoke that I was walking the Trail of Tears. An old-timer sitting at the bar wanted to buy me a beer and mumbled that this is a first for him to see a woman to come such a long way! I tipped the bottle toward him for Thanks!

By ten o'clock I'm back into my cottage room. Stood in the ama-hole for a long time to shed the chills. Started to cry with no control to stop myself. Curled up in bed snuffling and staring at a flashing neon sign. Don't even know what it was speaking to the public!

*"No word from Princess."*

---

Rain had chosen to rest for awhile when I headed out the next morning, yet the clouds told me not to get my hopes too high! Now I could admire the beautiful country with its rolling pasture fields and nearby mountains! I stopped to have a chat with some Mama cow (wahga)! She seemed to listen to every word I spoke by flipping her ears or with a swish of her lion looking tail!

This day turned out to be of a short walk! The next thing I notice was coming out of my daydreaming and entering the little town of BERRYVILLE! Found a little motel on the left side of the road the way I always walk.

The nvda was shining again but the wind much cold. Still I wanted to walk the town and see what all it held! Everyone I met either waved or spoke for a minute! Then on the other side of the motel I found a warm welcome at a market-cafe! Had to watch my money (adela) because I was much low! Kahwi and a fish (ajaʔdi) sandwich (asdvhahli) was to be my main diet until I got to the place that I would meet Mr. Bill for Christmas.

Agasga set in on me again as I headed Northwest but it was more of a warmer rain. Don't know if this is good or bad! After topping the hill from the motel, I didn't realize just how big the town was! There were many business places on both sides of the road! I felt if a person wanted to retire this would be a right size town to live out the winter-moons of life!

Found a shed just as this heavy downpour caught me! I felt that I looked like a squirrel (saloli) curled in a tree trunk! A few drivers caught a glimpse of me and turned to take a second look! I thank the Great Spirit for only having to walk about a dozen miles to my Christmas destination in

EUREKA SPRINGS!

As the winding road was taking me higher, I wasn't sure where to stay! I wanted it to be a special place for me and Mr. Bill. I had forgiven him many steps back but that doesn't mean I won't ring his jaw if this foolishness of his thoughts and doings should come again!

A car stops! Its a nice family! "Where are you going lady!" the husband-man speaks with a big smile on his face!

"I'm walking the Trail of Tears but I want to find a special place to wait for my Mr. Bill so we can enjoy Christmas time together!"

"Hop in, I'll take you first to a place where you can feel the many spirits of your people and I know the exact hotel that you need!" The family was opening the door and readjusting themselves for me to find seating.

We all talked of many things en route to the Spirit Grounds. Down deep in this flat land between mountains, he turns the car around then stops.

"Now over there," he points to the left, "At least four hundred of your People died of everything a person could imagine!" I got out of the car and just started walking toward the distant field! I grew so weak in my knees, my heart beat much fast! I stopped! Turned around to the husband-man and asked if I was hearing things like whispers in the wind? Him and his woman answered at the same time, "NO!" They went on to speak that a lot of people hear whispers and cries!

I then spoke that in Mama's Cherokee Numerology, four (nvhgi) means death. He went on to show me the construction that was underway here to make a park for the Cherokee in the near future.

This made me much happy!

After I spoke a prayer to our Great Spirit, we headed

back up the mountain. Then he showed me the Rock-Castle! Seems this woman used hand-sized stones and built a large home for the return of her husband-man while he was away during the war! He lived to come home! One could only imagine the look on his face when he saw the hard work and labor that his woman had done!

After the tour, they take me all the way to the top of the highest mountain to the CRESENT HOTEL! Perfect!! I bid farewell to my new found friends and tourist guides, walked up the ancient steps into the hotel and became lost in mystery-spirits!

Call my Mr. Bill; he spoke that he would meet me at the Crescent Hotel tomorrow (sunale?i) near sunset time. He was flying into Fayetteville then renting a car and would find me!!! I'm so happy I care even less about the old flower story; that's in the past forever! Its been so long since I saw my Mr. Bill!

---

*Princess called! All is fine. I will fly into Fayetteville, Ark. and meet her. She's in Eureka Springs.*

---

When he shows my mouth is going a hundred miles a second! There's so much to tell him and show the things that Ayv have seen here in this certified haunted motel! Then I pull him to the window and point to the far high and distant mountain that has the largest statue of Jesus I EVER SAW!!!

For the next five (hisgi) days we covered much! I took him to the Spirit-Grounds but never spoke of the story.

"Princess, what is this strange feeling that is around here? Listen, did you hear that?" turning to face me with a confused look upon his face. There I spoke of the Burial-Spirit-Grounds and the sounds were of the crying-spirits! He shivered then held me close and spoke "Princess, I am growing to know and love you more each day. You are different and I want to show you that I respect your People's past and your dreams. I want you forever Princess!"

We held each other for the longest while near the Spirit-Grounds then went to the mountain top so I could show him the strength of a white-woman that had built the hand sized stones into a castle for her husband-man!

We had a perfect Christmas dinner in the Crescent Diner! The staff were always so pleasant! This one woman made sure that me and Mr. Bill had a good supply of dry burgundy wine!

One night we went Spirit-Searching in the Crescent Hotel! I found many places of sadness. The giant Jesus statue kept calling me so we venture to that mountain. The story that it told was most beautiful!

One night we met the chef that is the blood of Chief John Ross! Mr. Bill invited him to our room and we talked long hours of the past and the Trail of Tears! He spoke that he lived alone up in the woods and used kerosene lamps for his lights. I spoke that I was raised like that then later in life went back to that way to live!

Eureka Springs was filled with every kind of motel and shop that one could imagine in a resort town but we had the best, the famous Crescent!

The morning that Mr. Bill had to leave, we took our time to repack. Sadness filled the room and tears filled the eyes. He spoke that his cancer surgery was scheduled on January (Unolvtana) 28th. We prayed for his safety and my safety so we could be together on his operation day. We left the hotel together so he could drop me back off onto the Trail that was route 62, I didn't like that number because when I add them together I get 8 and that speaks "Beware".

Right before the turn off, someone had some little gilas for sale. "Can I have one Mr. Bill, PLEASE?" Using my Indian-Scarlett voice

"Princess, you would have to carry that little puppy and your pack is already heavy! Let's wait until you come home okay?" smiling at me!

"Well since I have to wait, can I have two?" I chirped!

"Yes, Princess, you can have TWO!!"

Time to get out on the "Beware" road. We both tried to be strong but we weren't very good at it! He kept waving from his rolled down window and I waved until a curve took him out of sight.

---

*Finally got home. We had a good Christmas. Princess wanted a puppy. She hasn't left any messages on recorder.*

---

Weather isn't too cold today! Hope to make good time but many cars fly by me going off the mountain and there in no shoulder to walk on. Some of the places are so steep that I have to lean backward! Then I'm going back up another steep mountain. But I'm much lean and getting near (naˀv) my journey's end (alsgwadiˀa)!

By the time that I had reached ROGERS, I was hungry and cold. I had dodged traffic so much it seemed that I had walked the same distance from Eureka Springs to Rogers twice! Walk off the busy trail just far enough to knock on this door and ask if they knew where I may find shelter for the night? The man of Autumn-years starts to speak something but his missus appears only to speak that they don't know of a place! I just stare at her for a minute and walk away. I know that I looked like a bag lady with a backpack but she could have at least offered me the back of the house!

About another mile the darkness is setting in and I find this can be my friend (unali?i) at times! I spot this deserted filling station, go around to the back, make sure that nobody sees me as I turn the broken knob on the battered up door! "Oh Thank You Great Spirit," I spoke aloud as I checked out my new lodging!

No ama in the sink spouts or ama in the toilet! The floor was torn up with tile missing but my sleeping bag would cure that problem! I leaned the backpack gently against the door so if someone tried to come in, I could hear the sound of scooting. Curled up in the far corner and fell asleep in the middle of my prayers!

---

*Goodnight Princess. Where are you? Still raining.*

---

Heavy traffic awakened me. I was much cold so it didn't take me long to find my way south. Since I was coming into a four lane, I had to find the alternate route! Found a secondary road that promised to take me to Fayetteville!

At one place I went through this cow pasture and when Mr. Bull (jukanvsdena) followed me with his big watery eyes, I prayed that he didn't want to have a close conversation! This bit of journey was much interesting since I was making my own path. Wondered If I should have walked down the big road but trying to keep my eyes on the heavy traffic was one thing and I thought the Law might get upset due to the "Don't Walk, Ride A Horse or Drive A Tractor On This Highway" signs!

By late afternoon I found my way around FAYETTEVILLE! Where do I stay? This question was answered when I found Route 62 again. There to my left was a warm feeling hotel that seemed to beckon me!

Since the day had turned out to be more warm than I

expected, I was all sweaty as I tried to step into the lobby with as much grace as possible! Half afraid that I may be treated like I was in Nashville, I gave a big smile and spoke that I was walking the Trail of Tears and would like to spend the night!

The many clerks behind the desk thought I was much brave to do this and gave me a much needed welcome, plus a discount! Got a few stares from other guest as I was finding my room but I just smiled real big and held my head much high! The backpack did the part of holding my shoulders back!

Once inside the room, I could hardly believe it! There was a king size bed, desk, huge bathroom and the biggest ama-hole! First (igvyiʔi) thing Ayv did was jump in the ama-hole! Then had to doctor that damn blister as I gave those moon boots another piece of my opinion for the "can't count that far time"!

The next thing I remember it was ten p.m. and I was starved. Called room service, which was closing but they were kind enough to bring me two B.L.T.'s and a pot of kahwi!

Called my Mr. Bill; he was worried because I hadn't called last night but I explained that the deserted filling station wasn't with ama let alone a telephone!

---

*Princess called. She's in Fayetteville. Blister is back on her foot. Hates her boots.*

---

I was up for the night! Had to enjoy this fancy room and wash my clothes, then repack for tomorrow's walk. My backpack had torn loose again which meant that I must use the last piece of rawhide to mend it.

One of the ladies at the desk gave me many Band-aids!

There was a baby sewing kit in the room; just what I need to keep the blister under control!

After all my chores where done, Mama come to my mind so strong! I called the front desk to ask what day it was. They spoke that it was the twenty-eighth day of December (Vsgihyi). That was IT! If Mama was alive this would be her Birthday. In a way, I felt that Mama was walking this Trail with me in the Spirit World way! Tears begin welling into my eyes and feeling that I must fight this, I thought of a song that she had given me the idea to write! Some lady had come to Mama for Council because her boyfriend had left her. Instead of pity to give the woman, Mama spoke that old lovers just pass on by in our lives and take it as that! Well I was sitting in the living room having a glass of wine! Mama picked up the guitar and we made up this song for the heartsick woman. By the time she left, her outlook was better as she went out the door humming the tune to Old Lovers!

OLD LOVERS

Well old Lovers ain't real.
And old Lovers ain't true.
Old Lovers are memories just passing on through!

An old Lover called me today,
Asking how I had been?
Said I'm just fine an' back on the wine,
An' a hell of a lot better without him!

This friend of mine came by today,
She spoke, "I'll die without him!"
"Ah, you'll be just fine; have a glass of my wine,
'Cause you're a hell of a lot better without him!

'Cause old Lovers ain't real,
And old Lovers ain't true.
Old Lovers are memories just passing on through!

Remember that song Mama! ? We sure turned that woman's mind from weakness to good wine! I wiped the tears away that meant sadness and happy too; speaking to Mama that we didn't have too far to go and we would be at the end of the Trail!

Don't recall falling asleep. But agasga was beating against the window! Thought once that I would stay another day but it was 70 degrees! This would be much good for me if I don't walk too hard and sweat to where I may get the flu! I thank the hotel staff and head toward Prairie Grove!

The warm misty rain felt soothing to my face!

Was making real good time except these many people kept stopping to ask if I wanted a ride! "Thank you kindly but I am walking the Trail of Tears!"

This one little Christian woman that had her Bible upon the dashboard spoke, "I never pick up walkers, but I'm a Christian and if I was to be killed then its supposed to be! Would you like a ride?" smiling to me with this glow about her!

"Thank you my Lady. I feel the same about helping someone and finding that to become their death warrant! But I'm walking the Trail of Tears and I must not ride!" speaking softly back to her as I leaned up against her car for the short (asgwalaˀi) rest!

"Honey," she went on speaking, "It looks like a long ways into the town of Prairie Grove but it isn't and the people are really nice and you might check in the Cafe and Cottage Inn! Its just up the bank and on the left! Be careful and I shall Pray for you!"

I patted her frail shoulders as she drove from sight, thinking if only there were more like her that stopped to help a stranger and proudly displayed her Bible upon the dash! Was a little after 2 p.m. when I came to the Colonial Motel! Planned to stop and have some warm kahwi and puff a couple of jola but these two nice ladies started speaking to me in such admiration of walking the Trail that time slipped away!

Erma and Guy Matthew owned the restaurant and cottage lodging! Bernie, the waitress, served the best coffee, soup beans and cornbread, plus the best onion around! The ladies called this Woman Reporter, Lynette! She takes a picture of me setting at the counter with a big smile on my face and holding Bonnie! We ladies talked about everything!

Soon it was becoming late in the evening so I rented a Cottage for the night. Took another bowl of beans (tuya) and went to rest. Sleep did not come fast. Maybe the good people that I met had my blood running too fast! The agasga set in around two a.m. that finally put me to sleep!

---

*Princess was supposed to call.*

---

Hard rain was coming down at seven a.m. so I walk to the restaurant and have kahwi with Guy, Erma and a local friend. We sat there and talk about the sadness of the Trail of Tears as we stare out the window at the rain...

They pointed out the park that was well known as one of the most bloody battles during the Civil-War. I wanted to walk about the Battlefield but strange energies prevented this. I felt no welcome from the spirits.

Around one in the afternoon the rain stopped but left cold wind to face. I bid farewell to my new friends that I had met then found my way through the quiet and peaceful little town!

I admired the clean rock bottom creeks and the healthy livestock that made a turn around to check me out!! Again I did the little act of "Class turn to page seven in your books!" One big mama bellowed; speaking that she wasn't in the mood to play any games and I best be on my way, "That fence isn't that strong you know!"

Stood to admire the sight of this man riding his cow pony much fast to herd certain ones into the next pasture! Wish I could have mounted up a horse and helped him! I don't think he ever saw me.

Came to this APPLE-TOWN. There were all kind of signs and a big store that was now deserted due to the Winter Moons and the icy road that I now was sliding on! But I chose to skate across the ice porch to take my boot off again and give that damned blister a good forking with my new needle! People that drove by took a third look! This was not a normal sight to see; some crazy woman out in the sleet with her boot OFF! Couldn't help but admire those fine wooden barrels! They sure would come in handy back in my Kentucky hills! Not that we don't have plenty, its just that revenuers like them too!!

I was about to freeze out when I saw this bar! Had to fight the devil with that thinking! Held my head high and walked right on by! Just as I did, this car stops and I have a nice talk with this friendly couple! We laughed when I told her the old devil was trying to get me in that bar! She agreed and told me to keep strong! Soon I would be at the end of the TRAIL!

## LINCOLN

My face and body were so numb when I walked into Lincoln, I didn't know if I was cold or much warm! A sign spoke that it was 23 degrees!! The inside of my moon boot had ripped, I would think so it had more room for that BLISTER!

I was just starting across the street to walk toward the LINCOLN INN when this couple pull over and talk. They were really sincere Christians. They spoke that they where on their way to the market to buy a few things then go home and make some homemade chili! They invited me to their home for supper and to see their farm! I hopped into the pretty van, praying that I didn't smell too much.

The farm was a picture! I loved on the horses and enjoyed their kindness. The chili was the best I had ever eaten! Once I tried to make some but my chili had so much grease in it that I had to strain it! But I didn't speak this to the missus! I think she knew that I was no Betty-Crocker! After the chili, she served her homemade banana bread! There was no end to this woman's talented hands.

We talked a lot about the Bible, morals and family. I felt warm and welcomed in their fine home that was all decorated with manmade Christmas adornments! They asked me to spend the night because their children would be there the next day to open gifts and have a family dinner. I thanked them kindly but I didn't want to be in the way of a family gathering so I just spoke that I might as well stay in town. Late into the night, they took me to the motel. We bid farewell and they spoke that they would pray for my safe arrival in Tahlequah.

As I checked into the motel, the owner-man spoke that he didn't have telephones in the room so I called Mr. Bill and left a message on his machine that I was in Lincoln and have a Happy New Year! Then skidded on the ice to my room!

---

*Princess left message. I took the Grandsons skating.*

---

The temperature had dropped down to 15 degrees and I thanked Our Great Spirit that I was safe and warm. I prayed that Mr. Bill would be free of this devil cancer just as soon as I get home and get him to the Doctor-Man. Then I am crying...

Had the television on and this Announcer comes on to speak that the many Cherokee that started on the Trail of Tears on Turkey Day had just arrived in Tulsa! This dried my eyes much fast! Was this the same group? Am I that slow of a walker? Is this another group that I hadn't heard about? Oh, well, whoever they are, I am much glad that they made the Trail with safety!

The Owner-Man knocks on my door to speak that Mr. Bill is on the telephone! Can't run due to the ice so I S-L-I-D-E!! We give each other a kiss (atawedoʔvsga) over the telephone and I feel much better now!

---

*Talked with Princess. called her at 12:30. We said Happy New year over the phone. Its freezing rain in Lincoln, Ark. Love you Princess.*

---

TRAIL ACROSS ARKANSAS *BENGE'S ROUTE

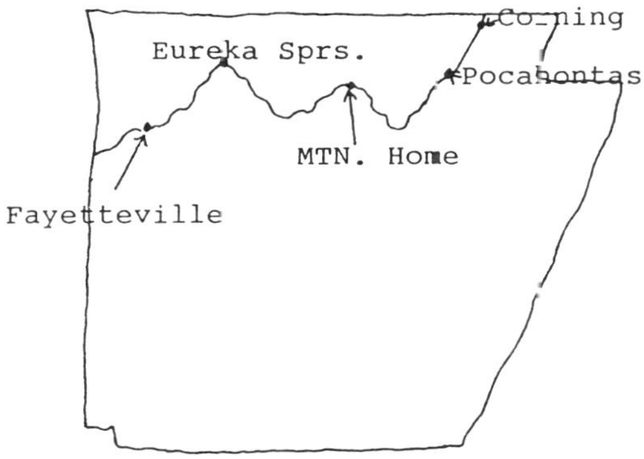


1. Corning
2. Biggers
3. Pocahontas
4. Imboden
5. Williford
6. Cherokee Village
7. Ash Flat
8. Horseshoe Bend
9. Brockwell
10. Melbourne
11. Calico Rock
12. Viola
13. Mountain Home
14. Bull Shoals Dam
15. Yellville
16. Harrison
17. Bear CR. Springs
18. Alpena
19. Green Forest
20. Berryville
21. Eureka Springs
22. Busch
23. Rogers
24. Springdale
25. Fayetteville
26. Prairie Grove
27. Lincoln

## OKLAHOMA

I MADE IT TO OKLAHOMA!!!!! At 11:16 A.M. I hugged the Oklahoma BORDER SIGN! I danced around that sign seven times! Oh, Thank You Great Spirit And The Maker Of Breath! If I never make another step I HAVE made it to Oklahoma! Thank You!!!

This is January (Unolvtana) the second and I'm in Westville! I'm plumb beside myself! As I walked through the town, praying that I would find a place to rest and doctor this damned blister, I ask this store man the best way to find a motel! He guides me in a very scenic direction, but it turned out to be three miles out of my way! The sky (galvloʔi) promised to rain upon me if I didn't rush my steps but the blister made me stop two times just for attention!

Finally see this junkyard of many cars and a sign that spoke MOTEL, but I am not so sure if the sign isn't for sale like the parts from the junk cars are but pain and rain drive me in from the 40 degree weather to find out!

I smell the beans cooking before I even get the door open! Boy, would I ever like to get my mouth close to that kettle. This big stout man appears from the back which is his home as well. He has a big grin, wipes his hands and speaks "What can I do for you Lady?"

"Well Mister," I'm looking all around, still wondering if that is still a sign for sale and this isn't really a motel! "Ah, do you like ah have ah. Is this a Motel?"

"Why yes" he laughs loudly. "Oh, I deal in a lot of junk cars and stuff but I think I have a room clean. Not sure but let's take a look!"

I follow back outside, limping like a little stray dog that somebody decided to throw a piece of cornbread to! The room was quite nice! Had the old-fashioned home touch.

Threw my pack on the bed, took off my boot and did blister surgery! Took a little of a 3O minute rest and decided I needed some food. From the motel door I could see an intersection that had a small market. With four Band-aids on this blister, it won't be too bad walking there but the two minute walk seemed an hour to my right foot.

Agasga caught me before I could enter the market! Everybody seemed nice and friendly. The lady had just made a fresh pot of kahwi and there were many sandwiches (asdvhahli) to choose from! Found me a little side table, ate supper and read the Westville Reporter!

When the agasga lightened up a bit, I headed back to the motel. Studied the map, looked like I had maybe thirty miles to go! Wonder how I will be treated? Will I meet someone to befriend me and understand (gohlga) this life long dream that Ayv have almost made happen? Does Tahlequah look (ni) anything like our Reservation in Cherokee, North Carolina? I pray (Adadolisdi) that Ayv make (gohlvsga) many (tsgwisdi) friends (Unaliˀi)!! None of these questions came close to (naˀv) getting half an answer! Agasga and a tired (duyawega) body (ayelvˀi) put me to sleep (gahliha)!

---

*Where are you, Princess? I love you.*

---

The crowing of a rooster was my alarm clock (waji)! Up quick! Brush my teeth, smack four (nvhgi) more Band-aids on the forever ruined ankle from those damned moon boots, gave Bonnie a check and was ready to go!! Much excitement rushed through my mind and body! I reach for the doorknob and my friend is there to speak good morning! Why its the agasga, which is much cooler now! A thought comes to mind; its the Third of January. Three means "News"! That's news of a good Message in the Wind!

Must stop again at the market! Needed a shot of kahwi then head on into Tahlequah! Sitting at the same little side table that is out of the flow of traffic when this sad looking yellow haired woman walks up to me!

"Miss, do you have a way to take me home? My friends left me behind last night and I have to get home to my two babies!?" She looked so pitiful and tired tears came into my eyes...

I motioned for her to set down in the opposite seat and patted her small milky looking arm. "Ma'am, I don't have a car. I'm about to finish my walk of the Trail of Tears but do you have anything to eat?" trying to lift her heavy heart with a smile!

"No, I haven't eaten since yesterday around noon!" keeping her eyes straight at me but her voice real low.

"OK, you see that batch of sandwiches over there? Get you a couple of the biggest! Now I can't tell you how to warm them in that fancy Yankee-oven that shoots lasers but make it happen and get much coffee and I will buy it for you!" She made a beeline to the food. I went to pay for it! At the counter this man was going to work in Sallisaw and that's where she spoke that she lived, so I ask him if he could give this young woman a ride!

"Sure, I'm doing some construction work down there. I'll be ready to go in about twenty minutes!"

"Thanks Mister!" then I shook his hand as I headed back to the table!

"Hey lady, you have a ride home!" I spoke with much happiness in my voice as I slide back into my seat!

She almost choked on her food; kept shaking her head in a "Thank You" way! After she had eaten and then rummaged through her purse, she comes out with a coupon for Motrin IB!

"Alethea, I collect coupons because I try to save all I can and raising two kids by yourself is hard! Now as you know I don't have any money but would you take this for the breakfast that you bought me?" speaking in a pleading low voice.

"Sure will! I really take Advil but I will maybe give these a try! Thanks much!" The working man motioned it was time to go. She hugged my neck thanked me many times and stuck the extra sandwich into her purse then headed for the door, waving the whole time! Her face looked as if a year of life was given back to her! "Good luck, little yellow haired Mama and take care of your kids and remove yourself from the so called friends that left you behind, I thought to myself.

The agasga had let up a bit, so the lady at the counter helped me with the heavy backpack and I headed for the next town! She spoke that the next town I would come to before I reach Tahlequah was Proctor, Oklahoma!

The narrow blacktop road looked beautiful! The Band-aids seemed to be doing the trick, plus the new box I had just bought at the market speaks that they will take me on to my destination! The homes were so neat looking. Many people stopped to ask if I wanted a ride! When I spoke the reason for walking, they smiled and promised that I was almost there!! This made me do a couple of skips! "Got this calf licked now!" I sang out loud!

Passing this one ranch, I couldn't help but admire the neatness and beauty. Saw the man working in his barn, quite a strong looking man. Oh, he caught me looking at him. This embarrassed (adehohisdiha) me, so I waved real big and he waved back!

Saw this little deserted turn off to my left and decided to take a break for a good (osda) taste of my jola Virginia

Slims! Found a dry (ukahyoda) spot beneath an ancient oak tree (higvʔi) and let my mind wonder if this same oak tree was here when my People were driven through? Just finishing the new four Band-aids on the red and pitiful ankle when this truck roars up!

"Howdy Ma'am. I'm the feller that you just waved at! Me and the missus figured you might want a good hot bacon sandwich, so she fixed this for you!" handing me a bag of food with a big smile for my dessert, then roared away!

"Thank you stranger!" speaking to myself! He moves too fast for me but I enjoyed the hot bacon sandwiches even though I had already eaten!!

Came to pass this little country school. Stopped and just took a long look. Got the most strange Message from this place. The school (junadehlohgwasdiʔi) seemed to speak of sadness to me!

Next I pass the Christie Baptist Church. Stood outside for the music of voices that sang two songs! For a second I thought I'd go in, then realized this is not good thinking. I wouldn't dare interrupt the sweet sound (ganohyvhlisdiha)!

A lonely, deserted ranch greeted me! One could tell that no human life was ever about anymore. Took a few minutes to rest and kiss the two horses (sogwili) that came to the sagging barbed wire fence to ask if I would like to ride? "No, thank you, but you sure do come to my eyes with temptation!!"

Crossing this little bridge (asvhdlvʔi) I noticed how clean and pure the ama appeared! It was so clear, I believe that one could lay down and drink from it! This little bridge led me to admire a stately home on the left, one on the right and many animals grazing in their nearby pastures!

Then I see this young boy about the age of ten (sgohi) or eleven. I spoke with a nod first then asked how far was it was on into Proctor?

"Oh, about two or three curves!" answering in a shy and low voice but keeping eyes of curiosity upon me!

"Thank you kindly, young man!" smiling as I mentally got a new burst of energy! Thinking just a few curves away and this may allow me to beat the agasga that had already left a few drops upon my face (ukatvʔi) with a promise to come much soon. Rounded the three curves! Now I've rounded seven curves! I don't think this boy can count curves very good!

Up a steep long bank; waved at a Forest-truck as it passed and waved back! Still I can see NO Proctor-Town! Top another bank; its time to find four more Band-aids! Then I spot a small town in clear view but its about a mile away! Who cares. Its there! This makes me skip a little! A horse speaks to me on the opposite side of the road, pressing against his fence! I'm a sucker for a horse, so I limp now over to him! "Seyo. Is that Proctor up there?" pointing in the town's direction.

He turns his muscular head toward my pointing direction then nuzzles my tattered and wind swept hair as if to speak "Sure it is. Do you want a quick ride there?" I give him a kiss and pat as he tries to keep my white (unega) headband (aligvdanosdohdi) for a play toy! I thank him for the information, cross the road (nvnohi) and rush my steps now to Proctor!!!

Quickness had left my feet again as I noticed the Proctor Baptist Church on the right and a big stone deserted school on the left. Then I pass a Post Office on the right and a little busy country store on the left that has just what I've been looking for, a TOILET!! Make a dash for the door and speak my prayers as I'm sitting on the old wooden seat!

When I surface from behind the skreeking door, I go

inside the much warm country store to be greeted by the smiling face of this beautiful young woman that is the owner! Asked where I could sit down and she leads me to the back at a table and speaks that I can remove my boots and put my feet up as long as I want!

I am enjoying this warm kahwi when the store lady brings her next door neighbor friend to me! We introduce as I am still sitting due to this blister that should be worn out by now. The happy smiling face of a woman about my age looks down at me and speaks "You are coming to my house! So get your things and come on! AND I'm not taking a NO for an answer!" Immediately this name for her comes to my mind, MS. LONGHORN!

This is the kind of cow that you admire the beauty of and it will allow you to be close to it but its not the kind that you want to butt heads with! I couldn't even think about putting those damned moon boots back on and she's not going to hear a NO from me! I grab my pack, carry those mean boots and follow her like a limping stray pup!

Ms. Longhorn's home is full of warmth with love and heat. She has a way to make one feel welcome by first asking, "What would you like to eat!" We talked for a long while as I spoke of my journey and met her hard working husband-man, her son Tall-Man, plus the grandchildren! There was LASSO, Tall-Man's son and MULE and HUNTER! They were her daughter's sons! The store-lady next door had a son that joined to meet this crazy Indian. I called him Dream-Catcher!!

As the evening grew into nightfall, Ms.Longhorn asks if I would like to attend Church with the family this evening? I was quick to speak, "Just let me jump in the water-hole. Do you have a baggy dress that I can borrow and would you happen to HAVE any worn out MOCCASINS that I could

PLEASE wear?"

Ms. Longhorn made it all happen for me! So here I am just sitting pretty in Church and when the Preacher led the opening prayer I thanked my Maker of Breath Great Spirit for allowing me to even get this far and for meeting these fine and warm people of this little town called Proctor!

Ms. Longhorn played the piano and sang two of the sweetest songs that one could ever hear! I kept swallowing hard to keep my tears under control. I thought of all the many things that had happened to me on this Trail of Tears and prayed that my Mr. Bill would soon be free of that devil cancer. Still as I set there in the third row from the front, I couldn't believe that I had made a life long dream come true by not giving up and by believing in our Great Spirit as my Mama had taught me. I felt that she was there in the congregation tonight singing as she so loved to do and speaking how proud she was of me. I have sixteen more miles to go, then my journey is finished...

After the Church-Gathering, Ms, Longhorn introduced many more Of her friends and relatives. I even got to meet the three-curve boy! We all had a good laugh about the incident! He was blushing as I was teaching him about the amount of curves it takes to make three miles!

Tall-Man was kind enough to give up his waterbed for a couple of days and took the living room floor! Working-Husband-Man gave me many pairs of his new socks and Ms. Longhorn gave me all the comfort, warmth and welcome that could possibly be known! I felt so grateful to meet such fine folk as these. This felt like having a beautiful rainstorm and the sun at the same time!

---

*Princess in Proctor, Okla. Staying with new friends that took her in.*

Later, after everyone was tucked in for the night and I lay in that fancy waterbed, the rain turning to sleet began to do it's dance against my bedroom window! I smiled, spoke my prayers again, curled up in this ama-bed that I'm not in knowledge of but the heater is in the water somehow! This let me know how good a groundhog (ogana) feels in the winter moons! "Tomorrow, I will finish my journey. Yes soon this will come to an end." Soon the dancing sleet closed my eyes to find rest so needed and I didn't even feel that ol' blister. A smile and heavy eyes brought to me sweet sleep...

# PROCTOR

With many THANKS to Ms. Longhorn Dee Patterson, Mr. Owen Scott, Mrs. Mig Hamilton and Mrs. Ruby Mayes for sharing much History of the four most active places that still exist in Proctor today and of the ways of Proctor's by-gone yesterdays. If not for these special people that now have become my new friends, I would be of much less KNOWLEDGE of this warm little town!

As one author wrote in the book called "History of Adair County", that was put together into 865 pages, along with endless co-authors, he spoke that Proctor didn't really become a Founded-Town, It JUST GREW!! The town received it's name after the man known as "Uncle Zeke Proctor". At one time Proctor had many businesses such as a Cotton Gin, many sawmills, a line of stores, several Restaurants, perhaps at least two Post Offices and this was all before the 1930's!

Its believed the first settlers were the Cherokee that moved here as the Volunteer Group before the Trail of Tears. Then later some of the forced Cherokee chose to live here as well as passing by Missionaries and the Stray-Folk that came to be as many moons passed over the skies of time...

The First Baptist Church of Proctor came from the remains of old camp-barracks! This was in 1949. The People needed $250 to purchase their Church-Dream and did so! Everybody pitched in to make the MONEY happen; not only the Church-Going folk but the non-Church-Folk. This speaks for itself meaning "Helping Thy Neighbor!" Reverend James H. Smith was the first Man of the Cloth to organize this sound establishment. He preached here from 1949 to 1951.

The old Schoolhouse was built in 1905 and remained active until 1968. Long ago workers that where called the W.P.A. built it's fence and bathroom. Mrs. Mig spoke that the last Principal of the School was Mrs. Tommie Ruth Coleman-Fishinghawk. Though the old Knowledge-Building has been without the sounds of the childrens' laughter for many moons, this is coming to pass. Soon, with enough donations, the building will have warmth and laughter again, due to the fact that its going to become Proctor's Community Center!

Now the only Proctor Post Office first opened in 1903. The first Post Master was Joseph McCarter. After many Masters and many letters passed over it's counter, we find that the first Post Mistress was Minnie M. Osborn...

The notorious little country store serves not only your grocery list, it's also a place to have a hot cup of coffee in the morning speak howdy to your neighbor, fill up the gas tank and draw the road to rest and meet good people that take you in or head you in the right direction!

Mrs. Ruby Mayes speaks that Leo Wilkerson built the store long ago! In 1938 Owen Scott's Father, Tom Scott and Owen's Uncle, Charley Sanders operated this store for awhile! During their partnership days an interesting event took place! Seems an undertaker that lived not far away was in debt. Well, to make his debt clean, he offered his HEARSE to even the bill! Mr. Tom went for the bargain since this allowed him and Uncle Charley to be so kind and deliver the store order to the folks home! After all, they did walk quite a ways to buy their groceries! Well, the partners would offer them a ride along with their groceries back to their homes. The answer they always got was, "No thank YOU, we ain't riding in that thing! Why IT hauled DEAD-FOLK"! The partners would just chuckle, take their "order" on home for them and wave as they passed the "walkers" still en route home!

Now this little "Proctor Country Store" has obliged many new owners over the years and made happen some great meals upon tables! Presently Treasa and Troy have the honor of carrying on this Proctor Tradition and I'm thankful for that toilet I first made a run for then walked into this STORE of warmth and met the lady that took me in. "If only that store could write It's own little book!!!

## LAST SIXTEEN MILES

On Monday the 4th of January the freezing sleet and rain held me at bay! Mrs. Longhorn spoke that I should just rest and we could visit many places of History and finish my journey tomorrow. I speak that this would be good for the number today is "4" and in Mama's numerology this means death. Tomorrow would be of a "5" and this means Surprise!!!

---

*Princess called. Not walking today. Probably tomorrow. Going to visit many sights. Love you, Princess.*

---

The old Christie School comes to our minds; this being our first stop. All the little eager faces met in the gym and I answered the many questions they and their teachers asked. Mr. Scott F. Davis from his Westville Reporter took many pictures of me and the Christie School and did a sincere interview. This one teacher, Burl Ford, was so kind as to give me a run-off Copy of "A GUIDE TO GATHERING AND USING CHEROKEE MEDICINAL HERBS" which was signed; From the Children and Teachers of Christie School, Thank you, Burl Ford."

This touched my heart much deep as I embraced each child and teacher! Then we all gathered in the lunchroom and ate together! No, there weren't a lot of fancy foods as so many schools have in many places. We enjoyed a filling and healthy meal of Selugada and Tuya (cornbread and beans)!

Our next stop was the Old Baptist Mission Church. This is where Ms. Longhorn's Great Great Grandfather sleeps in the ground...

We spoke our prayers there and wondered how the old Mission was of appearance when our Cherokee People where driven through. We remained in the "Resting Place" for a long while and imagined of this place many moons ago.

After many more historical visits and trading more stories of our life, the day comes to a sweet and prosperous end. I seek the ama-bed early tonight; had some thinking to do from deep inside my soul.

"Tomorrow I make (gohlvsga) the last steps of this long Trail of Tears. I am much happy but scared too! I have never been to Tahlequah (Daligwa) as my People that were forced to come here hadn't been either. Did many thoughts of wonder go through their minds too, from many questions to relief? Will I meet many nice people? Will anyone (yinigalsdihagwu kilo) greet me? Should I speak to the Newspaper people that I; Alethea Ann Adams have just completed my life long dream of walking (aʔi)?? I as a woman took the chance of danger and toil to find my own question answered that I had asked of my Mama long ago, "I will make that cry-walk one day, won't I Mama?" Well I am here now and so scared...

Will Mr. Bill know when I reach the Courthouse yard? What will Daddy think of me? Wish my sisters (udo) could be there! I can just see Little-Sparrow's face. She would stand quietly, whisper softly and embrace me. Demonzia would hold both hands up and look toward the Great Spirit and yell AMEN!! Two-Fist would give the grin of a wasa that ate the gold fish then speak, "Its about time you get here!" Little Sledge would give me a yona-hug and have two (taʔli) Virginia Slims lit and waiting for me! All the guards from Woodson Bend would be cheering! Mrs. Chieftain, Makahi, Handsome Buck, Broken Arrow, Mail Man, Wild Dog and Bronco would let me drive old White-Horse through the gate just to celebrate!!! The Dancing

Wolves would make a strideful circle with grace to celebrate. I believe my raccoon, Montana would hand me a piece of her dog-food!

I know Mama will be there because she has walked the Trail with me... But somehow I can see Dr. Quisenberry speaking a prayer with me, then handing to me a pen! "Start writing Alethea. Every time I read Shakespeare I think of you, "In my mind a Kingdom is". YES, that's it (Sgidv)!!! Well, in my mind they WILL be there!

Now I am rested with this settled!! Yet, as I lay here in this warm ama-bed of Ms. Longhorn's and hear the unole sing and whisper to me just outside her window, "Close your eyes and question no more. The sight that you will see tomorrow will be of much. Far more than you had ever dreamed of," I spoke my prayers out loud as my eyes grew much heavy for rest...

"Its time to eat walking-woman!" came the sweet voice and the smell of bacon from the large and warm kitchen! Seemed I had just fallen asleep a few minutes ago, but THIS is the MORNING that I have so waited for!

"Ms. Longhorn, thank you! Is it really time for the end of my journey this morning? I'm a bit nervous but I will feel better if you burn that pig meat and trade me your worn out moccasins for those mean moon boots!" Moving quickly, laughing as I try to get myself out of that moving-ama-bed, she laughs at me as I'm struggling! My thoughts? I would hate to be in this kind of bed on those spinning nights and need to get to the toilet fast! This kind of bed needs a bucket attached!

As we're eating and laughing, she speaks of today's plans! "Now Alethea, I am going to follow you in my car. Plus Muleskinner and Dream Catcher want to walk the last mile with you! Will that be alright?"

"The MORE the BEST!" trying to answer and eat pig meat like a pig "Will you walk some with me today?"

"Yes, I will walk at least a mile with you, probably as soon as you top Eldon Hill!" giving a grin that hides something. I have a feeling that Eldon Hill just may be a mountain!!!

Mixture of sun and clouds with a hint of rain for the last sixteen miles! I prayed for the misty rain to bring my journey to an end just as it had started me out. Today being the Fifth day of January (Unolvtana) would be the number of SURPRISE! To make this morning more better, I didn't have to carry my fifty-two pound backpack! No, I would be of freedom from weight! In no time I will complete this and I feel my Cherokee People felt the same way when the dog-soldiers spoke that there was only sixteen miles to the spoken Indian Territory.

Its been spoken that a few Cherokee told the soldiers they were close enough to the Government appointed place and they stayed in and around Proctor. Some just fled, speaking nothing!

Starting late, no use to be in a hurry! Feels so good (osda) to have these worn moccasins upon my feet with two pairs of Husband-Man's socks! Forever I will be free of those moon boots, thanks to the trade with Ms. Longhorn!

About a mile from Ms. Longhorn's, I cross into Cherokee County! I must speak that a smile touches my face! Thinking of 1838 and 1993, this speaks to me that we Cherokee have made our impressions upon this very land that we once freely walked upon. Our Name will always be somewhere just as other Indian Nations will have their names about many places! Many times we are sung about in songs!

Still a bit of coldness in the air when I come to this

intersection. Across the narrow hardtop I see this country treasure-store that has a small trail of smoke puffing out the chimney top. I feel this would be a good place to warm for awhile and good energies come from this treasure-store! Saw this old washing machine that used to set on everyone's back porch! Oh, I would love to own one!

Mama begged Logan for one once when he moved us into a three room mountain shack. He and Uncle Yomer somehow made some fire-wires work and though we had no furniture, Mama wanted this washing machine. Seems that Logan and Yomer had to steal a truck that night 'cause he needed a part from it so he could make this long moonshine run. Well, they got the truck part alright! And as dawn brought them in there was that white porch-washer!!! Mama was so happy! Logan spoke that since the owners of the truck were gone, he thought he may as well furniture shop too! We had so many fine pieces of furniture that we didn't know just what the real purpose of some were but Mama had that porch-machine!!!

Whenever it stalled on her she would speak,"Alethea come and speak to this machine that you have named. Its quit again!"

I go up to White-Night and speak good words to it! Then swish-swash sounds would begin again! Little Sledge wanted to play with those two round-rolls that made the water leave the clothes. Not listening to Mama's warning words, Sledge had a first hand lesson of White-Night's power when the rolls took her whole arm in!!!

Yes, Mama I will ask this Treasure-Store-Owner just how much this White-Night is!

This young man opens the door for me and welcomes me inside to warm "I have just built the fire but get close to the stove and pretty soon you will be warm!" I thank him kindly as my eyes search about the store that rattles (ujonata) memories again in my head (askoli)! As I walk about admiring the old horse-harness, cow-bell and the big backyard bell that used to serve to call workers in from the fields for noon-dinner or HELP, if you should hear the clang thrusting it's loud cry from in the deep Appalachians.

Soon the gentleman joined me by his old fire-stove and we spoke of the sad Trail of Tears and how his Treasure-Store somehow made a history connection with everything today.

I was just beginning to leave when Ms. Longhorn walks in the door. She had been looking everywhere for me then figured this is where I would be!

Once again outside, thanking him for the coffee and talk, I get a last look at that old porch-machine and the first look at the Eldon Hill! More like a mountain! I knew it! Feeling light-weight and lean. I gave a smile to the world and hit that mountain nonstop till the road became flat. Didn't even draw a second wind!

There I meet Ms. Longhorn coming toward me. She had parked her car a mile away so she could meet me then walk that mile with me as she had promised! We slowed down and took our time as we talked and admired the countryside as well.

Stopping again at Briggs Community area where she had parked her car. I head onward and she turns the opposite way to finish some chores that had to be taken care of, promising to see me again a bit later.

More clouds rolled into the sky as I came upon the Cherokee Campground and Baptist Assembly Church. Noticed how clean and well kept the place was. Stopped to admire this view and pat somebody's little gila that spoke there would be a gathering tonight if I would like to go!

Wonder how many times that Chief John Ross rode his horse down this road? He was so admired by the Cherokee People that he was asked by the People to hold office as their Chief for ten times every four years! His biggest plan for his people was for an extra star to be upon the United States Flag that would speak "The Cherokee have a State of their own!" I somehow felt this State of Oklahoma, if Chief Ross had gotten his way, would have become the Cherokee State! He fought for his People so hard. Even after this bloody removal, he kept his heart open for the Cherokee only to lose his battles with the Government, due to his death in August (Gaʔlohni) Moon of 1866. What I have studied about Chief Ross; he was barely one-eighth Cherokee. This goes to speak for itself. It's not the amount of Indian-Blood that one may have, it is the love and strength that one keeps in their minds and heart.

This truck kept coming closer and slower to my side, yet the two men acted as if they didn't see me. I crossed the road a few times to avoid meeting them, then just ahead of me, they stopped! I speak a prayer and cross again to the right side of the road where this tall man walks out to speak "seyo"!

"Are these men bothering you Ma'am? I have been watching them down the stretch here. Thought it best to walk out to you as if we had planned to meet!"

"Oh thank you mister," smiling up to his handsome and weathered face! "I was becoming concerned of their ideas and why they just kept close to me but wouldn't speak anything!"

"Well, don't worry none. I will keep you safe! Hey, everybody calls me Rooster-Man!" indicating by his outstretching arms toward the many proud roosters that were about his yard; the kind that a coon-dog doesn't even bother!

We talked for almost an hour. This allowed the two mystery men to go on their way and we enjoyed the company of sharing our stories about the Trail of Tears! Rooster spoke that he was most glad to meet a woman that believed in our Heritage so strong as to make such a dangerous (ganayegi) journey. We shook hands then I crossed the road to complete my Trail of Tears.

This is great! This down hill walk helps the mind and body, not to mention that a pit-stop would become of handy now! Just in front of me is this Phillips 66 station. Walk inside to warmth that rushes me toward the "ladies room, please!" and the smell of fresh coffee!

Later I find a seat in the back of the filling station market and eye these two large peanut butter cookies that I had just bought, knowing darn well that I should not even be thinking about cookies, let alone buying them! But I am near the end of my journey and this is a treat for myself! Besides nobody around knows that I CAN'T have sweets and I SURE ain't telling on myself!!

The sun is going downward in the big Oklahoma sky as I make sure that I eat every crumb that might have tried to escape! Time to go! Give my big long skirt a swish and head for the door.

Won't be far now! This lifts my spirits but only for a short time due to this pain in my belly. I KNEW I shouldn't have eaten those cookies! "Too bad Alethea. Now suffer and shut up!" Now I am swelling much! Glad I don't have Bonnie strapped around my waist, I would have to give up about three notch holes!

I wonder how many of our People that were prodded through here in 1839 had these pains too but not knowing that it was due to sugar poison? In many studies that archaeologists have found; the only ailing that the Cherokee had was arthritis. The incoming of the white-eyes gave us the sugar and fire-water, diseases and death. Do they teach in history that we Indians didn't know a damn thing about SCALPING although this is the word that we are related to. But our people learned this by watching the white men fight amongst themselves when they landed upon the shores of the big water (Ama-Utana)!!

I'm not pointing my finger only to myself! Nobody holds a gun to me to like the taste of brown liquor and every piece of sweet-making that I can get my mouth on!

I now come to a bridge that speaks,"The Illinois River". I think this is an odd name for a river in Oklahoma Cherokee Territory! As I stand upon the bridge and stare into the swift moving water, messages of Death-Spirits linger all around me. "Would this be the river that comes from the great north of Canada and flows to the big water through South Carolina? If so, that is why many death-spirits are about. They never stop flowing. This river is so long for it used to be the main source of food and dwelling for many tribes.

TAHLEQUAH (Daligwa)!!! I see the sign then make three circles around! This speaks NEWS, for I have made it to my long awaited destination!

"I AM HERE, I AM HERE!!! Does anyone hear Me?! I am now HERE!!!"

Honk, honk!!! I turn to see the warm and smiling face of my new Sister-of-Heart, Ms. Longhorn! She gets out of the car and runs to my side and hugs my neck!

"You have made it Alethea! Just think, you have really made your Trail of Tears!!" laughing and dancing with me! We didn't try to hide our tears of joy! The kids waiting in her car were as full of joy as we were!!! "Now just walk on up to the top of this hill, turn left and there at this little market, I will be waiting for you. Then Muleskinner and Dream-Catcher want to walk the last mile with you on into the Courthouse Yard!" wiping her tears and talking a mile a minute as we tried to regather our senses!

"Okay, I got it! I will watch for you! Be ready boys!!!" I still have tears in my eyes that won't leave me. I just allow them to take their own trail down my cheeks. They will become dry from the Tahlequah Wind!

Made the small hill in much short of time! Turned to the left and there I see Ms. Longhorn's shiny car! The boys jump out to greet me and each hug me closely, then one on each side, take my hand! We hold our heads high as if we were new appointed Chiefs of the Cherokee Nation and fight the traffic as we search for the well known Courtyard!

We come to the last street crossing! "Kids, hold my hands tight, for we are just a few steps away!"

"Yes, Alethea, we will and we are right here with you, aren't we!"

"Yes you are, my little men, yes you really are." Then I wondered if they could feel the sweat that was hot and sticky inside my palms as I clutched their small but strong hands maybe a little too tightly, as I felt a different "Message in the Wind!?"

Ms. Longhorn was looking at her watch as we crossed the street and walked upon the lush green grass of the Courthouse. "Alethea!" She yells, "Its five o'clock!"

As the little men release my watery hands, I drop upon my knees, look toward the darkening skies that are filled of clouds that I feel is a blessing!

"Maker of Breath, as I understand you and as you understand me, I thank you! I thank you for allowing me to hear every whisper on this Trail of Tears as you sent them by the unole.

Because of you, I am alive today, this very minute to speak these words of many thanks to you. I am glad for the friends that I made along the way. The ones that turned me down, I feel truly sorry for...

I thank you for my Mr. Bill. Please rid him free of that devil cancer.

For the time that I was much lost from the Trail, thank you again, for there I found medicine. The spirit-picture that only I can see now, I thank you. Everybody is here! I didn't expect such a grand gathering. Oh, how I thank you for this!!! I am much filled with joy to see that everyone has gathered to join in this Spirit-Time with and around me!

Bless the little men that walked the last mile with me and thank you for that mean blister, that little country store in Proctor and the way the steps led me to the smiling face of Ms. Longhorn and her family of warmth!

Teach me, my Great Spirit, to always walk the many roads to ways of Wisdom as you speak to the winds and they bring me your Messages. I will forever follow. I now have learned from everything that I see, feel or hear, there is your Spirit in all! Thank you. Please see that I find the safe road back to Kentucky, there I may have your strength to fight the many devils that still bring bad dreams to my mind and leave troubled sleep. Forever and ever I thank you for this life long dream that has finally come true and knowing that Mama shared this too! Thank you for the "MESSAGE IN THE WIND!"

## "THE LAST JOURNAL ENTRIES OF MR. BILL"

*Jan. 5, 1993 - Went to give blood for my surgery. princess finished her walk at 5:p.m. I'm proud of you Princess.*
*Jan. 6 - Princess still in Proctor with Ms. Longhorn and her family.*
*Jan. 7 - Called Princess. me & Gypsy going to get her.*
*Jan. 8 - Gypsy & I left around 6:p.m. to get princess. It was 800 miles. Got there around 6:a.m.*
*Jan. 9 - Left Proctor around noon. Got home around 4:a.m. Sunday morning.*
*Jan. 10 - Snow, ice and rain all the way. Princess is home safe now. The end of the Trail.*
*Thank you Great Spirit!*

END OF THE "TRAIL OF TEARS" IN TAHLEQUAH OKLAHOMA

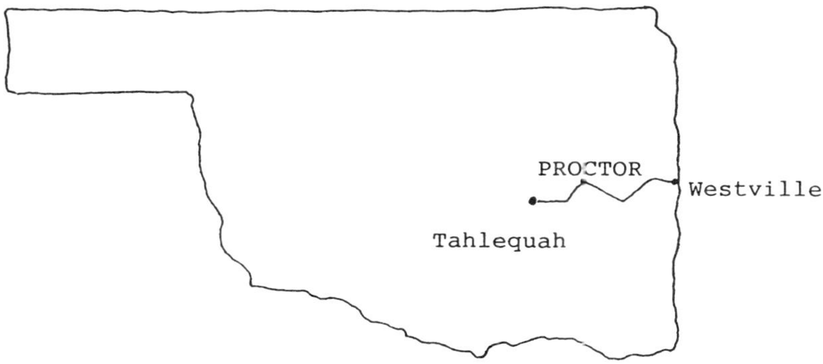


1. Westville

2. Christie

3. Proctcr

4. Eldon

5. Tahlequah

(Arrived and Ended the "CRY TRAIL", Steps of MY DREAMS!

# EPILOGUE

I left on a day of NEWS (3rd) and arrived on the day of SURPRISE (5th). Finally I have lived my life-long dream to walk the infamous but always remembered "Trail of Tears".

The following Saturday the 9th (meaning GIFT), my Mr. Bill and his cousin Gypsy, came to Ms. Longhorn's to take me home. We gifted Ms. Longhorn with that Calling-Bell from the Treasure-Store then headed for Kentucky. We had a snowstorm all the way.

Twenty hours later we were safe at Mr. Bill's cabin door. I have had to fight many devils since I walked the Trail of Tears. Finally removed the brown-liquor devil. Even named my truck after it; WHISKEY, to always remind me that I am the winner!

The sugar? Oh, I still fall in that bucket every once in a while! Get a little crazy and have to sleep it off!

Lard Department? I have found the middle of the road there! I gained some weight but only into the 130's. Pray I never see the weight of the 140's as I once was. Still crave those double cheeseburgers but I can control the urge unless I am in bad need of the famous estrogen shot.

Lost control of my nerves a time or two but a slow walk in the early morning hours tend to be my medicine.

The cancer devil? He has been removed from Mr. Bill and we keep a close eye on it to make sure that he never takes a hold again.

Walking I recommend for eveyone! Many poeple ask me the art to walking. I just speak, "Take it easy. If you get out of line with your steps, your body will teach you how the hard way!"

The gila I sometimes hated when I didn't even have any? Well I have two now; Sleeping Bear and Black Feather.

They were a wedding gift from Mr. Bill. Nelly Bly got her dream just as I did. She married another Tennessee Walker and a proper foal is ready!

I am now Mrs. Alethea Adams-Wells and we live a simple and happy life upon his Bath County farm. I am much wealthy with new friends I have made during my adventure, especially Attorney Scott Hall and his missus that now have become newly proud parents to their beautiful baby daughter. The warm arms of Tennessee State embrace them, just as my heart does.

From my study window, the Seasons pass and I admire the different shades of clothing that Mother nature displays. I've yet to become the perfect Susie Homemaker or Betty Crocker but I'm working on the many recipes that Mr. Bill's Mama: Ms. Chief and his sister, Turquoise send to me! Daddy speaks that I need to learn how to can the vegetables that Mr. Bill grows in his garden! I think Its best that Daddy just move in for the canning season, especially since I have in the making, this other adventure I had when I lived in the mountains for seven years! There, I did a lot of walking to learn how to deal with the passing of my Mama. Far into these Eastern Kentucky mountains, I was better known as the wild and crazy Indian, the "Lady of the Moon"!

So, let's go for another long, long walk. I still can hear that "Message in the Wind"!

# DEDICATION

To: MY MAKER OF BREATH as I see him and understand. Me and the maker have our own way of COUNCIL...

IN MEMORY: Of my Mama, Mary Katherine Hall, whose words and wisdom I still need and use every day of my life...

TO: My Mr. Bill that made this life long dream happen and come to pass. He never gave up on me and supported me mentally and physically. When tears I cried, he wiped away and held me when I wasn't strong. You are my Foundation of Love Mr. Bill.

TO: Willow, the lady that taught me how to cope with modern ways for the last five years and how to turn this machine ON!!

TO: Mr. Talking Leaves (Doug Mefford), that answered my plea for knowledge! He walked the Trail with me; placing commas, periods and all those other point values that one should learn!

TO: Daddy; Ernest Hall (Hank), Jr. that always knows my Messages in the Wind even before I do!

TO: My Four Sisters, Little Sparrow, Warm Demonzia Earth, Two-Fist and Sledge. I have driven them crazy, insisting that each one must listen to my DREAM!

TO: Mr. and Mrs. Hiwassee that showed me the way to the Sacred Grounds and Water at Rattlesnake Springs, Tennessee, where the Trail of Tears first began. They introduced me to Mr. Cattleman that allowed me to camp upon the very spot that my People were of prisoners ...

TO: Ms. Longhorn that was there to see me reach the end of the long Trail of Tears. Introduced me to a wise woman, Ms. Ruby.

TO: ALL the people with warm hearts that either took me into their homes or allowed me to stay in their barns. The ones that fed or doctored me. I thank you with all my heart and prayers...

TO: Brewsky who tried...

TO: Dr. Quisenberry, your words have always haunted me and sometimes made me behave!

TO: Linda Frahm that discovered my speaking...

ESPECIALLY TO: All the nice people that I have yet to meet, that read my story of a long awaited JOURNEY ... Thank YOU!

WADA To ALL!!!

# BIBLIOGRAPHY
## BOOKS AND MATERIAL I FEEL YOU SHOULD READ

Trail of Tears (Rise and Fall of the Cherokee Nation)
By: John Ehle, Publisher: Anchor

Walking the Trail, By: Jerry Ellis, Published: Delta

Myths of the Cherokee and Sacred Formulas of the Cherokee, By: James Monny, Published: Charles Elder Bookseller, nashville, Tennessee

The Bell Witch of Tennessee, By: Charley Baily Bell (A Descendent) Published: Charles Elder Bookseller, Nashville, Tennessee

Encyclopedia Britanica, North America, Britannica Center
310 S. Michigan Avenue, Chicago, Illinois 60604

The Cherokee One Feather (Newspaper)
P.O. Box 501
Cherokee, NC 28719

The South Eastern Indians, By: Charles Hudson, Published: The University of Tennessee Press

Concise Encyclopedia of the American Indian, By: Bruce Grant, Published: Wings Books

CHEROKEE AMERICANS, By: John R. Finger, University of Nebraska Press

American Indian Medicine, By: Virgil J. Vogel, University of Oklahoma Press

After Columbus: The Smithsonian Chronicle of the North American Indians, By: Herman J. Viola, Published: Smithsonian Institution

CREATION'S JOURNEY: Native American Identity and Belief, Pub. Smithsonian Institution Press

History of Cannon County, Tenessee, By: Robert L. Mason, Pub. Cannon Co. Historical Society: Lancer Printing Company, 220 South Spring St., Murfeesboro, TN

History of Adair County, By: Adair County History Committee, Pub. ARC Press of Cane Hill, Arkansas 72717

Walk In My Soul, By" Lucia St. Clair Robson, Ballantine Books

The Walking Magazine, Walking, Inc., 9-11 Harcourt Street, Boston, MA 02116

Bury My Heart At Wounded Knee, An Indian History of the American West, By: Dee Brown, Pub. Henry Holt and Company, New York

The Westville Reporter, 122 S. Williams Street, P.O. Box 550, Westville, Oklahoma 74965